LOCAL
MONEY

LOCAL
MONEY

HOW TO MAKE IT HAPPEN
IN YOUR COMMUNITY

Peter North

First published in 2010 by

Transition Books
an imprint of Green Books
www.transitionbooks.net

Green Books
Foxhole, Dartington
Totnes, Devon TQ9 6EB
www.greenbooks.co.uk

© Peter North 2010
All rights reserved

Design by Stephen Prior

Printed in the UK by Cambrian Printers.
The text paper is made from 100% recycled post-
consumer waste, and the covers from 75% recycled
material.

All photographs not otherwise credited are by Peter
North. The images on page 6 and page 143 are
courtesy of Jason Houston.

DISCLAIMER: The advice in this book is believed to
be correct at the time of printing, but the authors and
the publishers accept no liability for actions inspired
by this book.

ISBN 978 1 900322 52 2

CONTENTS

"Where oil is the king, where global warming is ignored, where the very end of life is the place we're heading toward, where it's more than just a metaphor the flooding of the dike, and if we don't stop this madness the whole planet will be like – New Orleans."
David Rovics, *New Orleans*

"This planet has – or rather had – a problem, which was this: most of the people living on it were unhappy for pretty much all of the time. Many solutions were suggested for this problem, but most of these were largely concerned with the movements of small green pieces of paper, which is odd because on the whole it wasn't the small green pieces of paper that were unhappy."
Douglas Adams, *The Hitchhiker's Guide to the Galaxy*

ACKNOWLEDGEMENTS

Thanks to Ben Brangwyn, Mark Burton, Helen Dew, Oliver Dudok van Heel, Marie Fare, Christian Gelleri, Noel Longhurst, Bill Maurer, Molly Scott Cato, Tim Nichols, Josh Ryan-Collins, Rolf Schroeder, Martin Simon, Susan Witt and Mathias Zeeb for contributing to and commenting on sections of the text – and for their good humour in the face of my misunderstandings and time constraints.

From Green Books, thanks to Amanda Cuthbert and Alethea Doran for their close reading of the text and invaluable editing support. From the Transition movement, thanks to the very unique and inspiring Rob Hopkins. All were unfailingly patient and supportive. Despite their best intentions, errors and omissions are of course all mine.

Thanks to all my friends in the local currency world over the years, too many to mention by name – but you know who you are.

To Bev, Polly and Gabriel – especially for you, kids!

To my fellow Liverpool Transitioners: Claire Connolly,
Clare Gillott, Kaz Lucas, Mark Shooter and Nat Uomini.

FOREWORD

THE POWER OF HOLDING YOUR COMMUNITY'S OWN MONEY

September 2009, Lambeth Town Hall, Brixton. On a beautiful evening with just the first hint of autumn in the air, hundreds of people are packed into the large room for the launch of the Brixton Pound. In the days running up to the launch, the media was full of stories about the currency; it even made the front page of the BBC website on the day. Alongside explanations of how it is intended to work and interviews with advocates were mainstream economists who, somewhat patronisingly, assured readers that this could never really work and that it was all tremendously naive and foolish. Clearly that was a sentiment that those gathered in the hall, and the 70 traders already keen to accept the notes, had chosen to overlook – or, more likely, would fervently disagree with. This event was both a celebration of the new currency and, perhaps most importantly, of Brixton itself.

Derrick Anderson, the Chief Executive of the local council, which had partly funded the initiative, told the audience that he would be using Brixton Pounds, that he hoped they would become 'the currency of choice for Brixton', and that he was delighted that this was a good news story about the area. When I spoke to him later, I explored with him how deep the commitment of the council to this new currency would actually run. Would it accept the currency in payment of Council Tax? Would it accept rent from stallholders in Brixton Pounds? The answer to both questions was yes: a national first.

At the end of the evening, the notes themselves were unveiled to rapturous applause. Each note featured a prominent Brixtonian, chosen via a community-wide 'Vote the Note' poll. They showed Vincent Van Gogh on the £20 note; C. L. R. James, a local historian, political theorist and cricket writer on the £10 note; Gaia theorist James Lovelock on the £5 note and Olive Morris, Brixton Black Women's Group founder, on the £1. Morris had died at the age of 27, and some members of her family were present to see this extraordinary memorial to her life and work.

At the end of the evening, people brought the first notes into circulation, and the Brixton Pound was now a reality, ready to take its place in the tills of Brixton. But is this legal? Will it work? And, perhaps most importantly, why would anyone bother?

The emergence of Transition currencies

In 2006, I attended a talk by economist Bernard Lietaer at Schumacher College. He said two things that stuck with me: firstly, that localisation was impossible without having a local currency; secondly, that that local currency had to be designed in such a way that businesses would use it. I was familiar with models such as time banks and Local Exchange Trading Schemes (I had been a member of a few different LETS schemes), but I left Lietaer's talk thinking that something else was needed. A few days later, I visited a local film company whose offices used to be the Totnes Bank. Lovingly framed and hanging on the wall was an 1810 Totnes banknote – a beautiful handwritten document, which had been legal tender in the town. What would happen, I wondered, if we printed some new ones? If we got a few shops to agree to take them and just ran it for three months and saw where they went? Would we be allowed, or would we suffer dawn raids from the Bank of England and be stuffed into a small and rather unpleasant room in the Tower of London reserved exclusively for those who print their own money? The answer to all those questions was a big 'no idea', but in the Transition movement that is rarely a reason for inaction. From the moment when 150 people first sat in St John's Church waving their freshly minted Totnes Pounds, the first for almost 200 years, the idea of communities printing their own money has, as Peter North so lucidly narrates in this book, grown rapidly.

First came Lewes in Sussex, then Stroud, then Brixton, and now several other places have their own schemes on the drawing board. Each currency learns from the previous ones in a wonderful iterative way, and each currency is fiercely of its place. They are all bold, thought-provoking and charming, and they all embody an important principle of not waiting for permission to initiate the process of relocalisation. They couldn't have come at a more timely moment.

Why do we need local money?

In spite of the Queen's musing aloud in early 2009 as to why no one had seen the economic meltdown coming, many people had been only too aware that economics, as currently practised, is designed to draw money upwards, does nothing to stop the poor getting poorer and everything to help the rich get richer, and has no loyalty to communities or individuals. A common national unit of exchange – sterling – is, of course, extremely useful, as it enables national trade. Yet its weaknesses are such that it needs a complementary currency running alongside it. Some transactions can be in one; some in another.

The very thing that sterling is designed to do, i.e. enable and stimulate trading between people and businesses, it often fails to do – especially in times of economic contraction. Money often feels like something 'done to' communities. The large corporate chains that now dominate the nation's high streets are like mining operations, extracting the potential wealth of communities and siphoning it away to shareholders and executive bonuses. It is a vicious cycle: people buy from chain stores, less money goes to local businesses, less money circulates locally, local businesses struggle, and we end up with identical high streets up and down the land – what the new economics foundation calls 'Clone Town Britain'. A local currency is an intervention that can, it is hoped, start to reverse that trend, building trade for local businesses, creating a mindfulness that means people start to choose local shops over chains, and encouraging them to get out and discover the independent traders in their community.

Money and resilience

Central to Transition is the concept of resilience. This is the concept, originally from ecology, that systems – whether businesses, settlements or entire nations – tend to be more or less able to withstand shocks from the outside. Although just-in-time distribution systems allow us to have access to a dazzling array of foodstuffs and other goods (much of which our great-grandparents wouldn't have even been able to name), we are left with an economy with little inbuilt resilience. The whole system is highly oil-vulnerable. Price volatility, or worse still, actual shortages, are things we are hugely unprepared for and could be devastating.

In the middle of the nineteenth century, when there was no welfare state and some business owners still paid their employees in a far less ethical form of local currency, one that could be spent only in their own stores, the question of 'plugging the leaks' in local economies was not hypothetical: it was, for many communities, a matter of survival. The Cooperative movement emerged, inviting people to invest inwards into their communities; to invest in local jobs and local businesses. It was hugely successful, and its legacy is still with us today. As the scale of the UK's debt, incurred through years of living beyond our means and the 2008 bailing out of the banks, becomes clear, and the scale of the cuts in public spending that they will necessitate also emerges into reality, we find ourselves needing models and approaches to do the same thing again. Communities will find themselves needing each other again, after years of being able to get by without knowing your neighbours and the very idea of community being pilloried.

Where all this might lead

So where might all this end up, if local currency becomes a key element of our daily lives? One could imagine a situation where several of the approaches Peter outlines here sit alongside our ongoing relation-ship with sterling. A significant proportion of our weekly shop would be done with local businesses, which, in turn, would encourage them to seek out local suppliers, leading to an explosion of local market gardening and other local manufacturing.

Alongside the printed currencies, we may also make use of time banks, and we may be members of a local credit union. For loans, we may talk to the credit union, or we might visit a website such as zopa.com and borrow direct from other people, with no bank in the middle. Any surplus money that we want to invest, we are now able to invest in local shares or bond issues, which raise the capital for our locally owned energy company to begin installing renewables, or for local food-growing initiatives to secure access to land. There may well be all kinds of evolutions that we can only speculate on at this stage, such as local electronic cards or even the idea of currencies that are stored on our mobile phones. Perhaps there will be regional currencies, as can already be found in Austria, Germany and Switzerland. What is key is that as humanity begins its inevitable shift away from energy-intensive, globalised, corporate economics to a more human-scale, localised version, the way we 'do' money will need to catch up. This book identifies a number of possible tools, and doubtless there are many more yet to be thought of.

The Cheerful Disclaimer

What Peter has done here is write a book that is a clear and deeply researched practical guide for you to get started, laying out of some of the tools that increased economic localisation will need. He brings to this project many years of insight and observation of local currencies around the world, and I hope that you will find the result both fascinating and thrilling. It is important at this stage to bring in what we call 'The Cheerful Disclaimer'. If you are reading this book thinking that local currencies, the Transition idea, projects like the Brixton Pound, are all tried-and-tested things that we can guarantee will definitely work, think again. Transition is an iterative process, a collaborative process of learning as we go along, of sharing successes and failures, of people being bold and trying things out, and learning from what has gone before.

At this time in history when things are changing so fast, this kind of innovative thinking and creativity is something that can really come only from communities, who are able to innovate and experiment in highly imaginative ways. Although this book does not come with a guarantee of success, it does come with the firm belief that what we need to do, what has the most chance of enabling a successful Transition, is to harness engaged optimism. What does engaged optimism look like? The currencies discussed in this book are all just one approach; perhaps just initial experiments from which other, better-refined, approaches will emerge. What they do, though, is give a physical form to that sense of engaged optimism: a tangible statement of a community's intent.

Moving forward

The Transition movement has developed a power and a speed to its vital momentum around the world. As I write, there are well over 200 formal initiatives and thousands more at earlier stages. Will they all produce their own currencies, and indeed do they need to? Probably not. What they will no doubt do, though, is continue to innovate, and it is that spirit of innovation that we hope this book captures. Having attended the launches of the Totnes, Lewes and Brixton Pounds (I was unable to make the Stroud one), I was struck by the fact that they were all characterised by being incredibly energetic and dynamic occasions. You get a sense at these events of a latent power that governments can't tap, but which rather can be 'unleashed' only by those communities themselves.

This book was preceded by *Local Food*, which set out an array of things that Transition Initiatives can do to start building resilience around food, seeing this as an opportunity to rethink many basic assumptions in a very creative way. It sought to give Transition food groups the best possible start and save them reinventing too many wheels. This book does much the same,

capturing from across the Transition network, as well as from the many projects that preceded and which run in parallel to it, best practice as it is currently understood in relation to alternative currencies.

You don't need to wait for anyone's permission to initiate local money. Its potential as a tool for relocalisation is something we are only just starting to grasp. One of the key things for a successful local currency scheme is trust. People use sterling because they know it and they trust it. Without trust, money is meaningless. However, the process of building trust in the currency is also one of building trust in local traders, and of local people learning to trust one another again.

Ultimately, the best thing about these schemes is simply that they are more fun; they feel better. Shopping with 40 Brixton, Totnes, Lewes or Stroud Pounds, you still return home with £40 worth of shopping, but what you leave behind you is a far more virtuous cycle of money cycling around locally, supporting local businesses, local traders and so on. Local currencies are, in effect, 'mindful money'. Our daily actions can make a huge difference, and local currencies can become a very powerful, and far-reaching, fact of everyday life. This book celebrates those who have taken the first steps to create them.

Rob Hopkins, Transition Network
April 2010

INTRODUCTION

THE VISION

Money as belief

Money, it seems, is everywhere. But we never really think about it. We worry that we don't have enough, or that someone else has too much. But it is taken for granted. It has always been there, we have always used it. It's like oxygen, or driving on the correct side of the road. We need it and worry about it, but do we ever think about new forms of money that we might create to solve our problems? Often not, as we believe that money is something we have to earn, a 'thing' we need to get hold of that we can't change. But actually, it isn't – it's a system of belief.

Believe it or not, the 'money' we use has value only because we all, collectively, agree it has value, and our experience *is* that it has value. Essentially, a five-pound note, a Euro or a dollar is just a security-marked piece of paper with certain writing and pictures on it, and a ten-pence piece is just a stamped metal disk. 'Money' might just be a figure on a bank statement or a computer screen; no more than a few pixels or a piece of computer code. But from the day we are born our experience is that with this piece of paper, disk or pixel we can get useful things – pay our bills, buy food, whatever we want. When we don't have access to enough of it, we feel we have a problem. Often we do!

We are told all the time that we can't do something because 'we haven't got the money'. 'We can't afford it.' 'We must pay off our debts.' This can affect a whole country – we are all told that after the credit crunch we will have to live with austerity, much as we did in the late 1940s after the war. We are told that if we print too much money, as they did in Germany in the 1920s, Argentina in the 1980s and in present-day Zimbabwe, we will cause inflation. It's true – if I just printed off thousands of forged five-pound notes, I'd destroy the economy (the Germans planned to do this to the British economy in the war). All I'd print is waste paper. Pretty soon, people would work out that the money had been devalued and start to use something else. Or the Bank of England would change the design of the banknotes I had forged, as the Northern Irish banks did when millions of pounds' worth of banknotes was stolen by terrorists.

But the fact remains. Since we left the gold standard in the 1930s (the USA in the 1970s), the money we use is what economists call 'fiat money', money that is just money because someone makes it so by 'fiat' – by *saying* it is money. If I go to the Bank of England with my five-pound note and ask them to pay me, on demand, the sum of five pounds they'd either look at me in a funny way, throw me out, or direct me to their museum. A pound has value just because we are told that it has value – there is no other reason. Someone says it is money, and it's our experience that he or she is right. We can spend the money, when we want to.

Does it then follow that if someone – states, banks – can point to a piece of paper or metal disk and says 'this is money' and we believe them and can spend what they call money, other people can point to other pieces of paper and also say 'this is money'? Shops create their own forms of money – the points we earn at supermarkets, book or record tokens, gift vouchers – which we can later exchange for the things we want to buy. Air miles are the same. Do you remember green shield stamps?

We believe that storecard points have value, as we find that we can spend them. So it's not just states that can create money – businesses can too. They can because we trust them, and our experience is that they keep their promises. Would we trust a bloke standing on street corner with a suitcase if he offered loyalty points or a voucher? Probably not.

So can individuals, groups or communities create money? Trusted states, banks and businesses can say 'this is money', and as long as we experience them honouring it, it *is* money. What is sauce for the goose is sauce for the gander. If we trust the other members of our community, and our trust is borne out in practice, we can create money as long as we don't create too much of it in comparison with the real resources we want to share, and work we want to facilitate. We must all honour our personal 'promise to pay'. We can't just print money if we don't then back it up with our labour, and the production of, and exchange of, real, tangible things.

. . . but isn't this forgery?

As long as the money we are creating does not look and cannot be construed as looking like a pound sterling or a dollar, and as long as we obey benefit regulations and pay our taxes on time in pounds and

dollars, money is a private matter between individuals that the State has no interest in. All the State says is that we must offer and accept legal tender to pay our bills and to settle disputes in court. 'Money' and 'legal tender' should not be confused.

The painter J. S. Boggs was famously tried at the Old Bailey for painting pictures of banknotes without the Bank of England's permission. He used to pay for his meals by drawing pictures of pound notes and dollar bills, which the waitress gladly accepted and then sold on. He never sold his pictures, or tried to pass them off as money – he just exchanged them for meals. He estimated that he had spent around $100,000 in his own currency. Boggs's error was to produce art that *looked* too much like dollars or pounds.[1]

In contrast, Ralph Borsodi, founder of the anti-inflationary Constant currency, was asked by a reporter if what he was doing was legal. Told to ask the US treasury, the response was "we don't care if he issues pine cones, as long as it is exchangeable for dollars so that transactions can be recorded for tax purposes."[2]

We can, then, create money as long as it doesn't attempt to look like national currency banknotes. If it does, it's forgery. It's also not legal tender – in a dispute the courts will enforce payment in pounds or dollars if the loser cannot or will not resolve the dispute in local currency. A contract is a contract, irrespective of the involvement of a local currency.

'We can't afford it!'

If we can create money, it follows that there is no longer any need to say 'we can't afford to – we don't have the money' when faced with problems – such as addressing climate change and resource depletion. What matters is not if we can afford to or not, but if we have the time, resources and knowledge to solve our problems and then the willingness and ability to commit this time, resources and knowledge to the task. It's crazy that we have unemployed builders and inefficient homes leaking heat and burning oil to keep us warm or cool, but the Government says we can't afford to fix the problem because 'we don't have the money'. Money should lubricate, not govern this process.

We know that climate change and resource crises are clear, urgent, present fundamental challenges to the survival of the human race and to biodiversity generally. To meet these challenges we need to focus on the skills, enthusiasm and resources we have in our communities and use money to utilise these to the full. If the banks are so big, so central, that they cannot be allowed to fail and money is created to pay for corporate welfare, then we can also say that the ecosystems we and other species depend upon are too important to be allowed to fail.

This puts money in its real place – as a store of value and unit of measurement. Saying 'there isn't enough money' is like saying 'there aren't enough inches'. Inches are a way of measuring – there isn't a limited supply of inches somewhere, and it would be nonsensical to say 'someone else has all the inches; there aren't any left over for me'. Money is just a way of measuring the value we have created, and saving that value so we can use it later, with someone else. While it would not make sense to produce hundreds of abstract 'inches' disconnected from something to measure, neither does it make sense to say 'there isn't enough money' when we know money is just a way to measure and store value. What matters is the work we need to do and the time we have, not the existence or non-existence of money.

Local, community money

Complementary currencies, created by communities, businesses and voluntary organisations, can do things that national currencies can't. They won't ever replace pounds and pence, dollars or Euros and cents, but they can help build resilient and inclusive local communities and economies in ways that relying on national currencies will never do. We can't expect too much of them too soon. If we do, after an initial burst of enthusiasm we might feel that their performance is disappointing without really having given them a try. Creating a local money scheme that really works is a marathon, not a sprint.

But the fundamental fact remains: You, I, we, *can* create our own money that actually works. We can spend it, and do things we couldn't do before. This book shows you how.

> "What if we just went ahead as though the revolution were over and we had won?" **Rudy, Twin Oaks Commune, 1970**[3]

The Transition movement

Our life today is unbelievably energy-dependent. We need energy to heat our homes and businesses; to travel to work, school and to the shops. The goods that we buy – clothes, furniture, CDs, computers, books, food – are increasingly produced abroad, meaning that even eating a salad for lunch can demand high levels of energy usage. The trouble is, our energy-dependent lifestyle can't continue for two, rather serious, reasons.

The first reason is climate change. The more energy we use, the more we destroy the natural environment and pump trillions of tons of carbon into the atmosphere of our rather small, busy and crowded planet. The greater the emissions, the greater the scale of destruction to our planet. We need to move to a way of life that generates lower quantities of dangerous greenhouse gases or we are in danger, literally, of making the planet unliveable for our children and grandchildren. If we make the necessary changes over the next ten years we can avoid the worst.

The second reason is peak oil. Simply put, we are running out of easily extractable supplies of oil. Peak oil does *not* mean that all of the oil will run out very soon. It means that existing oil fields will soon reach, or may even have already reached, a peak of production, after which their rate of production will begin a steep decline. This will result in huge increases in the price of oil, and reductions in its availability. That said, even if new supplies are found, or we turn coal into liquid fuel, climate change means that the planet cannot absorb the carbon we are releasing into the atmosphere. We need to find new, low-carbon ways of doing things. Climate change means we *should* change track for the benefit of future generations. Peak oil means we have *no choice*.

Of course, we could wait for governments to act, for technological gizmos to get us out of this mess, or support pulling up the drawbridge and looking after ourselves, or wars over oil. But there may well not be time. The Transition movement is a growing body of people whose view is that, although governments must act, we shouldn't wait for them. Technology will no doubt provide some solutions, but we can't assume it will. On our own, we can't make much difference, but working locally with other like-minded people, and with local and central government and businesses when they begin to understand the depth of the problem, we might just get through it.

It's not all doom and gloom. As a species we were incredibly creative when we built our oil-based economy. We can use the same creativity as we move to a post-carbon world where we live in more convivial communities and make a living in ways that we enjoy, and which don't cost the Earth. We can plan the process of weaning ourselves off our addiction to oil and growth, through what Transition Initiatives call 'energy descent pathways'. We can develop new skills that will help us live more enjoyable lifestyles through relearning long-lost, useful skills, such as how to grow, fix and make things that we need locally. (The relearning of these skills is known among Transition Initiatives as 'the great reskilling'.) And local currencies will play a key role in facilitating the move to a more localised lifestyle and economy – supporting the growth of grassroots networks of trade and interaction. In the Resources section of this book you will find some reference material to help you explore Transition issues in more detail. A detailed exposition of the oil-dependency problem and the Transition vision is given in *The Transition Handbook* by Rob Hopkins.[4]

The wider potential of complementary currencies

Although this book is published under the imprint of 'Transition Books' and is a contribution to the wider task of helping with the transition to a post-carbon economy, it's important to recognise that alternative currencies can be attractive as part of the solution to a number of problems.

Many people feel isolated at home. They don't know their neighbours, and want to meet like-minded people who will become new friends, and will help them out. Some people want to work, but can't find a job for a number of reasons. They would like to live in a world where people are valued for who they are and what they can do, not how much they earn. Others feel depressed, scared and alone, but would feel much better for a chance to get out and about and meet new people. Joining a local-currency network can provide feelings of community, and sources of help.

Some people have an idea for a new business, but don't feel confident enough of their skills or business acumen to launch it straight away on the open market. Some people regret the demise of our high streets and small, individual local businesses in the face of supermarkets and other facets of what the new economics foundation calls 'clone towns'. Small-business owners will want to find ways to get more people through the door. Local currencies can help to protect small businesses and local economies, especially in hard economic times.

While not a panacea, in different ways, different forms of local currency can contribute to addressing many of these problems. You do not have to be a member of a Transition Initiative to get involved.

A vision for the future

Assuming you are attracted to the vision of a resilient local, low-carbon economy, imagine ten or twenty years down the road, when we are much closer to our goal. What does the economy look like? Where do local currencies and the other local financial organisations that we discuss later in this book fit in?

In our imaginary local economy of the future, more of the food a community needs is grown locally and sold in locally owned shops, cooperatives and markets. More of its electricity is generated locally, and delivered by community-owned local power companies. Seeing the benefits in cash, and feeling a sense of local

ownership, short-sighted people who would have protested against windmills as a noisy blot on an otherwise pristine natural landscape now see them as 'angels on the hills', as beautiful as the sixteenth-century windmills protected for their heritage value, or a dry-stone wall.

More and more people work for themselves, part-time, for a mixture of local and national currencies. They do not see their livelihood coming from a nine-to-five job, but from a mixture of things they grow and produce themselves, things they exchange, share, recycle and repair, and things they buy and consume much as we do today. But far more of the things we need are produced locally than they are today. Those that we can't produce locally, perhaps because of local climatic conditions or because it makes sense to produce them in bulk, are still exchanged globally, but not on the basis of price alone. We choose what businesses we want to see in our community, and whom we exchange with.

The ability to meet more of our needs locally didn't just happen, since before the economy had its own local currency everyone accepted that globalisation was inevitable, unstoppable. They didn't think you could do anything to stop money leaching out of our community to head offices elsewhere. But from small acorns – a Local Exchange Trading Scheme and a time bank, then, in time, a local paper currency – a mighty oak grew. The local currency became an accepted part of the local scene. First seen as strange, perhaps wacky, perhaps backward (doesn't everyone use the internet and credit cards now?), it has become a normal part of the way people live their lives alongside, but not replacing, pounds, dollars or Euros. People concerned there might be a run on the bank have found their fears to be meaningless.

A local currency is not run in isolation. Much of the business we do is still conducted in pounds and dollars, but far more of these pounds stay local, circulating between locally owned businesses and cooperatives that produce for local needs. For ten years, a local purchasing and local distribution project run by the local chamber of commerce has been putting local businesses in touch with each other. One business's waste has been identified as a useful resource for another. Local businesses regularly collaborate with each other to identify ways to work with each other, design new projects, and share best practice. Larger firms work closely with their suppliers to ensure that the firm gets the supplies it needs locally, when it needs them, and in the right quantity. This is hugely profitable, as the costs of transporting materials and goods around the planet for no sensible reason have been eliminated.

No one feels the need to spend money, emit carbon and burn fuel by lifting human bodies into the air now that teleconferencing is so easy. People still travel, but less, more slowly, and stay longer. Once avoidable travel was cut out, we were surprised that we could travel more than we thought – but not as much as we used to in the irresponsible old days. Carbon emissions have plummeted and resources are not being depleted in the way they used to be, but no one feels worse off. What has been cut is the waste, the pointless globalisation based on cost and profit; not what is valuable.

The local chambers of commerce, development agencies and councils had all got fed up with the banks' continuing refusal to finance local businesses, no matter how many times those banks were bailed out. New small businesses in poorer parts of town were developing interesting new environmental products, but they had no track record, so could not get credit. Following the examples of councils in Birmingham and Essex, credit unions and local financial vehicles such as Aston Investment Trust, more and more local authorities set up local banks, often in the same premises that had housed local banks a century ago but had later housed wine bars. These local banks and revitalised branch networks of larger banks replaced the poor service, anonymity and poor working conditions of the twentieth century's call centres. Captain Mainwaring was back, and in charge again.

These local and municipal banks provide much-needed employment for those bank workers who had not been responsible for driving their former employers into the ground, but who had paid the cost when downsizing kicked in. Some banks specialise in developing green products, some in developing the range of services provided locally, and some in funding green power generation. They work with the Ecology Building Society and the Triodos Bank, which have a track record in this area. The UK is beginning to look more like the USA, which had never lost its local banks.

There is a renaissance in building societies and savings and loans. Not the big building societies that were demutualised in the 1980s, but new, small, local building societies run by and for their members, funding house purchases and the development of new, ecological building designs. The Bradford and Bingley Mutual serves Bradford and Bingley. The Halifax works in Halifax. Zero interest banks such as Sweden's JAK Bank, and Islamic banks, offer finance without usury. Credit unions have grown from places for the unbankable to get small, low-interest loans to more robust local institutions offering loans for small business start-ups. Credit unions in the UK have begun to look more like those in the USA or Ireland.

As the requirement for deep cuts in carbon emissions intensified, more and more councils had to upgrade their ecologically disastrous Victorian housing stock. Sure, some of the owners could afford to upgrade their houses themselves, but most people couldn't – they were stuck in fuel poverty. Some could get loans from the new mutuals. In the days when house prices were rising, some councils had loaned homeowners the money to upgrade their homes at low interest, with the money paid back when the house was sold, but as house prices no longer automatically rose, that approach had its limits. Councils needed to act fast to meet their carbon-reduction targets.

Eventually councils recognised that it is senseless having so many builders out of work, fuel bills so high, and emissions continuing to rise. Leaving it to individuals is not enough. So they went back to another old practice, one open to local authorities until Mrs Thatcher cut their wings in the 1980s. They issued local bonds to finance the great home upgrade.

Given that the big banks no longer trust each other, and savings interest rates are so low, local bonds have become an attractive proposition for the pension funds. Our savings have stopped funding wars and unsustainable forms of growth, and become part of the solution. Just as they did in the nineteenth century, local bonds also finance the upgrading of local power generation, street lighting, gas and electricity supply, and the introduction of modern waste disposal – and we realise that addressing climate change is not rocket science, but more like addressing cholera and overcrowding in nineteenth-century cities.

Solving climate change isn't Albert Einstein, it's Joseph Chamberlain.[5]

Does this vision sound utopian? Probably. But if we are to avoid dangerous climate change it's the sort of future we need to start building now. To ensure that the optimistic scenario above is played out there will be a need for a diversity of alternative currencies and new financial vehicles to fund what we need to do to build secure, resilient local economies. This book explores how a diverse ecosystem of community-generated currencies and local institutions can fill the gap.

Transition money – the options

The points outlined so far can be summarised as follows.

- Local communities have visions, skills and enthusiasms, but they do not have the sterling, Euros or dollars necessary to build a resilient local economy themselves.

- We can create money that values everyone's time equally.

- We can create currencies that build community feeling, not cut us off from each other in a competition over limited resources.

- We can create money that doesn't travel too far away, so it circulates around our community. It helps local businesses, and stimulates local production.

What would this community-created local money look like? There are basically four options that you could choose between – or mix and match the models to suit your own local needs.

Local Exchange Trading Schemes (LETS)

LETS schemes use a currency with a local name that is exchanged between members using cheques, with account balances held on a computer. The currency is valued in relation to national currency with a recommended hourly wage. Users of the currency meet each other through a directory, and negotiate their own prices.

Time banking

This is a virtual currency whereby one hour's work is worth one 'time credit'. Account balances are held on a computer, and there is no negotiation on price. Users of the currency contact a broker who puts people in contact with each other. State benefits are unaffected, as there are no businesses involved.

'Hours'

These are paper-based currencies that are denominated in time, not in relation to conventional money. They aim to value everyone's time and work equally.

Transition pounds, BerkShares, regiogeld

These are paper-based currencies, denominated in relation to conventional money. They circulate in a small community or a region, but not outside that community.

To these four options we can add a number of financial innovations, such as credit unions, local bonds, microfinance and local banks. In this book I discuss how they might all be weaved together to form a rich platform to aid our transition to a community-based, low-carbon economy.

Diverse forms of money as an ecosystem

We all know that in agriculture, monocultures don't make sense. Growing just one variety of crop means that it is vulnerable to disease, and doesn't replenish the soil or support the vibrant ecosystem of bird and insect life that keeps crops healthy and the soil fertile. If you are dependent on one crop, you are vulnerable if the price of your crop crashes, or demand for your produce fails. We need a variety of plant and animal life that supports and nurtures the whole system, making it resilient.

Resilience

What would happen to you if something unexpected occurred? If you lost your job, split up with a long-term partner, or got sick? Or if it rained so much that the drains, clogged with carrier bags, all failed to cope and your house was knee-deep in unmentionables? Or if the rains failed, year in year out? Or if you were in New Orleans when Katrina hit?

Could you cope? Would you be resilient? Could you handle a shock to the system? How much of a shock? What could you cope with, and what would put you under?

As with ourselves, so with our communities and local economics. Could our economy stand the loss of demand for a key product we made or the disinvestment of a large employer – or climate change? Or the end of cheap oil and gas ('peak oil')?

A local economy that can handle shocks and that is able to reproduce itself again and again over the years, without depleting the ecosystem on which it depends, is resilient.

In *The Transition Handbook*[6] Rob Hopkins argues that as well as cutting emissions, we also need to build resilience to handle future challenges from climate change and peak oil. Cutting emissions without building in resilience (or more accurately rebuilding resilience), he argues, is futile.

It's the same with money. If we rely on just one form of money, and a form of money that we don't control, we are vulnerable to pathologies in that form of money and to the supply of it drying up. That is not resilient. We might find that it does not nurture parts of our community that we value. It may be good for setting up businesses, but not for valuing the environment, community and conviviality. It may create wealth, but puts us on a treadmill. Just as we need diverse agricultural ecosystems, so we need a diverse financial ecosystem.

A diverse ecosystem of alternative currencies and local financial institutions

Imagine a future scenario where a community has a long-established LETS scheme involving a few hundred ecologically minded members of the community. In the inner city and on the estates, local people help each other out using the time banks. Both LETS and time banks are used to facilitate community exchanges as people share knowledge, gardening tips, seeds and cookery skills; repair, reuse and recycle things they don't need; and help each other to make their homes more energy efficient. Local businesses regularly use the local paper currency, which delinked from national currency after five years. Loans are given out to help develop new local production.

The result is an explosion of local employment in small businesses, providing face-to-face services to a local market. Everyone recognises that this diverse monetary economy is more resilient than the old financial monoculture, where problems in one part of the world were transmitted across the entire global economy at the press of a button, while profits flew to where they could get the greatest return rather than to where they could best be used to build the low-carbon economy.

"Give me a one-armed economist!"

President Harry S. Truman once demanded "give me a one-armed economist". He did listen to advisers, but quickly lost patience with those who gave recommendations heavily hedged with caveats: 'On one hand, on the other hand.' He wanted clarity, not a long discussion of the advantages and disadvantages of a particular course of action. His academic advisers wanted to stress the unknown, the doubts, and the problems – to put in the caveats and let others take the decisions. I'm afraid I'm such an academic. I'm going to put in the caveats as I see them and let you decide what to make of them.

I'm an academic by occupation and sceptical by temperament, and therefore critical of my own and others' work. I think that the sort of life we enjoy on this planet is in real danger from dangerous climate change and multiple resource crises, that we need to radically change the way we organise our lives and economies, and that the problems we face are serious. I'm convinced that a monoculture of money, just like a monoculture of crops, is not resilient.

Much of what follows in this book, therefore, is based on my own research or, where indicated, on that of others. Some of the research – on LETS, on Argentina and time banks – is more extensive than that on some of the newer currencies, especially BerkShares and the Transition currencies. Some of the currency models now have enough of a track record that we – you the reader, me the author – can be fairly confident about what works and what doesn't. BerkShares, regiogeld and the Transition currencies are newer, more pioneering in character, and although the wider literature on money helps, it's too soon to draw firm conclusions. Where things are new and tentative, I provide pointers to the relevant websites so you can follow the stories of these pioneering currencies as they emerge. This is *not* an academic book, but it is built on my research and that of others which I hope to make useful to a wider audience. My research, and that of others, says that some forms of complementary currency do have real benefits, but they also have their limits and are unlikely to be a complete solution to the problems we have or ever completely replace national currencies. They can have a place in Transition strategies, and this book describes what the different currency models are, their strengths, and their weaknesses as I see them. I don't see problems as insurmountable barriers but as interesting issues to grapple with.

But I also believe that there is no point in praising things that don't work, or following dead ends. I try to avoid polemic. I am aware, in particular, that local currencies are, to coin a phrase, 'never knowingly undersold'. In questions of finance, there are snake-oil salesmen, crooks and con artists out there as well as well-meaning but misguided people and really knowledgeable, inspiring and sensible pioneers. The wisdom is in knowing the difference.

I don't think it is to anyone's benefit to avoid hard questions. We don't want to build on sand, but on the

'Path dependency' and 'lock in'

QWERTY keyboards were first designed to slow typists down to a speed that a mechanical typewriter could handle – something not relevant now. VHS won the battle with Betamax for videos, even though Betamax was a superior product. There is no point in producing videos or tape cassettes now that we have CDs. Soon, we won't have CDs – we will just download music.

As we learn more and technology develops, the adoption of one way of doing things and new technologies can close off other options, or make us not consider them. This is called 'path dependency'. We are now dependent on following a path that ensures all keyboards are QWERTY and we use CDs, not videos and tapes. We are 'locked in' to using these technologies even though, like QWERTY keyboards, they are suboptimal. We ignore the alternatives that have been discarded on the way, even though they might be better.

The trouble with this is that we assume that what worked in the past or somewhere else will work now, and that, conversely, what didn't work then won't work now. We assume that we build on accepted knowledge, and that as we get more experienced our store of knowledge is built up cumulatively over time.

Another way of thinking about this is to envisage an oak tree. It has strong roots, a tall, thick trunk, then branches coming off the trunk that form the canopy. From an acorn, roots emerge, then a tiny sapling with a few leaves grows up from the soil. As the tree grows the trunk gets thicker and the canopy more verdant. The energy flows one way – acorn to roots to sapling to trunk to canopy. Here, the process of building up knowledge and experience is hierarchical. It flows one way.

Now think of spots of oil on a film of water or spores on a Petri dish that spread and coalesce. Each drop of oil or spore exists in its own right; is as good as the other. The spots emerge and coalesce at different times and in different ways, but that doesn't matter. Here knowledge is egalitarian.

The point I am making is that you should think 'spores or spots', not 'trees'. Betamax, not VHS. Just because Totnes and Lewes have decided to run a paper currency, that is not necessarily a good reason for following them. One of the other models of currency, or a new one entirely, might be better. The Totnes Pound, or LETS, are not the trunks of a local-currency tree – they are different spots of oil. All of the currencies I discuss in this book have their strengths and weaknesses, and all are equally valid. What matters is what you want to do with an alternative form of money, and the nature of the place you are from. Don't be path-dependent, or locked in to an unnecessarily narrow range of options.

solid foundations of past experiences. I think that research matters, and practical work that isn't reflective can lead to a lot of heat and light but no movement forward.

I aim to be an 'honest broker', telling the stories of those at the coal face developing alternative currencies as I see them, using my research experience as a resource on which to build our understanding. The suggestions I make about what works and what doesn't are backed by research and 'co-produced' with those with whom I have worked over the years. I hope you will find the ideas in this book a valuable tool for Transition. If you want to follow up the academic research, you will find source material in the References section at the back of the book.

Transition money in a nutshell

- Alternative currencies have their specific strengths and weaknesses. There is no one size fits all, or silver bullet. To understand what works and what doesn't in different contexts, you need to understand what makes good and bad money, and why. This is covered in the first two chapters, so it's worth reading them first and bearing them in mind as you read the rest of the book.

Local currencies and the Transition process

Alternative currencies help to transition our local economies and develop ways to make our livelihoods enjoyable, sustainable and resilient in a number of ways.

Early days

Alternative currencies help us mobilise the hidden skills, time and resources of our community. Through alternative currencies we can create the money to finance this process.

LETS schemes are very easy to set up in a Transition Initiative of around a hundred members – an easy, quick win.

LETS or time banks could be useful tools to facilitate 'the great reskilling' – relearning the skills we need to meet our needs more locally and look after ourselves once we can no longer rely on goods shipped halfway around the world, fuelled by cheap oil and with the carbon cost ignored.

Time banking has been shown to be a good way of building community feeling and involving more socially excluded members of our community.

Put next to our unemployed builders and unused building materials, time banking could be used to help upgrade our energy-inefficient homes, and to train more people in these valuable skills.

Paper currencies can work well for small, locally owned businesses that are able to get their supplies and make some of their sales locally, or where the proprietors are able to spend small amounts of local currency on their day-to-day needs. They can generally give out small volumes of a local paper currency in change.

Deeper Transition

At present few businesses can handle large volumes of a local currency, as the things they sell are not sourced locally. The world we live in today is just too globalised and supply chains are too long. This is a structural barrier, a wall you will hit quite quickly. The objective is to develop more local production so this changes.

- Look at what your community's needs are, what its resources are, and think about what you are hoping to achieve with complementary currencies. Use the form of complementary currency that best suits your community and meets your objectives.

- Building on what has been done before, work out for yourself what's best for your community.

- Given the above, don't go too far the other way. Don't think like a tree and try to slavishly impose any single model upon your community. Think spots of oil (see 'Path dependency' and 'lock in' box, page 23). Tweak the designs, mix and match, to fit local conditions. Then, as the model develops, let it go where it wants to go. You might come up with something completely different that we can all learn from.

- Remember the 'Cheerful Disclaimer' (see Foreword) – this is an experiment. We don't yet know if it will work.

Deeper Transition could be facilitated by using local currencies to build a more localised economy where more of the things we need and use every day, including food and power, are produced locally. Loans in local currencies could help develop local production.

Long term, new models of special-purpose currencies could be developed to fund new locally owned cooperatives providing community power generation and local food production.

Long term, a monoculture of money is not resilient. A well-functioning, respected local currency network that is rooted in our local community and economy could be a useful insurance policy. We are lucky in that some local currency schemes now have fifteen to twenty years' experience, and are accepted parts of the local scene. We can learn what works and what doesn't from experience, not just basing our ideas on hopes or declarations of what 'should' be. We are not working in the dark any more.

Some Cheerful Financial Disclaimers

Do not assume, in advance, that a local currency is a necessary component of your Transition strategy without being clear about what you want to use a local currency to achieve. It could be that a resilient local economy can be developed using the forms of money we already have, mobilised by new institutions such as local banks or credit unions, or through issuing local bonds. The involvement of local councils and other agencies will be necessary here. In the long term, a community that does not control its own money will never be truly resilient, but you can do a lot in the short term using the money we have in interesting ways.

You can also get a long way by just sharing the things you have, without using money at all! Some people object to bringing money into relationships built on trust and sharing.

In matters of money, 'here be dragons'. There are crooks out there, and peddlers of quick fixes. Remember that if community-based exchange in a LETS or time bank goes belly-up, it's not the end of the world. But don't play games with someone's business, with their livelihood. Running a business is hard, and a brave thing to do. Respect and listen to local traders, and don't make things more difficult for them than they are already, especially in a difficult economic climate.

$$1 $$1

48.50.N **SALT SPRING ISLAND** 123.30.W

www.saltspringtoday.com

ONE DOLLAR

*"How I wish that somewhere there existed an island
for those who are wise and of good will! In such a place
even I would be an ardent patriot."*

Albert Einstein

Henry Wright Bullock
1866 — 1946

BU   00320

Date of Issue   Sept. 15, 2001
Expiry Date   Dec. 31, 2003

Robert McGinn   *Eric Booth*

ISSUED BY THE SALT SPRING ISLAND MONETARY FOUNDATION

PROMISE TO PAY HERE TO
BEARER ON DEMAND

GRAPHICS: WARREN LANGLEY PAT WALKER   © 2001 SALT SPRING ISLAND MONETARY FOUNDATION

ONE   ONE

50 FIFTY
BERKSHARES

NORMAN ROCKWELL 1894-1978

MONEY
WELL
SPENT

FOR PURCHASE OF GOODS AND SERVICES
FROM PARTICIPATING BUSINESSES IN THE BERKSHIRE REGION

PART ONE:

THE JUSTIFICATION

"The process by which banks create money is so simple that the mind is repelled." **John Kenneth Galbraith**

"If you want to know what God thinks of money, just look at the people he gave it to." **Dorothy Parker**

"Lack of money is the root of all evil." **George Bernard Shaw**

"A bank is a place where they lend you an umbrella in fair weather and ask for it back when it begins to rain." **Forest E. Whitcraft**

"Only when the last tree has died and the last river been poisoned and the last fish been caught will we realise we cannot eat money." **Cree Indian Proverb**

"Money can help you to get medicines but not health. Money can help you to get soft pillows, but not sound sleep. Money can help you to get material comforts, but not eternal bliss. Money can help you to get ornaments, but not beauty. Money will help you to get an electric earphone, but not natural hearing. Attain the supreme wealth, wisdom, and you will have everything." **Benjamin Franklin**

CHAPTER 1

THE MONEY WE HAVE

If we are to transition our local economies and provide new ways to make a living that do not cost the Earth, money will become more central to the process. I hope this book will be a resource to help us understand how money works, and what makes good and bad money. Perhaps the place to start is to ask: Why bother? Why set up a local currency? What's wrong with the money we have now?

If you have enough, probably nothing is wrong, and the money we have isn't going anywhere anytime soon. Complementary currencies are complements to, not replacements for, the money we have. As we see in more detail later, to use a complementary currency you don't have to have a critique of money at all. Many people can and do see them as a way to help others out and use their skills. Many businesses see them as just another promotion, as a way to get footfall through the door. They don't see complementary currencies as a tool for building resilient localised economies as a response to peak oil and climate change.

You can also, of course, opt to do good things with the money you have. You can invest in and buy ethical products; spend it with sustainable and local businesses. You can avoid spending money with unethical or exploitative businesses, or on environmentally damaging products or things produced under oppressive working conditions. The money we have could work better.

But as long as there is grinding poverty next to extreme wealth, financial crises that destroy livelihoods and ruin lives, and needs being unmet even though we have the skills and resources to meet them, it's hard to argue that everything is rosy and the type of money we have today can't be improved upon. It has its problems.

Money is artificially scarce

Conventional thinking has it that the basic problem of economics is: how do we decide between competing demands in a world of unlimited wants and desires and deep, engrained problems, given finite resources – including money? Would it be better, Bjorn Lomborg[1] argues, to spend our limited amounts of money on fixing malaria now and leaving climate change to richer future generations? Nicolas Stern,[2] writing for the UK government, argues pretty conclusively that the costs of doing nothing about climate change seriously outweigh the costs of doing something. It is a debate about priorities.

Perhaps it's a false debate. Lomborg and Stern both assume that the argument is about how to allocate money between competing options, when money is a limited resource. If we spend it on climate change, they argue, we can't spend it on solving malaria. There are two possible responses to this.

First, at times, we solve our problems before worrying about whether we have enough money – times of war or emergency, when we go into hospital with a life-threatening problem, or when the banks fail. The UK health service does not depend on our ability to pay when we turn up at a hospital. Given the extreme severity of the climate crisis, we should be doing all we can to solve it, not being limited in our response by the amount of money we have in the first place. That's what our leaders did when they had to bail out the banks – they created millions and millions of new pounds and dollars at the touch of a button.

Secondly, this way of thinking sees money as a 'thing', not a relationship or a tool for measurement. Money is seen as a stack of coins. It needs to be *there* before we can spend it. This view does not see money as a way to lubricate the exchange of what really matters: our time, skills and resources. Money is not a 'thing' but a relationship with a 'thing'; with our knowledge and ingenuity. It is limited only by the amount of knowledge, ingenuity and resources we have.

Money that is more like knowledge and ingenuity is something we can all share and use to help to cultivate and grow the world we want to see. We *all* have knowledge and ingenuity. It's not limited. My knowledge and ingenuity is not at your expense: we both have it, and can use it again and again. Why don't we develop forms of money that work this way? Of course, this does not mean that we can just print money seen as a 'thing' willy-nilly. We can only create as much as we need to enable us to do the things we want to do. If we print too much, out of proportion with our skills and resources, it would be just waste paper that most people would not take seriously, and it would not solve our problems. But we should see money as a way of facilitating the work we need to do to solve our problems using the resources we have, not a 'thing' we need in advance that limits us.

Problem: Although we don't always have the money we need, we can't just print it willy nilly. It would be worthless.

Solution: We need to concentrate on whether we have the labour power and the (non-financial) resources we need to solve our problems and meet our needs, not on whether we have enough money in the first place. Money should facilitate our lives, not dominate them. We should have forms of money that people back with their time, knowledge and resources, rather than waiting for governments to create the money we need first.

We are not in charge of it

Money is a central part of our life, but we are not in charge of it. The amount of money in the economy, how it is regulated, and who has access to it is controlled by an elite of private bankers and politicians, and this gives that elite huge power to enrich themselves and control the rest of us. Beginning in the seventeenth century, ordinary people were forced off the land, where they met their own needs, into the hell of the early factory system. In many places in the global South this is still the case: people leave the countryside to go to work in poor conditions to make the cheap goods that we in the North benefit from. Sometimes they go willingly; sometimes they have little choice.

Even in the global North, we are not free. The need to earn money to feed and warm ourselves and pay our bills means we still have to take jobs that we might not like. We may have to work for low pay and in poor environmental conditions. We don't have a free choice in how we live our lives while we are compelled to earn money in its current form, a limited resource controlled by someone else. Given that money should just be a way of lubricating trade, of measuring, this is unfair and unjust. Why do we put up with it? Having no control over a key part of our economic health is not wise. A central part of resilience is controlling those factors that affect us. We should have democratic, not elite money.

> **Problem:** We are forced to take jobs we might hate to earn money.
>
> **Solution:** We need money that we create, to meet our needs in ways we find fulfilling.

Money rewards people in grossly unfair ways

Some people earn a phenomenal amount of money, while others have the choice of going hungry or working very long hours for low pay. Why does the money system value some people so highly, when their work might not add that much to human happiness – for example, the bankers who developed the complex financial vehicles that regularly get us into financial crises? Why is hard manual work, care work and childcare so poorly paid? Why do women, younger and older people generally earn less than middle-aged men?

> **Problem:** We are not treated equally.
>
> **Solution:** We need money that rewards people fairly for the work they do. This is a key argument, particularly for time money (see Chapter 6).

We value money too highly

We need to see money as a way of making sustainable, convivial, enjoyable livelihoods possible, not an end in itself. The parable of the talents suggested that money should be used for production, for good – not seen as a commodity itself. Worshipping money, we put it before happiness. We are on a consumption treadmill, which is carbon-intensive and built on cheap oil. People often do not have time for each other, for their families, or for their children. We need money that lubricates real production, not something that we covet for itself.

> **Problem:** We value money too highly and it makes us unnecessarily competitive.
>
> **Solution:** We need a more convivial form of money that helps us live at the pace we want to, earning the living we want to. We don't want to have to chase after money, or to covet it. We need to see money as a tool, not something of value in itself.

Issuing too much money – or too little

In the Great Depression, bank after bank crashed as those in charge of the economy believed that prices must be allowed to fall to their 'natural' market level. 'Liquidate, liquidate, liquidate,' those in charge of the economy said. The result was that too little money was issued, and the economy collapsed.

In contrast, in the 1970s across the Western world many economists felt that *too much* money was printed, causing inflation. F. A. Hayek, Mrs Thatcher's inspiration, consequently argued that the creation of money should be privatised, put in the hands of what he called 'men (sic) of a conservative temperament' rather than 'profligate politicians'.[3]

It is thus no coincidence that the Depression saw an effervescence of 'soft', unbacked paper 'scrip' currencies designed to encourage people to spend them. At the other end of the scale the inflationary 1970s saw the development of 'hard' alternative currencies backed by baskets of locally valued commodities. These were hard currencies designed to maintain their value. When should you use a soft currency, and when should you use a hard one? What is 'too much' money, and what is 'too little'?

We want to develop currencies in enough quantities that we can solve our problems using them. Money needs to be seen as a lubricant that helps things happen. But we don't want unlimited, 'waste paper' or 'monopoly' money that just loses value.

How on Earth do we get the balance right? Central bankers get this wrong all the time, which is why Mervyn King, Governor of the Bank of England, once commented that managing the UK's money supply is like 'driving with only a rear view mirror'. It can take months for changes in the money supply to affect the 'real' economy.

Problem: How much is 'enough'?

Solution: This is a hard one. The only solution is to constantly review how our money system is working by talking to people who use it, watching prices, and monitoring how much money is in the system. We need to issue the money in predictable, transparent and logical ways, with the consent of those who use it. Don't issue money arbitrarily, informally, or behind closed doors. That way we can have a democratically controlled form of money that we can fall back on if (or more likely, when) politicians and bankers mess up the economy again.

Usury is fundamentally unsustainable

When we lend money out at excessive levels of interest, we are living off unearned income and force the economy to grow unsustainably. While economists will argue that interest is a payment for the use of someone else's money so you can do now what you would otherwise have to wait for, or compensation for accepting the risk that you might not get your money back, for others the amount of interest paid is out of all proportion to the value gained from using someone else's money.

Credit cards and mortgages for those who cannot afford to pay them back, who regularly miss payments and pay penalties, are hugely profitable for the finance companies. The last thing they want is the person who always meets their payments, who pays off the credit card in full each month. Some citizens' organisations are therefore campaigning for rates of interest to be legally limited to 8 per cent.

Why should someone setting up a new business, which might be of great social value, have to bear all of the risks of the business failing, *and* pay interest on a loan to set the business up? The person making the loan wins twice – if the business works out he gets his interest; if it doesn't, he gets his interest. A failed business can leave the entrepreneur with a debt and no income. A community and its citizens should take collective responsibility for the sort of businesses and livelihoods it wants to see.

Worse, high rates of interest and climate change don't mix. As charging interest means that you need to earn more money than you borrowed to pay back the interest, then you must grow your business – and the economy inevitably grows as a result. It seems hard to reconcile this with the need to cut carbon emissions by at least 80 per cent by 2050. Interest and a steady-state economy are incompatible.

> **Problem**: Interest and sustainability don't mix.
>
> **Solution**: We need sustainable, zero-interest (or at least very low interest) forms of money. Interest should at best be a small fee for using someone else's resources, not a means to super profits or a way to live off your money. The long-term rationale for the new local currencies is to get to a stage where they are all seen as normal parts of the economy that we control. We can then make loans at no interest in our currency to support the sort of businesses we want to see in our community.

Money leaves our communities – and we can't spend it again

If I go and buy my food from a supermarket chain, the money I pay mainly goes straight off to head office. Some of it will stay local – money for wages, local taxes and locally sourced produce. But most of it will leave. Once it leaves the area, we lose it.

If I buy locally produced food at a locally owned shop, farmers' market or co-op, it is more likely to circulate locally again and again. Lots of people can get a living from the same money re-circulating around our community many times – what economists call a 'local multiplier'.

Now you may argue that money that flows out of our community isn't a problem if it flows to another community and benefits them. One community's outflow of money is a resource for another community.

But the point is that national or international money flows to where it makes the greatest profit, not where it is most needed. Scaled up, whole countries and economies can be destabilised by international financial speculation or by irrational herd behaviour on the part of money markets. We need to control where our money flows to, not assume that connection is always good. If the connections are mutually beneficial and do not involve the emission of too much carbon, we keep them. The point is, we have a choice over when our money stays, and where it goes.

> **Problem**: Money leaches out of our community.
>
> **Solution**: We need money that circulates locally.

www.pluggingtheleaks.org has a toolkit for communities to conduct their own 'PTL' workshops, including slides.

... why not do without money completely?

So – money has its problems. We can do better. So why not do away with it completely, and just share? This has been the dream of anarchists and socialists for years – a society based on pure cooperation.

In practice, however, we find that people have different wants, needs, skills and time to share, and that these needs are not always compatible – and we discuss this 'incommensurability of wants and needs' next. Money is useful as it helps lubricate exchange in a world characterised by difference.

Understanding this helps us design forms of money that work better than those we have, and facilitates the development of more convivial and resilient low-carbon local economies. But not all forms of money work as well as others. If we are to design and use our own forms of currency and avoid mistakes, we need to spend a little time thinking about what money is, how it works, and who can and cannot successfully issue it.

When times are hard, people find ways to help each other out. An alternative currency market in Buenos Aires, Argentina.

CHAPTER 2

WHAT IS MONEY – AND CAN WE CHANGE IT?

Imagine we are at a Transition skills-share event, and I have brought along an old chair I don't need that I would like to be re-furbished and reused. You have brought along some homemade pasties. They smell and look so good, and have been ethically produced from local ingredients. As I'm feeling hungry I'd love to buy one. But neither of us have any money. We need to exchange a chair for a pasty.

But you don't need a chair. If you did need a chair, how do we decide how many pasties should be exchanged for a chair? I only want one pasty, so paying a whole chair for one pasty is a bit steep. You would rather buy some of the cards that Jayne is selling, but she doesn't want a pasty. What if you don't want to buy anything this week, but might next week – but you also know that next week you won't have time to make any pasties to take to the next swap? Unless we all think 'to hell with it' and just share, exchange based on barter alone breaks down very quickly. We are all sunk by what economists call 'the incommensurability of wants and needs'.

To get over this, we need a token of some sort that helps us to measure the value of the things we wish to exchange, break down the measurement into exchangeable units, and if we have no wants today, store these valuable tokens for the future. We need money.

The economist W. S. Jevons[1] said that the best form of money should have all of the following characteristics.

- Portability (I can carry it around)
- Indestructibility (it lasts into the future)
- Homogeneity (I can exchange my money for yours easily)
- Divisibility (we can use it to count)
- Cognoscibility (we can understand it)

If I had one great big brass coin, 20 feet wide, weighing a ton, it would be indestructible, homogeneous (if other people also had a big coin) and cognoscible, but it would not be portable or divisible. How can I buy a pasty with a one-ton coin? As I can't lift it, it's not portable. But I can safeguard my wealth very well with a one-ton coin – or a block of gold. That's one reason why so many people buy gold or wear gold jewellery.

At the other extreme, a tub of ice cream would be divisible (provided that the scoops were uniform), but how many scoops do I need to buy a car? Assuming we could find a way to divide ice cream into cars (which is a struggle in itself), we would need quite a large amount of ice cream, which would not be portable. It would melt, so it can't safeguard my wealth, and it's hard to work out values in scoops so it's not cognoscible. We would laugh if someone tried to pay us in ice cream, unless we had a very large freezer and liked a lot of ice cream!

But, if you had an economy in crisis, where people are worried about the future and save rather than spend, melting money (which you have to spend or it's gone) might make sense. This is why the money reformer Silvio Gesell proposed *demurrage*. Not quite melting, but certainly 'rusting' money. Transition Stroud has developed a local currency based on a German model that loses value if it's not spent (see Chapters 9 and 13). This is money like ice cream!

> Money should therefore be:
> * a means of exchange
> * a unit of measurement
> * a store of value.

Money should bear some relationship to concrete things, to 'stuff'. I need to know that I can go and buy something useful with my money or I can get someone to work for me with it, otherwise it's just a piece of monopoly money or a metal disk. I need to know that it is divided into small enough units to let us assess the value of, say, a pasty as two units, and a chair as fifty. And I need to know that if I don't want a pasty today, I can sell my chair, get money, and in the future can spend it.

In other words, money needs to have, for want of a better word, 'moneyness'. I need to have confidence that I can exchange, measure and store value with it. It needs to be seen as valuable, so we use money with intrinsic value in the form of precious and rare metals, or we design a piece of paper so it looks important, and is protected from counterfeiting so others can't just print a load of it off themselves. It needs to have an elusive characteristic of 'valuableness'.

This, then, is money. Seems simple enough. Can we use these principles to design better forms of money, or is the form of money we have that which has won out in the historical battle of ideas? Is the money we have the best there is, and is anything else a step backwards? Can other people create different forms of money?

We can untangle this if we delve a little bit more into how economists and others have thought about money. Thinking a little more about how money works helps us understand how we can design better forms of money as part of the Transition process.

Where does money come from?

People have thought about where money comes from in a variety of ways.

* Is it just 'out there', has always been 'out there', and we have to work with what we have inherited, even if it isn't perfect? Or can we make it anew?

* For some, money evolves over time and we can develop new forms of money as part of this process. You and I, or our community, are just as competent in doing this as anyone else. Others argue that money should be related to limited and valuable commodities, or is created by states, so our power to create it is more limited. 'They' can do it because they control the commodities that give it value. 'We' don't control those commodities, so we can't create forms of money that anyone will take seriously.

* Some say that money controls us; others say it sets us free; while a third group argues that we are very good at differentiating between situations where money is useful and where it is illegitimate.

If we understand these debates, we can create better forms of money and avoid mistakes.

In this chapter I mainly use what I regard as reputable academic sources to explain how money has come about. Any search of the internet will provide you with many, many alternative, perhaps more radical, views about the nature of money. But remember that in the realm of money, conspiracy theories and snake-oil salesmen abound. Personally, I find some of these more esoteric ideas interesting and fun, but they are not a solid basis on which to build a real alternative to our unsustainable world.

For reasons that will become clear later, if you are going to use the ideas in this book to set up a local money scheme it's best to be a little conservative (with a small 'c') in your thinking about what sort of money you and your community can create – even if you are using the new forms of money for radical ends.

> "The propensity to truck, barter and exchange one thing for another is common to all men, and to be found in no other race of animals." **Adam Smith**

Money evolves over time

Adam Smith,[2] often regarded as the father of economics, saw money as a 'natural' tool that has evolved over millennia as a result of characteristics inherent in humans. For Smith, humans are social beings who trade with each other to get what they need – no other species does this. Money evolved to facilitate this innate tendency in humans.

The Chinese started with cowrie shells, and the Lydians minted the first coins. Many different tokens, objects and metals were tried out and discarded – markings on clay tablets, shells, tobacco, furs, coins,

precious metals – in a process of evolution that led to today's paper money. The form of money we have today is that which has won the evolutionary battle. In this view, any other form of money would be a 'backward step.'

> "Man is an animal that makes bargains: no other animal does this – no dog exchanges bones with another." **Adam Smith**

Others would argue that the money we have is just its latest, imperfect incarnation. It's not the optimum, fully evolved form of money. Evolution has not stopped. We can still do better.

If money is constantly evolving, then community-based currencies might be the next innovation in forms of money, along with air miles, store 'points' or carbon credits. Who uses a chequebook now we have debit cards? Might paper and coin money soon have had their day? Companies such as Mondex are trialling completely electronic forms of money. The evolutionary school, then, would say that there is nothing set in stone about money – in fact innovation and evolution are key to money's continuing success. It changes over time, and can change again as we move to a post-carbon economy.

> "This is completely neutral – a bank account . . . like store budget vouchers or air miles. If we can say to people, 'have a card that saves you cash', do we have to educate them, morally? No. Do they have to understand the system? No. They have to understand that it's saving them cash, and if they understand that, they're happy, and I'm happy."
> **LETS designer Michael Linton**

Commodity money

The commodity money approach[3] argues that this evolutionary process was not open, as forms of money that are related in some way to 'stuff', or commodities, are intrinsically better than others. The best form of money is a universally exchangeable but by its very nature scarce commodity, like gold, that acts as a *proxy* for and a method of valuing other less easily exchangeable and more commonplace commodities (cars, chairs, ice cream, DVDs).

Gold is believed to be one of the world's most valuable commodities. There is a limited amount of it in existence, it does not tarnish, and it can be melted down into coins for exchange or ingots for storing value. Jewellery made from it looks nice, and wearing it is a good way to display your wealth and status. This is why it is more attractive than any other commodity. Given, in this way of thinking, that people will always want gold, the likelihood that it can be exchanged for any other commodity in the future is increased. Will I trade my car for ice cream, or gold? A no-brainer.

Commodity money can be the commodity itself (a gold coin), or a token that I can exchange that acts as a proxy for that commodity (for example, a pound sterling banknote issued when Britain was on the Gold Standard). If I so choose, I can take the proxy and get the real thing by taking my pound sterling banknote to the Bank of England.

The 'commodity school' argues that money unconnected to a scarce resource, for example paper money, can easily be over-issued, so there is too much money about in comparison with the goods and services in the economy. The result is hyperinflation.

Of course, the other side of the coin is that if the supply of the precious commodity that money is made

from increases faster than the supply of goods and services you can buy with it, again, you get inflation. We saw this when the Spanish began shipping the gold and silver of the New World over in the sixteenth century, and again in the nineteenth century when South African silver was discovered. You are left with a symbol that you *think* is intrinsically valuable but that is actually disconnected from what really matters, the 'real' economy of goods and services. The Spanish found out the hard way that finding more gold does not necessarily make you more wealthy, even if you have rooms full or shiny, beautiful objects to look at. You can't eat gold or power a machine with it.

The important argument here is that money *should* be limited; that printing paper money is potentially dangerous if too much is issued. The commodity school would argue that if a Transition Initiative issued its own money at irresponsibly large volumes the result would be inflation, loss of confidence in the currency, and 'Gresham's Law' whereby 'bad money drives out good'. People would save their sterling or dollars and try to spend the new 'funny money', and the supply of valuable money would dry up. People holding this view on money might well automatically reject what they see as naive and outlandish ideas, especially if they are perceived to have come from the 'alternative' community.

Advocates of commodity money argue that it should therefore be backed either by a valuable commodity like gold, or by being linked directly to a hard currency that is backed – for example, Argentina's currency in the 1990s which was 'pegged' to the US dollar, or BerkShares or Transition Pounds, which are backed by national currency held in a bank account.

On one hand, the implications of this are not good for Transition:

- If money must be limited to have value then it might not be possible to issue the amounts of money we would like to in order to meet our needs. All we would do is set off inflation.

- If money is connected to scarce resources held by others outside our community – for example, gold – then we can exchange that money for a more local variant, but we would not be able to produce our own currencies in large quantities.

Alternatively, we devise another form of backing:

- Our time and our commitment to do work in the future (the backing of personal credit money such as LETS and time money), or

- Commodities in the form of resources that better represent the value of local ecosystems. As we will see, there have been proposals for alternative forms of commodity money – the 'constant' valued against a bucket of local resources such as wood, corn or oil, or the energy-backed kilowatt hour (see Chapter 16 for more details).

But the message of the commodity school is that if you just create money not linked in some way to 'stuff' that we actually need, all you do is kick off inflation. It needs to be backed with 'stuff', time or labour. You don't need to be a Thatcherite to accept this – it is pretty much common sense. But it is surprising how much common sense is ignored!

Money as belief or 'credit'

"All money is a matter of belief." **Adam Smith**

"The judicious operation of banking, by substituting paper . . . (for) . . . a great part of gold and silver . . . provides . . . a sort of wagon-way through the air." **Adam Smith**

Advocates of 'credit money' argue that we have gone beyond commodity money, which is too limited a form of money. If we don't have enough of the commodity that we use as money, then we cannot do what we need to do. We no longer accept this restriction on our ability to create wealth and solve problems.

The Spanish thought they were wealthy because of the immense wealth they dug out of the 'silver mountain' at Potosi. When they set up the world's first banks the Florentines developed a different conception of money – credit money – which the United Provinces (present-day Netherlands and Belgium) then used to finance their war of liberation against Spain. The Dutch did not have the gold they needed to wage the war, so they issued 'promises to pay' – promissory notes which evolved into bank notes – to buy the weapons they needed. By the end of the eighteenth century, this idea was formalised for the first time by Britain's Dutch king, William of Orange, in the fractional reserve system operated by the Bank of England,[4] while gold-rich Spain went into a long decline. Spain never regained the pre-eminence it had in the sixteenth century, despite all its gold.

The Florentines and the Dutch invented the idea that money does not have to be discovered and then dug up and minted: it can be created in the form of bank loans. We can create money and thereby create wealth, not just divide up the money and wealth that already exists in different ways. We can issue a note promising the bearer of that note that when they come back to the bank they can get gold. People can use these pieces of paper to pay each other without anyone ever having to go to the bank to get the gold. If they believe they can get the gold if they have to, they don't worry about it. The pieces of paper become valuable.

Consequently we no longer use gold as money, or even paper that we could exchange for gold as money. We use money that is just a piece of paper or disk of metal that has little or no intrinsic value beyond our confidence that we will be able to buy 'stuff' – useful commodities or services – in the future.[5] Our money is not based on a commodity but on a 'promise to pay' (i.e. to receive goods in the future) issued by a trustworthy institution. No commodity needs to exist before the money is issued, as long as whoever issues it is confident that one will exist when we want to buy something. Our confidence in credit money comes from our experience that this has always been the case, and that the money has been issued by a reliable source. The origin of the word 'credit' is *credo*, to believe; when something unexpected happens, we still say 'would you credit it!'

This is a more flexible form of money than the more limited commodity money, which Keynes called a "barbarous relic". A bank can create credit money by issuing loans and mortgages beyond the value of that held in its vaults in the form of savings, as long as it is sure that not everyone who has savings will come to get them out at the same time. If they do, they cause a bank run and the bank collapses.

This is the basis of the right of banks to issue new money, seemingly out of thin air, out of the money we deposit with them, and, crucially, out of the money we borrow from them in the form of mortgages, credit cards and loans. The banks call the money we have pledged to pay off the loan an 'asset' that they lend new loans against. They even buy and sell these assets, creating more money.

Much, but not all, of the money we use is created this way by the banks. And all of it is based on our trust that we will pay the debts back, and that at the end of the day we can get real 'stuff' for this credit money. When in 2007 the banks started to doubt the extent that these 'assets' really were assets, and began to doubt that people with sub-prime loans could be relied upon to pay them back, the whole system crashed.

> See the animated film *Money as Debt* for an enjoyable, if sometimes rather conspiracy-theory-laden, explanation of how credit money is created out of our deposits and debts.
> **www.moneyasdebt.net**

If banks can create money that others trust, so can other institutions or people, as long as *they too are trusted*. Do the people being asked to accept this money *believe* that they will, in future, be able to exchange it for real goods and services, and do their experiences back up this belief? As we see later, this is the secret of the success of North American scrip notes such as Ithaca Hours. 'Hours' are not backed with conventional currency (like BerkShares or the Transition currencies) or in any other way except by the trust and the experience of users that those responsible for issuing 'hours' are honourable people who will not over-issue them, and that they can buy what they want with 'hour' notes.

Is bank lending always wrong?

Some people have a problem with banks creating money to loan to us, but, if they don't charge extortionate interest, that's no bad thing. Frank Capra's *It's a Wonderful Life* celebrates American 'building and loan' associations, small-town banks that enable ordinary people to own their own homes.

When frightened members of the community start a bank run, local Building and Loan manager George Bailey tells them that their money has been lent out to provide them and their neighbours with good, affordable homes.

He tries to calm the mob by saying that all that will happen if they follow through on the run is that the rapacious local bank owner, Potter, will buy the Buildings and Loan at a knock-down price:

"You're thinking of this place all wrong. As if I had the money back in a safe. The money's not here. Your money's in Joe's house; that's right next to yours. And in the Kennedy house, and Mrs Macklin's house, and a hundred others. Why, you're lending them the money to build, and then, they're going to pay it back to you as best they can. Now what are you going to do? Foreclose on them?

Now wait . . . now listen . . . I beg of you not to do this thing. If Potter gets hold of this Building and Loan there'll never be another decent house built in this town. He's already got charge of the bank. He's got the bus line. He got the department stores. And now he's after us . . . he wants to keep you living in his slums and paying the kind of rent he decides.

Joe, you had one of those Potter houses, didn't you? Well, have you forgotten? Have you forgotten what he charged you for that broken-down shack? Here, Ed. You know, you remember last year when things weren't going so well, and you couldn't make your payments? You didn't lose your house, did you? Do you think Potter would have let you keep it?"

Bailey was imploring his fellow citizens to have faith, to *believe* that their money was safe. The problem we have is that the banks we have are more like Potter's, not the Building and Loan. When, in real life, the banks really did take over the Buildings and Loans and the Building Societies, they did hike interest rates, gave loans to people who could not pay them back, then foreclosed on them. We need more George Baileys and more local banks. This is discussed in Chapter 16.

Money, love and reciprocity

While Adam Smith saw money emerging through the 'natural' human desire to trade – through economics – sociologists see money as emerging through society or politics. Anthropologists Bronislaw Malinowski[6] and Marcel Mauss[7] examined gifts and potlatch as non-monetised forms of exchange and reciprocity through which the giver achieved status through their generosity. Mauss pointed to the prevalence of gifts and reciprocity in modern life in phenomena such as weddings, Christmas, valentines and get-well cards. Otherwise valueless objects, Christmas cards are fundamentally just pieces of paper, inscribed with value through the process of giving and the sentiments that inspired the act of giving. This is the other side of the coin from the conflict that can and does occur over money if I want to buy as much as I can and pay the lowest possible price, and you want to sell your products for as much money as you can.

This suggests that we can make otherwise valueless pieces of paper valuable if they are given as marks of love or respect, or to indicate that you are thinking of someone. Forms of local currency that celebrate the local community draw on this to give them value, as do names of currencies like 'thanks' or 'favours'. If the experience is that I can then exchange these tokens inscribed with love for other people's time and commitment, then love and the gift economy can, actually, make the world go round!

Money inscribed with love and reciprocity can help overcome a second 'incommensurability of wants and needs'. What if I need regular childcare, and don't like to ask for favours? What if I am old, and need someone to clean the house for me? Between lovers and families, we might not count favours too much. But what if you need nothing from me, and I need lots from you? We may care for each other, but you might get fed up and I might not want to ask. With money designed to foster feelings of love and reciprocity, we need not feel this way. Local money can be a symbol of reciprocity, of caring or of love, an acknowledgement or a 'thank you' – not a desiccated way of keeping score.

Money and freedom

Whereas some would argue that money is king, that those with money can dominate those without, and that more and more parts of our lives are being turned into something that can be counted and exchanged with money (commodified), the sociologist Georg Simmel[8] argued that the opposite is true. Having money makes us free, he argued, by liberating those that have it from social restrictions. If I pay for a service with money, the obligation ends there and then. I can be free to move on to the next exchange without being tied up in complex webs of favours or obligations.

For example, a peasant who is required by his lord to provide a bushel of wheat has to grow wheat, whereas a peasant who has to pay tax in money can make his livelihood as he sees fit, as long as he pays his taxes in money. In the UK, Henry VII (1485-1509) systematically started monetising what was previously a feudal system of obligations in which peasants had little use

for money. It was the start of the modern world.

Money, Simmel argued, is objective and fair. I do not need to like you to trade with you, I just need your money and my money is as good as yours. If I do not like someone I can take my money elsewhere, and this ability to change our relationships, lubricated by money rather than favours, hierarchies or obligations, makes us free. Social class, status, tradition and what we think of each other are all irrelevant clutter that can be cleaned out through use of money. Strangers can get what they need from each other if they can pay for it. We get what we need from a complex interdependence based on what people can do, not on their personalities, morals or status.

Simmel also saw money as a tool that allowed us to calculate the benefits and costs of different courses of action in our heads. Money is a token that enables us to apportion value and play 'what if' games in deciding what to do and get the best value from our transactions. In these analyses, then, money is a tool of modernisation and rationality.

When is money appropriate, and when inappropriate?

In contrast to Simmel, for Viviana Zelizer[9] money is diverse, not universal. Focusing on how people give value to and use money, she rejected it as tool for rationalisation and calculation to the extent that everything is turned into a commodity to be bought and sold, or 'commodified'. She accepted Simmel's arguments about the usefulness of money in helping us decide between options, but she also felt that this potentially harmful rationalising tendency is limited by people's ability to decide, for themselves, which parts of their life money is appropriate for, and which parts it is not. We do not just make a desiccated cost–benefit analysis in

A 'sympathetic critic'

Simmel's views are reflected in the following friendly critique of the Totnes Pound, reminding us that being able to spend your money where you want is one of our freedoms.

"Personally I may not be a great proponent of it, because for many years I was a collector of trade tokens which are a local currency . . . and the history of trade tokens was a way of keeping the workers down. The local mill would be issuing their own token because at certain times national coinage was hard to come by, so it was partly to fill the gap, but partly also as a way of restricting where their workers could spend their money. They could only spend it in the company shop and one or two other shops who got a rake off and so on.

So the introduction of a national currency to me was one of the greatest advances in freedom, allowing people to be free in what they did with their money. I think a national currency is a wonderful thing. I can sympathise with the principles of wanting to keep spending locally but . . . I say the other side of the coin is that it restricts what you can do with your money and I know from history it's not a good thing to do that." Douglas Cockbain, Arcturus Books, Totnes

deciding how we want to live our lives. Sometimes, using money is just not seen as appropriate. Some things can't be bought with it.

For example, can we buy love, give money as a gift, charge a hitchhiker for a lift? Would you go out for a romantic meal on a first date and insist on dividing the bill by exactly how much each of you had eaten, and give the object of your affections a crisp fiver to show how much you liked them? No – but why not, if money is universally accepted? It is because we do not allow money into parts of our lives where we think it is inappropriate. Money does not make us free, because you can't buy some things which can only be given freely. You can buy sex, or a show of intimacy, but not real intimacy, not love.

Money gained unfairly or illegitimately might be seen as tainted. It can be 'ill-gotten gains' or earned through 'honest toil'. It can come from currency speculation, or from investing in socially useful production. It can be earned fairly, or unfairly. How we think it has been earned affects how we see it. For example, does a church accept the mafia don's gift, knowing where it

came from? If I am against drinking or smoking, do I accept commercial sponsorship from a drinks or tobacco company?

We also don't give similar amounts of money the same value. We 'earmark' the money we get, with money earmarked for essentials – the rent or mortgage, food and to pay the bills – seen as more valuable than money earmarked for treats. If I have to forgo one of these pots, losing money for the bills would be a disaster; losing that for treats merely an inconvenience. Money, then, is not universal and all-conquering, but used for some things and not for others, and we all make our subjective choices about when and where it is appropriate to use money.

Three examples from complementary currencies illustrate this.

1. Many people who advocate complementary currencies say they want to put the relationships back into economic life. 'When I trade with someone, I want to have a relationship with them' they say. They want to reject the rationalising side

of modern life that Simmel liked, and see people they are trading with as people, not sources of commodities. But your wish for a relationship might not be reciprocated. What if the other person wants a quick, utilitarian trade so they can go off and do whatever it is they want to with their life? We can't assume everyone wants a relationship all the time. They might want the freedom *not* to have a long chat!

2. The second example concerns a single mother in a LETS scheme who wanted childcare. She got it, but found that half the time her babysitters did not bank the LETS cheques she gave them, or tried to refuse payment. They liked her and wanted to help her out, do her a favour. They didn't want payment for their favours, as they felt it was inappropriate. In contrast, she felt patronised, wanting to 'pay her way like everyone else does'. One person felt money would pollute a gift, while the other wanted the freedom to pay their way.

3. The third example is of a Steiner School in Gödöllõ, a small town just outside Budapest, Hungary. A group of parents were refurbishing the school. One of the parents got upset about what he regarded as the chaotic and inefficient way the work was being done. People turned up when they wanted, did what work they wanted to when they wanted to. Some people worked hard and efficiently, others slowly and convivially. He knew about alternative currencies and tried to introduce a currency scheme to quantify and 'clean up' what he thought was a chaotic and inefficient system. But everyone else felt that 'paying' them, even with an alternative currency, devalued their contribution. They preferred a more easy-going reciprocity, even if some people ended up overloaded or disappointed.

Zelizer had some insights that are useful here. She argued that money and friendship, love and sentiment were neither completely separate nor inextricably mixed. Paying with money is not completely different from sharing, giving, loving. Rather, she argued that any relationship will be based on a negotiated mixture of sentiment and monetary exchange.

Any household needs money to pay for food and pay the bills, but the work that goes into running the house will not be quantified. My wife and I do not pay each other to cook meals or do the laundry, and we don't charge the kids room and board. But money does flow through our relationship, not least as we don't own the house, grow our own food, or generate our own power. We need to remember everyone will have a different take on what to pay for and what to give freely, and a different conception of what is the right balance between the two.

> You load sixteen tons, what do you get
> Another day older and deeper in debt
> Saint Peter don't you call me 'cause I can't go
> I owe my soul to the company store.
> *Sixteen Tons*, Merle Travis

Money, the State and society

To read some accounts of the role of money in the world, you would think that a coalition of bankers invaded Iraq in 2002, not the US and British governments. Obviously the relationships between corporate power and governments are complex, and beyond the scope of this discussion, but it needs to be remembered that at the end of the day our economies and the form of our money is decided on by governments, not by big business alone.

The Chartalist school of monetary analysis[10] therefore argues that the form of money is a political, not an economic, decision. Someone had to decide how to measure the value of different goods, how to quantify this 'valuableness', and how exchange should happen. Someone decided what the currency would be, and it was states that conferred the quality of *valuableness* on what emerged as money. Chartalists argue that this was states, not Adam Smith's businessmen.

Money emerged, Chartalists argue, not from an inherent tendency to trade, but from states. Some forms of money emerged from communal, Celtic and Gothic tribal societies as *wergeld*, a way of quantifying 'worth' when making compensation for wrongs, insults and injuries. When the English paid Danegeld, a bribe to stop the Viking marauders, the price was calculated in *wergeld*. Other forms of money were created by emperors and kings, who put their images on coins as symbols of their power. They stipulated how the coins should be denominated. Later, money was established by states to facilitate long-range trade, to gain control of national territory, to raise taxes to pay for wars, and for collective goods (roads, bridges, hospitals, lighting). This is why money generally circulates within nation states rather than in economically determined spaces.

Money thus has a political and cultural history that gives it value, which is hard to recreate. This is something obviously true of old currencies such as the pound sterling or the US dollar, but also true for newer currencies such as the Euro, which is legislated for and backed by the European Union. Money, along with stamps and a flag, is used to create national consciousness, and that is why feelings are so high about money as a symbol of national sovereignty. For this reason, it seems unlikely that the British people will give up attachment to their pound.

Against this, while it is true that just about every state has its own form of money (national symbols remain even on Euros), and therefore thinking about money without considering the State seems inconceivable, it is also true that while states can legislate about the form of money, people will actually use it only if it fits with deeper social and economic realities. States can legislate that the legal tender in the UK is the pound, but not how much a pound is valued; how many bolts of cloth a pound buys. Consequently, while states may declare what money people must pay taxes in, they cannot give it value or ensure that everyone will use it.

Where the money-legislating power of the State is weak, for example in contemporary Argentina where the provinces have the right to create their own currencies, and the national State does not have a good track record in producing money that works, state-issued money might be ignored or replaced. In the former Yugoslavia in the 1990s, for example, no one trusted Serb, Bosnian or Croat money, so everyone used German marks. In turn-of-the-century Ecuador, the US dollar replaced the national currency. In border areas, the national currencies of two or more states might circulate just as easily as each other.

Some would argue that international financial crises and speculative currency markets suggest that nations no longer fully control the nature of money in their territory. Currency market traders / speculators can spectacularly bet against national currencies, as incidents such as the UK's ejection from the European Exchange Rate Mechanism in 1992 graphically show. Long-term trends in the growth of international capital markets disconnected from real production, and the growth of international forms of currency such as the Euro and dollar suggest that the era of national domination of money – if it ever existed – is over.

The question then arises as to the extent to which the end of State monopolies of money creation opens up space for others to create new forms of money – or whether, in practice, only national states are trusted enough to give 'valuableness' to money and to enforce its acceptance. We will know the answer to this only when we have more experience of creating and using new forms of money than we have now. At the moment, we don't know. But we should not be too surprised when many people raise a quizzical eyebrow at the idea that anyone but a state can create real, serious money, and that it can be backed just by trust.

So what does this mean for Transition money?

1. Money has evolved over time *and can continue to evolve as new forms are designed. We can also design new forms of money.*

2. Money needs to enable us to get 'stuff' at some point – it needs to be related to a hard commodity *so we can back our alternative forms of money with conventional cash, or other, more useful commodities such as food or fuel.*

3. Money is a form of credit that we trust will enable us to get 'stuff' at some time in the future – as long as we experience this to be the case, we trust it even though it is not backed by anything more than trust. *As long as we don't over-sell what people can buy with alternative currencies, and do back it with our commitment to provide goods and services in the future, trust and confidence in an unbacked currency can be maintained.*

4. Money either gives us freedom, or is something that we make decisions about in our day-to-day lives. Our lives are a mix of connections; some involving money, some not. But we do not live lives where we keep money and sharing, caring and loving in different compartments. Different people will organise their lives in different ways. We need to be aware of this and respect people's choices. *What matters is not a perfect design for money, but what the person using it decides to do with it. The ghost in the machine, not the machine.*

5. Money is created by states, *states being trusted institutions. Other trusted institutions can create it as well – examples are supermarket loyalty cards and air miles. The trustworthiness, openness and integrity of the alternative currency system is paramount. Avoid the problem of overselling your currency, breaking trust, and looking like snake-oil salesmen.*

CHAPTER 3
LOCALISATION

We need to build more sustainable, resilient, localised economies where more of what we need is produced closer to home, not where it can be produced most cheaply. We can no longer assume that the price of oil will always be so low that it makes sense to make widgets in China and ship them around the world, ignoring the carbon emitted from long-distance travel.

If we are to build localised, more resilient economies for our communities we will need to engage with local businesspeople. To convince them, the arguments we will need to make will be different from those we might hear in a Transition meeting, made to the already convinced. We will need to talk about how reducing emissions and producing more locally reduces costs and boosts town pride.

We will also need to be able to meet objections – 'localisation sounds like protectionism, everyone knows that protectionism is bad' and 'but I don't buy anything locally, and sell all over the place'. This suggests that we need to know why localisation today is not like 1930s xenophobic protectionism, and that we need to be clear what we mean by 'local': do we mean our town, the county, region, within a hundred miles, the bioregion, or even the country?

Localising economies

First, let's revisit the arguments for localisation outlined in Chapter 1. If I spend my money in Asda, owned by Wal-Mart, the money I have just spent goes straight off to Wal-Mart's HQ in Arkansas, making the family that owns it exceedingly rich. True, some of it comes back, in wages for the store workers and for anything that Asda sells that is produced locally, but the majority of it leaves the local community. When we spend money in stores owned by someone who lives locally, and that sells things made locally, it stays local. It circulates round the local economy again and again, being spent many times over – what economists call a 'local multiplier'.

Against that there is a strong argument. Money that leaves one community provides an income for other communities – one community's output is another community's input – and if we are all equal and trade with each other on the basis of what we do best, then we can all be better off from so doing. We can't all pull ourselves up by our bootstraps, cut off from each other.

In reality, there are a number of problems with this. Money always tends to leach away from poorer, less well-endowed communities to the richer ones, so some communities always seem to win, and others always lose. The game is not fair. It's not the case that every community has something unique that they are good at or that they make that they can specialise in and trade with others. Some places are just poorer, less well-endowed. Can Mali really be expected to trade on an equal footing with New York? New York has global finance, while Mali has . . . sand. OK, Mali has some great world music, but you see the point. Mali always gets to lose; New York always gets to win. So, if you are one of the regular losers, you might want to stop the leaks, especially if the leaks mean that money leaches out of your poor community to a richer one.

The chaotic nature of the global 'casino' marketplace is another strong argument for localisation. Sometimes the global market loses confidence in a particular place, and the flow can turn into a flood, ruining a local economy overnight. Just ask anyone in a community that has lost its key industry! Or talk to someone in a country that the credit-rating agencies have declared a financial risk, and that the speculators have abandoned. We discuss this in more detail when we look at the situation in Argentina, in Chapter 8.

In *The Life and Death of Great American Cities*, Jane Jacobs[1] contrasted 'cataclysmic' with 'gradual' money. Cataclysmic money flows into communities, raising house prices and forcing out local people who can't afford the new prices. It can just as quickly flow out of communities, leading to slums and the destruction of jobs. In contrast, 'gradual' money stays in our communities and helps us to develop it. We need more gradual money, and less cataclysmic money.

Protecting your local economy

We look to the police to protect us from crime, the government to protect us from being invaded, and health and safety rules to keep us safe at work. For the same reason, we need to have some level of protection of our local economy. If goods are produced somewhere where employment and environmental standards are lower, wages are lower, hours of work are longer, levels of exploitation are higher, and the goods made are of poor quality, the goods will be cheaper. But this means that a poor employer or place with lower standards can undercut a better employer or a place where regulations and wages are higher. You get cheaper goods, but at what cost?

We outlaw child labour as it's immoral and bad for the community and the economy in the long run, even though we could have cheaper goods if children made them. We protect children from work, sending them to school. We don't expect them to compete in the labour market at the age of five – but we do at eighteen.[2] Citizens and communities need to decide what sort of businesses and standards they want, and support them.

It's a case of getting the balance right. Someone else may be just better at making something than you are, everything else being equal. It makes sense for you both to do what you are best at, to specialise. You both get better-quality goods, and work that you are good at and enjoy, provided the costs of transporting those goods does not cost the Earth. If we stopped people who make a real innovation from capitalising on it and selling it out of their locality, perhaps displacing an inferior local product in the process, we would cut out much of the innovation of the modern economy, including innovations that might help with climate change and resource depletion. We would protect lazy, backward, inefficient businesses producing inferior products just because they are 'local' – that does not make sense.

Against this, however, we must consider when a producer has an unfair, immoral advantage. They get their advantage by undercutting others and providing an inferior product produced in exploitative and unsustainable ways, driving the superior but more expensive product out of the market. You get a cheaper product, but at the cost of the bad employer and poor-quality product driving out the good. The two scenarios could not be more different.

Responsible local ownership

A third scenario recognises that decisions about what to make where are not made on a level playing field. If a business gets into difficulty, and its owners are based elsewhere, they can close it without having to see or suffer from any of the consequences of their decisions. My own city of Liverpool suffered terribly in the 1980s, as most of its industries were owned by people who did not live here. The city's elites all focused on global trade, and did not invest in their own city. When things got rough, they put thousands of people on the dole, ruining lives with impunity. Living elsewhere, they did not see

the consequences of their actions. Liverpool felt as if it had been abandoned.

If you live in the community that is affected by your economic decisions, you are more likely to act responsibly and be in it for the long run, not just try to maximise your profits in the short term and to hell with the consequences. Your neighbours will point out the error of your ways, and you will have to live in the environment you have created. There will be none of what economists call 'externalities' – problems that one business creates for which others have to pay the

Publicising Dunedin's 'Buy Local' campaign, Aotearoa/New Zealand.

cost, such as the packaging that supermarkets expect local authorities to dispose of.

Local money as information and feedback

In *Cities and the Wealth of Nations*,[3] Jane Jacobs explained that a national currency like the British pound, or even worse a continental currency like the dollar or Euro, means that a local economy does not have the economic tools it needs to manage its economic future, or respond to changing economic conditions.

The performance of the pound internationally reflects the overwhelming influence of the UK's 'elephant city', London, and its financial services. What works for London finance penalises, for example, Liverpool manufacture. In Jacobs' terminology, places like Liverpool became 'passive' economies 'jerked around' by energy emanating from elsewhere. National currencies consequently provide fairly good 'feedback mechanisms' for stronger cities, allowing them to measure *their* economic health. Other, smaller, communities and regions need their own feedback mechanisms in the form of their own currencies that enable them to monitor the health of the local economy.

Regaining control of what jobs and businesses your economy has

If local economies had their own currencies that reflected local conditions, more jobs could have been provided to meet local needs by replacing imported goods (over which the community has no control) with goods it produces itself (and thus has control over). This is not a total replacement. A local currency might sit alongside trade. During the Middle Ages Hanseatic city-states all had their own currencies, but trade between them was still vibrant. Once a local economy begins to produce more locally it imports different things. Local currencies mean that imports are not based on price and low standards alone. It does not mean that a border post will be put outside every

locality, trade will be completely cut off, and inefficient businesses will be protected just because they are local.

Can the planet stand free trade?

Finally, the global vision of every community trading with every other community on the basis of what they each do best, so beloved of Adam Smith and free marketers,[4] makes sense only if transport is cheap and doesn't emit carbon. When oil is cheap, and carbon emissions are not counted, it might make sense to produce things all around the globe. But peak oil and climate change are bringing this era to an end, and we need to start to localise economies to cut avoidable carbon emissions. The high price of oil and the need to count, not externalise, carbon emissions will radically change the economics of where we choose to produce things. They will need to be produced much nearer to their market. Even Liverpool shipping agents I have spoken to understand this.

Really localising an economy, making it resilient, means making it possible for the average person to meet their daily needs – for food, power, shelter and entertainment – locally. That means involving local businesses and developing local production by proactively substituting things that are made elsewhere, and transported around the world in unsustainable ways, for things that are made and sold in locally owned and controlled businesses, markets and cooperatives. This is the localised economy. But if things can be exported and imported in ways that do not entail unsustainable levels of emissions and fuel consumption, then trade will continue. The balance will change, but trade will not cease completely.

Tracing production and consumption chains

One of the advantages of using a local currency is that it makes visible what is and, conversely, what is not being produced locally. Businesses that sell products that are not produced locally for local currency quickly find that they can't buy new stock with the local currency they have earned. They have to exchange it for national currencies, which rather defeats the point. The answer is to use a local currency to show you what sort of things you need to start to produce locally, and, once it is an accepted part of the local economy, use your local currency to finance the development of new forms of local production, thus strengthening the local economy.

This will take time, but unless we do seriously involve local businesses in the construction of a localised, resilient economy, then the extent to which we have genuinely taken our towns and communities through the Transition process can be seriously doubted. Just circulating things around our locality that are made elsewhere is not good enough. Consumers and businesses will soon stop using a local currency that can be spent in only a few places. Why use a currency that you can spend in only a few places when you can use universal currencies that can be spent everywhere?

What do we mean by ' local'?

I'm a geographer, so when people talk about a local economy, my first questions are 'But what do you mean by local?' and 'What's wrong with connections between places?'

The core of localisation is a claim that economic decisions should focus not on profit maximisation and economic efficiency to the exclusion of all else, but on meeting needs as locally as possible. Michael Shuman, author of one of the first books arguing for localisation, *Going Local*,[5] argues that localisation means producing as much as you can as locally as you can. If you can't produce things locally, produce them as close as you can to where they will be used. Produce as much as you can in communities, towns, cities and regions firstly, then in countries, or groups of countries. It is an

argument for economic subsidiarity – doing things at as local a level as makes sense.

It would not make sense, for example, to make wind turbines, hydroelectric power stations or solar panels in every small town. That should be done at a national scale, or even in a nearby country. For a business, 'local' might mean using inputs from Britain rather than China, and selling across the UK rather than globally.

It might still be OK for fair trade cooperatives in India to sell us tea, if it is shipped here on a new generation of tea clippers like the Cutty Sark. It would take a little longer to get here, but that's just a matter of logistics. But it doesn't mean that India should just sell us tea, and we just educate India's graduates. India should produce for India, selling us what it chooses to. The process should be controlled, and connections consciously entered into for the benefit of both parties. They are not inevitable and not always beneficial.

The benefits of local ownership and control

Localisation is less about specifying any particular definition of what is 'local', and what isn't, than about maximising control over our lives and minimising emissions and fuel use associated with transporting things around the world that we don't need to. Produce as much as you can locally.

A place that does not control its economy cannot agree to cut emissions and reduce dependency on oil if those are decisions made in a boardroom far away. For example, what control does a small town in the UK have over what cars are made in car factories owned by Ford, an American company? Can the London-headquartered multinational Hong Kong and Shanghai Banking Corporation, HSBC, credibly call itself 'the world's local bank'? How can a place that does not control its economy be resilient?

Localising a local economy does not mean an unconditional end to all connections with other places. Localisation is not autarkic, or xenophobic. No-one is arguing that we should build a wall around our communities, and keep everyone else out. Rather, localisation suggests that we should not assume that connections and globalisation are always inevitable and always good. Localisation rejects the conception, asserted all the time by politicians, that globalisation is like fire, a natural process, an inexorable process, and that anyone opposed to globalisation is looking to go back to 1930s protectionism or is a closet member of the British National Party. But, built on cheap oil and ignoring associated carbon emissions, globalisation isn't inevitable and connections are not always good.

Rather, connections to other places should be consciously entered into, controlled, kept when they are sustainable and beneficial, and ended when they are damaging. We might want to provide alternatives to mass-produced unsustainable cheap goods imported from China, produced under poor labour and environmental conditions. There is a reason why that T-shirt costs one pound. Perhaps that's a bargain we don't want to take advantage of, just as we would not knowingly buy something produced by slaves or send small children to work in cotton factories in the UK. But we would be happy to trade on an equitable basis with communities around the world who can benefit from such trade and want to enter into it, where transport can be undertaken sustainably.

Localisation starts with an understanding that local diversity and local distinctiveness are good in and of themselves. We don't want to live in clone towns that all look the same, with the same shops that sell the same cheap, mass-produced goods. We want a say in what sort of businesses we want in our community, and a currency that does not leak out of it. If global trade means global sameness and the end of local difference, then we want to look after places which have a local distinctiveness worth defending.

Local resilience

Local economies should be diverse. People should make their livings in many different ways, not all work in one sector or firm. Economic monocultures are not resilient. In a company town everyone works for the same employer, which is boring but at least people have jobs. But what if that firm goes under? We saw the devastation that was visited in one-industry towns such as Britain's mining villages when the one source of employment goes. They are not resilient.

If people are employed by a range of businesses, employ themselves, work part-time, and produce more of the things they need themselves, the local economy is more likely to be resilient in the face of changes in demand or external shocks. If one part of the economy goes into decline or breaks down there are plenty of alternatives to take its place.

If places are *too* connected to each other and dependent on each other, problems in one part of the economy can be transmitted all around the world, seemingly instantaneously. We saw this in 2007-8 as problems that began with mortgages in America had repercussions all over the globe. If there were trips or breaks in the system that stopped money flowing in and out of communities at the flick of a switch, this would not be the case.

In the 1990s, when fans of globalisation argued for all countries to open themselves up completely to global trade with no restrictions on flows of money, countries such as Malaysia, which kept some measure of local control, fared better than those that were completely open when the inevitable financial crisis hit. As Jane Jacobs points out, if it's true for countries, it's true for local communities. We need the financial equivalent of electrical 'surge protectors'.

Developing local production

If we are just circulating goods made elsewhere around our community and are reusing and recycling things, we might feel good, but we are not really building a resilient local economy.[6]

To do that, we need to look at the goods and services our community needs, and the goods and services our community produces, and put them together. If we need something but currently needlessly pump tons of CO_2 into the atmosphere and burn fossil fuels importing it, we need to start replacing our imports with local production. If we are similarly exporting things that other communities could produce for themselves, then perhaps we need to replace what we export for things that we need locally. This is a well-known process of economic development, called 'import substitution'.

Sometimes clever people do come up with new products or invent new ways to produce things more cheaply, or to a higher quality, than anyone else. That's what we call entrepreneurialism, and it's what most people think drives innovation in the economy.

But if you examine how Japan developed its car or electronic industries, or how Latin America and China got any industry at all, it was by requiring that any business that wanted to locate there trained local people in new techniques, or by setting up their own companies to produce what they imported. If they hadn't done this, they would have stayed poor and continued exporting low-value primary goods to the rich North. It is how the global production system developed. But, as we know, this was an exploitative system that kept the poor poor and the rich rich. It was also built on cheap oil, and ignored carbon

emissions. Now we are at the end of the period of cheap oil, and need to count and reduce carbon emissions, we need to pull apart this global system by developing more local production.

There are two ways we can do this. We can't expect communities to have the resources or know-how to develop a windmill factory locally, so we could leave the development of a low-carbon local economy to the workings of the market. As businesses see the future, and adjust to carbon pricing and high fuel costs, they will start to move their production closer to where they sell their goods. This might happen, but we also know that the global market is a casino that seems to reward financial speculation above developing the new technologies that will address climate change and peak oil. We can't afford to wait. We have to work with local economic development agencies, councils and chambers of commerce, to *intentionally* relocalise the economy. For this, a local currency can be a great resource.

Practical considerations

That's the theory of localisation. A convivial localised economy is the objective that the Transition process aims to bring about. But what does this mean practically when you are thinking about what role local currencies might take in your Transition process? You will need to make a number of decisions.

Think about what you mean by 'local'

What is 'local' is a matter of negotiation between those who will use the currency, especially if you want to involve local businesses. It can't be imposed. Your moral, ethical, political or ecological conception of what is 'local' might not be the same as an economically sensible conception, given that we can't produce everything we need completely locally. Unless, of course, we plan to, or believe we will inevitably end up with, a much more simple way of life when the full impact of peak oil and the need to cut carbon emissions hits.

Irrespective of how you think the future will pan out, you need to consciously decide how widely your 'local' currency should circulate and what goods and services you hope to stimulate with it. Do you primarily want to share the skills and resources that your community already has? Do you want to involve local businesses? Do you want to actively and intentionally develop local production, so that far more of what we need is produced locally? The scale at which your currency circulates matters and depends on what you hope to achieve.

To some extent, how widely a currency circulates is a matter either for regulation or for the market to decide. If you have a currency scheme that you have to join, like a LETS or time bank, you can decide who is eligible and who isn't. You can stop people who are not local from joining. But if you have a paper currency, it's harder. You can't stop individuals from deciding to accept whatever form of money they want to accept. We discuss this in more detail when we examine what happened to paper currencies in Argentina (Chapter 8), and, more recently, in Brixton, when the national multiples wanted to accept the Brixton Pound (Chapter 14).

Think about your world view

People who use local currencies use them for very different reasons, and it is important to understand this.

Local money, or more money?

Transition Initiatives may want to set up specifically local currencies to strengthen local resilience and to help build a more localised currency that uses less fuel and emits fewer greenhouse gases. Some will be attracted to a local currency out of a political or ethic

commitment, specifically because they *are* local. They want money that stays local because their focus is sustainability, peak oil and climate change. They are happy to convert their pounds, Euros or dollars into a local currency, so their money doesn't leak out of their community. Their main focus is a currency that promotes localisation.

Others are attracted to the idea of complementary currencies because they don't have *enough* conventional money. Their focus is more on reducing poverty, or social justice. They want to be able to buy things they currently can't afford, and don't particularly care where they are produced. Millions of people in Argentina used alternative currencies in that country's crisis at the turn of the century, but they weren't all local currencies.

To maximise the number of goods and services circulating in your economy it might make sense to have a larger conception of the 'local' than the neighbourhoods that LETS or time money circulate within – perhaps a region, a bioregion, a US state, or a small country? Here we can look to Germany's regional currencies for inspiration (see Chapter 9).

People's money?

Some might be interested in alternative currencies because of their political views: they are socialists, eco-socialists, or anti-capitalists, or they don't like the hold that banks and finance have over our communities and livelihoods. Complementary currencies pay no interest on savings and demand none for loans. They are created by ordinary people, not banks and states.

For those with a focus on social justice the 'local' might not be so important – they are in favour of more international fair trade, especially trade in things that have a low carbon footprint and that are easily transported around the globe by internet or by sea without too high a carbon cost. They might even prefer to look after poor people and fair-trade businesses far away than comfortable people and exploitative local businesses that offer no observable benefit to the community. They might be attracted to ideas of rusting, interest-free money because rusting stops people making money from money. The Stroud cooperatively managed local currency (see Chapter 13) aims to engage with this debate.

Inclusive money?

Finally, some people use alternative currencies because they want to strengthen community feeling, so their conception of 'local' might be very local – a neighbourhood; a few streets. If a currency circulated in an area big enough for businesses, they might see this as too impersonal, too much like conventional, 'universal' money. Here, LETS or time money might make sense.

But it doesn't make sense to try to cover too large an area with a community-focused local currency, as in practice people won't travel too far for interpersonal exchanges. For example, Borders Exchange and Trading Scheme in Berwick, UK, has been going for eight years, but has recently relaunched on a more local basis as a result of concerns that the exchange had been trying to cover too large an area.

What do you want to be able to use your money for?

To some extent, this is a practical issue. If I want a babysitter or someone to help me paint a room, that person is likely to be local to me. You would not travel 10 miles, let alone 200, to babysit.

But what if I want to buy a wormery and the manufacturer, 200 miles away and still in my region, would be prepared to accept an alternative currency? Businesses might have a different conception of what is 'local' from communities. To get a diverse range of services available on your local currency network, and to get businesses circulating local currency amongst themselves, might mean that it would be better to settle for a wider conception of 'the local' than purists are comfortable with.

Decisions about how 'local' your currency is transmit messages about the 'valuableness' and 'moneyness' of your currency. A currency that circulates at a regional or national scale might be 'local' enough to cut emissions (when compared with global trade), while being attractive to businesses and thus enabling access to a wider range of goods and services.

A much more 'local' currency might be appropriate for community building and for small towns where a much more local form of resilience is the objective of your Transition Initiative.

As we discuss in Chapter 15, the solution might be a range of community currencies – LETS to build community feeling and unleash community skills, a time bank for the elderly and more vulnerable, and regional paper currencies to involve businesses in constructing more localised economies.

Now we understand the principles behind setting up a complementary currency, we can look at what has been done in the past, so we can build on experience.

Feeding The Swans
Watercolour by Carol Evans 1996

Date of Issue Sept. 15, 2002
Expiry Date Sept. 15, 2004

L$ 50

The Lewes Pound:
- **Supports Local Traders**
- **Keeps Money Circulating within Lewes**
- **Helps Cut CO2 Emissions**

For a list of participating traders and issuing points go to: **www.thelewespound.org**

For each Lewes Pound issued, 5p is pledged to support local projects. A 5p donation will apply from every Lewes Pound exchanged into sterling.

Supported by: Bill's, Harveys, Just Trade - Food Co-op, Lewes Town Council, Pelham House, Southern Solar and Transition Town Lewes

Transition Tow
LEWES

twenty one lewes pounds

21

Valid until: **31 August 2014**
© Lewes Pound 2009

PART TWO:
ALTERNATIVE CURRENCY
MODELS

"Those who have reflected on the nature of public revenue, and who possess minds capable of comprehending the subject, know that revenue has but one legitimate source: that it is derived directly or indirectly from the labour of man, and that it may be more or less from any given number of men (other circumstances being similar), in proportion to their strength, industry, and capacity." **Robert Owen**

"We have found that, especially in our area which is rural and contains many isolated villages, the scheme has built up a real community spirit. With little or no public transport those members offering lifts have been in great demand. We have a great need for such people as gardeners and handymen – as we all get older it is harder and harder to keep on top of the grass and weeds!"
Plume Local Exchange Trading Scheme, Malden, Essex

CHAPTER 4

A BRIEF HISTORY OF ALTERNATIVE CURRENCIES

Market economies such as ours can be creative, dynamic and resourceful, but they can also lose their collective nerve overnight. They go through cycles of boom and bust. Irrational 'herd behaviour' occurs when everyone does the same, perhaps daft, thing at the same time: 'sell, sell, sell', 'buy, buy, buy' echoes round the brokers' hall at the stock market. Bubbles are blown up and then burst.

Eighteenth-century financial bubbles and crises included speculation over tulips, the South Seas and Louisiana. In the nineteenth century, America saw bank crises in 1819, 1825, 1837, 1857, 1873 and 1893. In the twentieth century there were crises in 1901, 1907, 1921, 1929, 1973, 1980, 1987 and the big one starting in 2007. We saw recurrent problems in Latin America throughout the 1980s, such that that decade was dubbed the 'lost decade'. Mexico collapsed in 1992, Brazil in 1995, East Asia in 1997, Russia in 1998 and Argentina – spectacularly – in 2001.

It is worth exploring how people have responded to previous financial crises, as I think that what they did can teach us a thing or two. Before looking at a range of contemporary alternative currencies, let's spend a few moments examining lessons from the past so we can avoid other people's mistakes, and see further by standing on their shoulders. Think about what works, what doesn't, and what conclusions we can draw. Remember, though, as discussed in the Introduction,

to think spores and spots, not trees. We can examine what has been done in the past without becoming path-dependent.

Labour money: London, Birmingham and Liverpool, UK, 1830s

When capitalism was still young, Robert Owen showed that factories where the workforces were treated humanely were more profitable than those where they were exploited to the bone. He funded utopian communities in the USA that pioneered cooperative living.

During hard times in the 1830s, cooperative societies in London, Liverpool and Birmingham established Exchange Bazaars at which craftsmen facing destitution because they were unable to sell their goods on the open market could bring them to the bazaar and trade with each other using Labour Notes – money denominated in time. In 1832 Owen set up his famous 'National Equitable Labour Exchange' in rather splendid premises on Grays Inn Road, London.

Prices at the bazaars were calculated using a formula that took into account the cost of materials and labour priced in cash, divided by an average daily rate, which was set at ten hours at 6d per hour. The exchanges were, for a time, very successful, turning over

Robert Owen. Photo courtesy of the Robert Owen Society.

Robert Owen statue in his home town, Newtown, Powys. Photo courtesy of the Robert Owen Credit Union.

12-14,000 Labour Notes a week. The doors of the exchanges often needed to be closed, given the crush of traders. Owen's new dawn seemed a reality.

Owen's Labour Note – an early form of time money – was the first, faltering experiment with alternative forms of money. However, while utopian and inspiring, it was not a great success. The exchanges quickly ran into problems, from which we can nevertheless learn a lot.

It's important to remember that although Owen's experiment was short-lived, the movement from which it was generated lives to this day. In 1844 the Rochdale Pioneers established the modern cooperative retail movement from one shop. Elsewhere working people gathered together to create mutual insurance societies, and clubbed together to help each other buy homes. From these small steps the modern insurance industry and building societies developed into the mainstream organisations they are today. From small acorns mighty oaks can grow.

Lessons from Robert Owen's experiments

1. There was a lot of confusion over how to charge in time for work that was of different quality. If I work at a slower rate than you, is it OK for me to charge you six hours for a chair that you, perhaps more experienced or with better equipment, could make in half the time? Obviously people will often go for the cheaper or better-value item unless they understand why someone learning their trade might be a little slower, and act accordingly.

   Lesson: You can't go on price alone when using alternative currencies. You need to understand where the person you are trading with is coming from and the context within which the work was done. You need to have a personal relationship with the person, not a utilitarian relationship. This is what is called 'relationship trading'.

2. Many people found that they could not get the things they needed on a day-to-day basis using labour money. Complementary currencies will probably always run alongside conventional money, not replace it.

   Lesson: Avoid giving the impression that your money system will solve all the world's problems overnight, and that people will be able to live off the new money. Outside the special case of Argentina, this has never been the case. Don't raise unrealisable expectations, only to inevitably let people down later.

3. The labour exchanges challenged elites and the social order of the day just as capitalism and the factory system on which it is built was being created. Owen was viciously attacked by elite businessmen as dangerously communistic and atheistic, and the courts refused to enforce the labour exchange's rules.

   Lesson: We need to be aware that vested interests might not welcome an alternative currency scheme. You might see the political nature of what you are doing as one of its strengths (see the Stroud Pound Co-op, Chapter 13) or want to reassure them of the complementary, rather than revolutionary, nature of what you are doing (see the Brixton Pound, Chapter 14). Be ready for an attack from elites if you are too successful and provide an alternative to a job for low pay!

4. After a couple of years, trade unions exploded on to the scene, and took Owen's attention away from the exchanges. He began to think that local experimentation was not good enough, and that we need larger-scale changes in society. Trade unions were recruiting thousands of working people, and seemed a better use of his time.

   Lesson: We need to let our local currency experiments 'go where they want to go'. If people want to do something other than set up a currency scheme, then fine. Be prepared for key activists to lose interest and get stuck into the next big thing for social change. Plan for a sustainable organisation in which no one is indispensable.

The Owen Labour Note. Photo courtesy of the Robert Owen Museum.

Anarchist labour money: France 1840s, USA 1850s-60s

In the 1840s the French anarchist Pierre-Joseph Proudhon developed Owen's ideas into a fully fledged proposal for the organisation of society. He advocated 'Banks of the People', confederations of 50-100,000 artisans who would agree to issue exchange notes and guarantee their reciprocity, to meet social need, and without speculation or charging interest, which was condemned as usury.

Proudhon rejected an economy where, seemingly by accident, some received much more money for their work than others, irrespective of the quality to which the work was done. He envisaged an economy based on the exchange of goods and services between free producers, which, he argued, would develop into one based on mutual aid and real equality as an alternative to rapacious capitalism.

He was critical of money based on precious metals, arguing that the rich and powerful would inevitably control it in their own interests, such that "whoever can get control of the specie of the world can rule the markets with despotic hand, and may work his will upon communities and nations."[1] Proudhon argued that money based on labour issued by those who produced societies' wealth was democratic and equitable when contrasted with that issued by unaccountable private banks to support the factory system.

After the failure of the 1848 revolution in France, Proudhon found himself in jail for sedition and unable to implement his ideas (even though he had taken no part in the revolution, which he saw as authoritarian). But in the USA, Josiah Warren ran a time bank for three years in Cincinnati in the 1850s, and later set up two intentional communities in America ('Modern Times' and 'Utopia'), which traded labour notes. They both lasted twenty years.[2]

Lessons from Proudhon's 'Banks of the People'

Proudhon seemed to spend more time trying to develop the perfect scheme for the fundamental transformation of society than actually doing anything practical. Warren worked at a smaller, more practical scale and he was able to set up schemes that were more than short-lived ephemeral experiments. Practical, grounded alternative currency schemes *work*.

Fighting 'The Man': the Populist Revolt, South and Western USA, 1890s

The American Revolution was fought and won on a wave of paper money, unconnected to any form of backing beyond support for the revolutionary government and a wish to throw off British rule. Similarly, the American Civil War was financed by unbacked paper money by both sides: Greenbacks in the Union and Greybacks for the Confederacy.[3] Union Greenbacks largely kept their value, but Confederate Greybacks didn't. Greybacks did enable the Confederacy to put an army in the field, but when the Southern economy was strangled by a Union blockade and cotton could not be exported, the Southern economy collapsed. By the end of the war the Confederacy had suffered price inflation of 4,000 per cent, the Union just 60 per cent.[4] This is because Union paper money helped to lubricate a real economy and a real war effort, whereas the real Confederate economy collapsed. Printing money did not save it.

After the war the corporate financial elite in the east wanted to close down this 'irresponsible' emergency experimentation with paper money in favour of tight, limited money on the gold standard. The 'Goldbug' elite, as they began to be called, wanted to make sure there was a large supply of people who had no other options than coming and working for them for as low a wage as possible, so they maximised their profits and their private wealth. In contrast, people moving west into the frontier, taking up land grants and establishing family farms, wanted cheap money. They liked paper money.

This was the 'great compromise': hard, gold-backed money in the east; soft paper money in the west.[5] But in the former Confederate South, losers in the civil war, ordinary people laboured under the domination of 'The Man', the 'Yankee carpetbagger', who offered them limited credit at exorbitant interest, based on a call on their next crop.

The carpetbagger provided the sharecropper with seeds and food while his crop grew, and the debt would be paid when the crop went to market. Given that the next crop never ever raised enough money to pay off the ever-growing debt, the sharecropper was essentially a slave to finance. The following quote, from Lawrence Goodwyn's magisterial history of those times, captures it perfectly:

> *The farmer, his eyes downcast and his hat sometimes literally in his hand, approached the merchant with a list of his needs. The man behind the counter consulted his ledger, and after a mumbled exchange moved to his shelves to select the goods that would satisfy at least a part of his customers wants. Rarely did the farmer receive the full range or even the full quantity of one item he requested. No money changed hands; the merchant merely made brief notations in his ledger. Two weeks or a month later, the farmer would return, the consultation with the ledger would recur, the mumbled exchange and careful selection of goods would ensue, and new additions would be added to the ledger.[6]*

'That was the old days', you might think. 'It's not like that now.' But think how much you are working, even when times are good, to service interest charges from your mortgage and credit cards.

Think about how you pay for your house three times over at least, when you take out a mortgage. Who benefits from that extra money you pay? How can we reconcile a sustainable economy with the endless growth we need to feed the 'interest beast'?

Think about the bad times, when people lose their jobs and can no longer pay their credit-card and mortgage interest payments, until their house is repossessed or they are bankrupted.

That's not even mentioning people who can't get cheap credit, and who have to rely on violent, thuggish loan sharks or 'Rachman' landlords. Exorbitant and exploitative levels of interest are as much of a problem today as in the past.

In the Deep South, eventually, the lid blew off this financial oppression. The Texas-based 'Farmers' Alliance' denounced "credit merchants, railroads, trusts, money power and capitalists" in favour of cooperative buying-and-selling collectives, of which there were over 2,000 by the mid-1880s, with 100,000 members.

In Dakota a territory-wide cooperative exchange was established, while cooperative experiments spread widely across much of America between 1887 and 1892. Farmer lecturers travelled the length and breadth of the country spreading the message of cooperation, eventually calling for a network of state-owned banks, called sub-treasuries, which would provide cheap credit.

The movement saw mile-long processions of carts decorated with flags and evergreen to symbolise the 'living issues' of the Alliance, brass bands, crowds so large that four farmer-lecturers were needed to keep them occupied, and twilight meals feeding thousands. It eventually exploded into a full-scale agrarian revolt that spread like wildfire through the early 1890s, such that it seemed that, as Goodwyn puts it, there was "almost a universal conviction that financial salvation (has) come".

The movement became known to history as the Populist Revolt. We now think of a 'populist' as a politician who will say anything to get elected, an unprincipled crowd-pleaser with no intention of following through on his extravagant claims. American Populism was very different. It was a full-scale revolt against money power.

Things culminated in the 1896 presidential election, the 'battle of the standards', perhaps the only presidential election based on the nature of money. The Republicans called for limited gold-backed money, while the Democrats and Populists agreed to fight together in favour not of paper money (the preference of the Populists) but of silver money. Silver is softer than gold, but harder than paper.

The Republicans won, and in a wave of repression reimposed the domination of gold, hard money. The repression was such that it was not that surprising that the victorious Republican Presidential nominee McKinley was eventually assassinated by an anarchist.

Paper money in the Great Depression

While the repression of the Populists meant that protest about money was driven underground at the end of the nineteenth century, the chaos of the Great Depression saw it emerge, perhaps stronger than ever.

Many of today's alternative currencies were inspired by experiments in the 1930s.

Freework

The anarchist stream in money reform was continued by the Argentine-based German money reformer Silvio Gesell, who developed arguments in favour of the abolition of interest and for 'free money'. Gesell argued that extortionate interest was the main problem of the capitalist system, and consequently he advocated interest-free banking.[7]

After the First World War, Gesell inspired the German 'Freework' movement, which established the 'Wära Exchange Association' (a word compounded from the German for 'goods' – *wara* – and 'currency' – *wärung*). It issued its own currency notes, interest-free, as a response to Germany's financial collapse and experiences of hyperinflation.

With the arrival of the depression in 1929, the owner of a coal mine in Schwanenkirchen, Bavaria used Wära notes to reopen his mine, with the Wära passed on to local merchants, then to the wholesalers, then on to the manufacturers who returned to the coal mine for coal. It is estimated that during 1930-31 around 20,000 Wära were issued, with some two million people using them.

Gesell-inspired 'stamp scrip' notes issued by local authorities or business associations spread to other towns in Germany, Austria and Switzerland. In 1932, the town of Wörgl, Austria, used them to fund public works for unemployed people, who spent the notes with local merchants, who in turn paid the notes back to the local authority in local taxes. Local state employees were paid 50 per cent of their salary in scrip, inscribed with the words "They Alleviate Want, Give Work and Bread".

Stamp scrip utilised Gesell's ideas for *demurrage*, or 'rusting' currencies. Demurrage was intended to increase the velocity of circulation, as 'slow money' was regarded as the cause of the depression. When people are worried about their future they will pay off their debts or hoard money that they would otherwise have spent, and money leaves the economy. Local small businesses are the first to suffer from a problem that is as great in contemporary recessions as it was in the 1930s. Now we will pay off our credit cards rather than spend, but the effect is the same – a chronic lack of demand, and shops and businesses close.

"The money changers have fled their high seats in the temple of our civilisation. We may now restore that temple to the ancient truths." **Franklin D. Roosevelt, Inaugural speech, March 1933, just before signing an order closing America's banks for a 'holiday' and outlawing local currencies**

To address this there needs to be some mechanism to encourage people to spend, not hoard, their money. Each month or quarter the notes had to be 'validated' with a stamp purchased each week. If the note was not passed on, the holder of the note would still have to purchase the weekly stamps or the note would be worthless, so it was obviously in his or her interest to purchase something with it rather than hold on to it.

After 52 weeks the note could be exchanged for cash by the local authority, using the receipts of the weekly stamps.

Although these currencies were eventually outlawed by the fascists, the legacy of the Freework movement survives to this day in form of the Swiss WIR Bank. Swiss businesses that join the Wirtschaftsring (WIR

When money stops working, people die

The politics of the Wörgl notes are clear from the inscription on the back of the scrip:

To all. Slowly circulating money has thrown the world into an unheard-of crisis, and millions of working people are in a terrible need. From the economic viewpoint, the decline of the world has begun with horrible consequences for all. Only a clear recognition of these facts and decisive action can stop the breakdown of the economic machine, and save mankind from another war, confusion and dissolution.

Men live from the exchange of what they can do. Through slow money circulation this exchange has been crippled to a large extent, and thus millions of men (sic) who are willing to work have lost their right to live in our economic system. The exchange of what we can do must, therefore, be again improved and the right to live regained for all of those who have been cast out.[8]

Scrip issued by the city of Long Branch, New Jersey, 1934.

business network) agree to accept its money and to use it to trade with each other, and have access to interest-free loans. WIR is as much a part of Swiss society as Visa is part of ours. Seventy years on, the Freework tradition also inspired the development of regiogeld, German regional currencies (see Chapter 9).

American Stamp Scrip 1931-33

Gesell's ideas inspired other financial responses to the Great Depression of the 1930s. In 1931-2 a nationwide run on the banks in the USA dried up credit and very nearly caused the circulation of money itself to seize up completely. The banks just closed their doors for weeks on end, then months. Under these crisis conditions farmers began swapping their unsellable produce with each other. In time, with no end to the bank crisis in sight, the movement developed from informal one-to-one swaps to an organised system of barter exchanges facilitated by swap bulletins and newspapers.

Contemporary reports claimed that the 'Swap Movement' had some 50,000 participants in 400 exchanges across 29 states. Eventually, warehouse receipts were issued by the barter exchanges, and, when denominated in dollars, these began to circulate as and were loaned as money. As news of the European Scrip movement crossed the Atlantic, in no small part due to its popularisation by respected Nobel-winning economist Irving Fisher,[9] local authorities and business associations in the USA also began to issue their own local currency notes, denominated in dollars, and barter grew from an informal movement run by poor farmers into a more formalised stamp scrip system.

By 1932 so many American banks had collapsed or suffered from runs that the entire system seemed literally on the verge of collapse. The newly elected President Roosevelt grasped the nettle, declared a nationwide bank 'holiday', issued millions of Greenbacks (unbacked paper money that looked like dollars) and temporarily took the USA off the gold standard. Scrip was outlawed – or, should we say, nationalised. Some would say superseded.

Lessons from the Scrip movement

Conflict over money can, at times, mobilise millions. Elites who benefit from the way money works today will resist change, perhaps violently. But at times when elites do not act to solve major problems, solutions emerge from the grassroots. We do not need for 'them' to act when we can do things ourselves.

Social credit

In the UK, New Zealand and Canada a movement developed during the Great Depression that was based on Major C. H. Douglas's ideas for 'social credit'.[10] Douglas argued that the wages of those making any goods for an enterprise would by definition be lower than the price of those goods in the shops, if the business and those who got it to market were to make a profit. So, by definition, working people could not afford to buy the things they had made. If wages were high enough for working people to afford them, there would be no profit for the capitalist, he argued. The result is a chronic lack of demand in the economy.

To counter this he proposed that prices should be set 'rationally' and 'scientifically' (rather than by supply and demand), and that a national dividend or 'social credit' should be paid to everyone to make up the difference between wages and prices. Then workers could afford to buy what they had made.

Douglas relied exclusively on argument to explain to the powers that be the benefits of his 'self-evident' insight. Others argued that we need more muscular action to force the powers that be to change track. In the UK the 'Green Shirts' was a uniformed political movement organising unemployed people for social credit and in opposition to what they called the 'money power'.[11] They pulled off the sort of stunts we now associate with Greenpeace, such as defacing a wax statue of Hitler, painting the Bank of England green, throwing a brick at No. 11 Downing Street, burning an effigy of Bank of England Chairman Montagu Norman, and burning a sheaf of wheat outside a meeting of the Wheat Commission (with the slogan "They burn the wheat we want to eat!").

The Green Shirts should not be confused with the Black Shirts, the British Union of Fascists, to whom they were militantly and physically opposed. In contrast, Douglas, who opposed political organisation, did degenerate into racist, anti-Semitic conspiracy theories, arguing that the world economy was controlled by a conspiracy of Jewish bankers. We always need to be aware of unpleasant undercurrents in the politics of money reform.

Social Credit administrations were elected to power in two Canadian Provinces, and in the 1970s and 1980s the New Zealand Social Credit party had one or two

MPs. Douglas's ideas re-emerged as arguments for a basic income in the 1970s and 80s. More recently, arguments for cap and share as a way to distribute carbon credits (see page 209) echo ideas of social credit.

Some would argue that we now have a 'social credit' in the form of a family allowance and working families' tax credits, which make up the difference between low pay and being able to buy what you need.

From the 1970s to the millennium

The fifties and sixties did not see many grassroots alternative currency experiments. The crises that followed the 1973 oil shock and the crises of the 1980s and the 1990s led to the alternative currencies that form the bulk of this book. Ralph Borsodi developed proposals for an inflation-proof currency based on a basket of commonly used commodities. In 1987 Michael Linton designed the first LETS scheme, which he called the LETSystem (Local Exchange Trading

Greenshirt drummers and Greenshirt meeting, 1930s. Photos courtesy of the Kibbo Kift Foundation.

System), on Comox Island in British Columbia. Michael's ideas were refined over time and through experience, and the 1990s saw an explosion of LETS around the English-speaking world, with similar variations elsewhere. Scrip reappeared in the USA, famously as Ithaca Hours in upstate New York. Continued difficult economic times in eastern Germany, after unification, led to local money systems there. And in Argentina, after the crisis of 2001, literally millions survived – and I mean survived – using money they created themselves through barter networks. Transition Initiatives have created their own currencies, building on the E. F. Schumacher Society's BerkShares programme in Great Barrington, Massachusetts. There is, then, a strong tradition to build upon, which is described in more detail in the rest of this book.

An alternative currency timeline

1830s	UK	Robert Owen's Labour Notes
1840s	France	Proudhon's Bank of the People
1850s	USA	Josiah Warren's Labour Notes
1880s, 1990s	USA	Populism: mass struggle for cooperation or silver currency
1920s	Germany	Freework movement
1930-34	USA, Europe	Stamp scrip
1930s	UK	Social Credit
1930s-70s	NZ, Canada	Social Credit parties elected
1930s-date	Switzerland	Wirtschaftsring
1987	Canada	Michael Linton designs the prototype LETS, the LETSystem
1990s-date	worldwide	Green Dollars, LETS, SEL (France) Talente (Germany, etc.)
1990s-date	USA	Hours, BerkShares
1997-2004	Argentina	Mass use of barter
2007-date	UK	Transition currencies

CHAPTER 5

LOCAL EXCHANGE TRADING SCHEMES

LETS was the first of the community currencies in this book to really take off – in the 1990s – and much of what early LETS members did was as pioneering in its time as the Transition movement is now. We now have the models to choose from. Back then we didn't, and LETS members experimented with a number of issues around how to value your currency, what to call it, how the scheme should be run, and the relationship between a complementary currency and national money – issues that later local currency models learned from.

LETS has a lot to offer the Transition movement as a way to quickly manifest and mobilise the hidden skills in a community, to fund 'the great reskilling', and to honour and use the skills of those of us in our communities who lived before the age of cheap oil.

If you are part of a fairly new Transition Initiative you might want to consider LETS as one of your early projects. It's very easy to set up, it's a good way to build connection and community feeling amongst people who might not know each other, and it helps unleash the skills your community has. Embarking on Transition can be daunting – LETS is a quick and practical project to show that you are on your way.

Some LETS schemes now have 15-20 years' experience of grassroots organisation and development, using processes remarkably similar to the Transition movement. If they have not burned out or turned in on themselves, LETS will have skills and experiences to offer.

It's worth reading through the debates that follow, and learning about the diversity of types of LETS, past and present, to get a feel for the possibilities. Remember, don't be path-dependent or locked into any one design. Let it go where it wants to go.

What is LETS?

A LETS scheme is really just a network of people who agree to share their skills with each other by means of a local currency that they have created and agree to use. LETS was started by Michael Linton on Vancouver Island, Canada, in the 1980s, with the first Comox Valley LETSystem eventually growing to about 500 members. During the late '80s and '90s LETS spread around the world to Australia, New Zealand and the UK, while in Europe similar schemes included Tauschringe and Talente (in German-speaking lands) and SEL (Système d'Échange Locaux, also 'grains of salt') in France. Some LETS were small, local networks involving 50-100 people, while some included 300-500. Auckland Green Dollars in New Zealand briefly involved over 1,000 people. Schemes such as North London LETS, Sheffield, Ashley (Bristol) or Brighton LETS in the UK, or some of the New Zealand Green Dollar schemes, have been going now for over twenty years.

For more on LETS, including where to find your local LETS, contact LETSlink UK: **www.letslinkuk.net**

How does LETS work?

The system is simple. A group of interested people get together and list all the skills they have to offer and the things they want, together with their phone numbers, in a directory. The directory can be printed out, photocopied, or put on the web. They then agree to create and accept money from each other, which they back with their commitment to do enough work to pay this 'commitment' (not 'debt') off in a reasonable time in the future. LETS works as follows.

- If Dave wants someone to cut his lawn, he looks in the directory, and sees that Sarah is offering that service.

- Dave phones up Sarah, who agrees to come round at the weekend to cut Dave's lawn, and she says that she charges six LETS pounds an hour. Dave thinks that's fine.

- Sarah cuts the lawn, and Dave writes out a cheque for six LETS pounds, which he gives to Sarah. Dave doesn't need to have six LETS pounds in his account to start – he writes a cheque, thereby agreeing to earn six LETS pounds to pay off his 'commitment' to the community in the future.

- Sarah then 'banks' the cheque by sending it to the LETS treasurer, who keeps the accounts on her computer and sends out LETS bank statements periodically. Using the LETS software, the treasurer debits Dave's account six LETS pounds, and credits Sarah's account for the same amount.

- Later that week, Sarah asks Jim to give her a lift into town, and Jim charges Sarah six LETS pounds for the service, but before he can go, his car needs a clean.

- Jim asks Dave to valet his car, which Dave does, earning back the LETS pounds he has paid Sarah.

That's how it works – everyone has had their needs met, and been paid, without using any conventional money. You don't need any local money before you start – you just make a *commitment* to work for someone who asks you to in the future, and honour that commitment in return for the right to create the money you have just paid out, and you back it with your personal commitment.

The beauty of the system is that if you add together all the credits and debits held on the computer by all the participants, they balance out at zero. Over a reasonable amount of time, everyone is expected to personally balance the credits they spend with those they earn, so their personal account balance also hovers around zero.

Now scale this up to a community of 200-300, all paying for services with a *commitment* to provide services to others in the future, to earn back the money they have created. LETS is community credit money, backed by the commitment (the provision of work and resources) members make to provide to the network in the future.

That is the heart of LETS. Many other issues – what to call the currency, how to value it, how much or how little to regulate the network – are all issues for you to decide on locally, whereas for some other forms of complementary currency this is more prescriptive. A LETS scheme is easy to set up and might therefore be a good way for a Transition Initiative to start to experiment with alternative currencies.

Can you create your own money and pay yourself to set up a currency scheme?

The point about all balances adding up to zero matters. It's very important to understand that every unit of LETS currency issued *must* be backed by someone's work in the future.

So, for example, you can't just pay yourself LETS credits for running the scheme unless you are raising the credits to pay yourself from somewhere – for example, from a membership subscription. You can't just 'give' all new members of the LETS scheme, say, twenty units to get them started unless you take that money from another account that goes into commitment.

Everything going out of all accounts and everything going into all accounts must balance to zero. LETS schemes that have forgotten this have got into a mess.

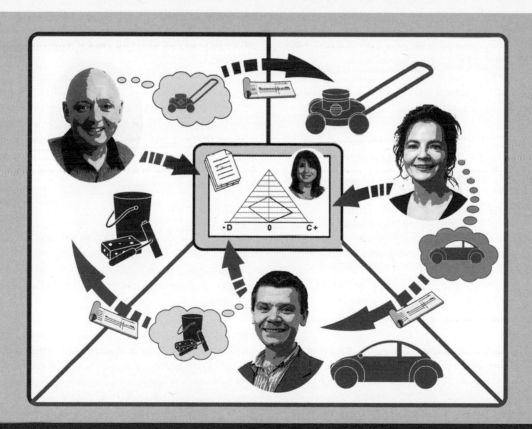

How LETS works. Thanks to Suzanne Yee, Department of Geography Cartographics Unit, University of Liverpool.

How do you set up a LETS scheme?

To get started, ask around members of your community or Transition Initiative to see if anyone remembers LETS, or if there is energy for setting up a complementary currency. Or just call a meeting. Most LETS started from existing communities who wanted to trade with each other: members of community and environmental groups, churches, people interested in alternative therapies and wholesome food and the like, and people interested in building local ecological alternatives. In other words they were just the sort of people who are now members of Transition Initiatives. You will find your Transition contact group a good resource, then it's a good idea to have a stall at local community and green fairs. Bradford LETS was set up with help from a government regeneration agency. Forest of Dean LETS grew from members of Friends of the Earth. More recently, Truro LETS has emerged from the Transition movement.

"Swindon LETS has been going for over four years and has over 100 members. Everything from organic veg, hairdressing and dog walking to computer training, languages and CV writing is offered using the exchange rate of £1 = 1 Sarcen – the Sarcen being the local rock found in fields in the area, which Avebury is made from. We take part in community events such as therapeutic gardening Open Days and have regular Open House sessions, where LETS members can trade. The largest item purchased was a polytunnel, but ongoing projects include major DIY renovations, garden makeovers and industrial quantities of jam making!" **Jo Heaven, Swindon LETS. www.fiohnetwork.org/swindonlets**

At the meeting, start by explaining what the money we use is (see Chapter 2, pages 39-40), remembering that the promise on a banknote (to pay the bearer on demand the sum of five pounds) really does not mean anything.

It can be tricky getting this right – you can look like a con artist. There are scams and con-men out there, so if you don't convince some people, don't worry about it. Hopefully you will have some former LETS people in your Transition Initiative. Use their memories and enthusiasms.

Do not assume in advance that you will end up with a LETS scheme after this meeting. The discussions you have might suggest that another form of currency is better for you. Again, let it go where it wants to go.

What sort of money do you want to create?

There are a number of issues to be considered here.

What will you call your currency?

The choice is between a neutral name, e.g. 'green pound/dollar' or 'Anytown Pound', or a more locally resonant name. For example, Bristol had Favours, Bath had Olivers, Bradford had Brads, Lewisham has Anchors, and Ilkley had Wharves (named after the local river). Letnet in Milton Keynes trades concrete cows! There are strengths and weaknesses to both options:

• Calling your currency a local pound, Euro or dollar makes it seem less controversial, more in line with conventional thinking about money, and less wacky. Businesses are more likely to accept it.

• But some more radical members of your Transition community might be put off by that. Why create a form of money the same as normal money, they might say?

• A locally resonant name for your currency can make it seem fun, interesting and different, and unlike national currency. You can enjoy experimenting with different ways of valuing the currency (see pages 73-76). Some people in the Transition movement feel very strongly that our economies and livelihoods *should* be more integrated within our ecosystems, and associating your local currency with local natural or bioregional features communicates this. But it can cause problems – see box below.

How will you value your currency?

There are really only two options: by reference to national currency, or to time. You could theoretically value the currency by reference to something else, for example a set quantity of local wood. But how do you calculate the value of the wood? This would either be its market value denominated in pounds or the time it would take to cut it down. As with the name of your currency, your decision here is important and communicates your perception of the 'valuableness' and 'moneyness' of your currency.

Linking to the national currency

Linking your currency explicitly or loosely to the national currency is probably the easiest. Very few recalculations of value are needed and people know

Manchester's 'Bobbins' – a cautionary tale

In the 1990s Manchester LETS was one of the world's biggest LETS schemes, with over 500 members at its height. Part of its success was the name of the currency, the 'Bobbin'. The name was chosen to show that the Bobbin was different from the pound sterling, and to reflect Manchester's spinning heritage. In spinning, the bobbin is just there for you to wind the newly spun thread on to, and is discarded once the thread had been used up. The bobbin has no value in and of itself, without the thread. LETS Bobbins similarly had no value, Manchester LETS argued. They were just there to facilitate trade.

But colloquially, the intrinsic valuelessness of the Bobbin was also imported into local vernacular. As anyone who has watched Coronation Street knows, Mancunians say 'that's bobbins, that is' to mean 'that's complete rubbish', or 'I wouldn't pay bobbins for that' meaning that a job has been badly done.

So calling your currency 'Bobbins' was funny, and those who got the joke appreciated it. But local businesses were completely unimpressed. Explicitly calling your currency 'valueless' takes it too far away from the intrinsic qualities of 'valuableness' and 'moneyness' that money needs to have if people, especially businesses, are to take it seriously.

The problem was drawing attention to the inherent valuelessness of the currency and to things that are regarded as valueless, rather than associating it with a local feature, say a river, mountain, waterfall or local dignitary, which carries connotations of value. Ilkley had no problem with Wharves, as the name of the currency conveyed a sense of 'valuableness' by association with a well-loved and precious river.

Calling a currency a 'favour' again suggests borrowing or cadging favours rather than 'paying your way' (as discussed in Chapter 2, pages 42-44, when we considered the 'money as freedom' perspective). Bath 'Olivers' is again witty and playful, but shouldn't money be seen as serious?

Others in Manchester decided that the Bobbin was 'beyond the pale' and created the Manchester Pound, which to those who liked the subversiveness and playfulness of the Bobbin seemed too conventional and too much like normal money.

The answer is 'horses for courses' – does your Transition movement want to shake things up and get people thinking about the contribution of money to our currently unsustainable world, or does it want businesses to join so they can contribute to Transition? The name of your currency matters and communicates your values to others, so think about it carefully.

how it works. If something costs five pounds, Euros or dollars it also costs, about, five 'favours' – thereabouts. The difference is that your currency is contributing to local resilience and helps build a local economy, reducing dependence on fossil fuels and greenhouse gas emissions.

Local businesses are more likely to be comfortable with it. They can easily offer to accept local money in full or in part, and do not need to change their prices. But others will object that it's not radical enough. Those who are highly paid in the conventional economy (say, lawyers) will continue to be paid more than others (say, cleaners).

Linking to time

Linking the currency to time is again simple and egalitarian, but this suggests that to use the currency you have to sign up to these egalitarian views. A lawyer might say that an hour of her time includes all her accumulated experience, where this is not the case for a cleaner – so she should be paid more. The cleaner might be outraged at the devaluation of his skills.

Another issue is how hard or efficiently someone works in that hour. One person might just be more efficient at something than another, so the slower person is effectively better paid. It might be that this is what you want. Why penalise a more leisurely, thoughtful worker at the altar of efficiency, you might say. These are political questions inherent in decisions about how you value your currency, and they send messages to people about your currency scheme's values and objectives.

Secondly, and more practically, it's easy to value labour in hours, but what about *things*? How many hours for a second-hand fridge or rental of a van? Connected to national currency, the calculation is easy.

A mix of the two

A good compromise is a mix. The currency is worth 'roughly' a pound (so you can pay someone more or less, as you see fit) and you suggest a recommended hourly rate, which provides a reasonable or non-exploitative living when compared with the minimum wage. This compromise does not set anything in stone. People can do what they want.

It is important to remember Simmel's arguments about money simplifying relationships in a complex world (see pages 42-44), and provide some guidelines. If you just leave it to individuals to decide for themselves in an unregulated market the result can be mayhem.

Should you mix LETS and national currency?

Should exchanges be entirely in the local currency, or should members be able to mix sterling and local currency when they trade? For some it's necessary for people to choose for themselves how to charge for their services. They might need a certain sterling income to make ends meet. They might have to pay for things that aren't supplied locally in national currency, or pay their taxes. This seems sensible.

But this can be pernicious if taken to extremes. There can be a tendency for some to reduce the amount of local money they will accept to such a low level that others might feel they are not really entering into the spirit of things, or that they just see the local currency scheme as a cheap way of advertising. Is just giving a 10-per-cent discount payable in local money good enough? No? What about 30 per cent? In time, everyone starts charging sterling and your local currency dies.

For example, some people in Manchester said a Bobbin is a pound, others that it's an hour. Others wanted to pay one Bobbin per hour or job (the Bob-a-jobbers) while another wanted to create as many 'Bobbin millionaires' as he could. Some said it's OK to mix Bobbins and pounds; others objected that it's against the spirit of LETS. The result was that people struggled to agree how to value the currency, and could not agree prices with each other. Some people left when they did not get their way, others felt hard

"South West Dorset LETS has been going strong for fifteen years and currently has nearly 200 members. We have had a LETS wedding and several personal events, including a baby-naming celebration. We hold regular socials. To mark our tenth anniversary the group took over the local Borough Gardens and made it a 'LETS only' area for the day. Cash could be exchanged for our local currency (NETS) to trade on the numerous stalls, including children's entertainment, face painting, glass painting and complementary therapy taster sessions. The stall selling home-made cakes and teas was very busy and we traded nearly 1,000 NETS on the day. The local Transition Town group has recently joined the LETS and has already started trading. Our relationship with other like-minded groups locally is also very strong and we are working closely together to develop a resilient local economy." **Deborah Bond, SW Dorset LETS**

LETS brochures and directories.

done by. Things stagnated until an agreement evolved – a Bobbin is 'like' a pound and the recommended rate was six Bobbins an hour. In South Powys LETS people charge eight Beacons an hour, but other members charge between 3 Beacons and 25 Beacons an hour, depending on the type of work.

What form should the currency take?
Again, choices here can add to or devalue the 'money-ness' and 'valuableness' of your currency. The very early LETS currencies developed in Canada, green dollars, had no physical form at all. Traders just phoned details of their trade through to the treasurer, who kept the accounts on a computer. Later LETS used chequebooks.

Writing cheques for small amounts can slow things down for high volume high-street businesses so much that they are likely to be reluctant to participate. But a nicely designed cheque is fine for interpersonal trading, which will be the majority of LETS trades in practice. Some LETS in New Zealand have printed scrip notes that are backed by a LETS account. At markets run by Golden Bay's HANDS ('How About a

Non Dollar System') exchange in New Zealand you can draw a LETS paper currency, the Exchange Voucher or EV, against your LETS account, which you can then spend with market traders. You can turn any unspent EVs back into New Zealand dollars.

It may be that in the future we will have local currency debit bank cards, but that seems some way off. As we see later, German regiogeld and business barter card networks already issue their members with debit cards charged with barter points, but this technology is probably beyond the abilities of a Transition Initiative unless it has a very friendly local bank, building society or credit union.

How closely should individual accounts be managed or overseen by the group?
Remember that LETS currencies are technically community-based credit currencies backed by the commitment of the person who issues the currency to honour it with work or goods provided in the future to other network members. Generally, best practice is that people should give and receive in roughly equal proportions, periodically taking their account balance

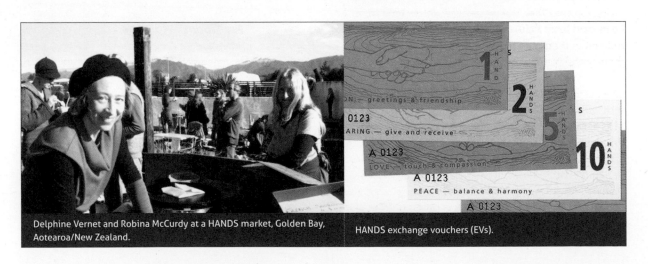

Delphine Vernet and Robina McCurdy at a HANDS market, Golden Bay, Aotearoa/New Zealand.

HANDS exchange vouchers (EVs).

through zero from credit to debit or vice versa, and they should be trusted to do this automatically as part of their commitment to the network. It's based on trust. But how closely should this trust be monitored, either by a management committee or core group or by the community itself? What happens if people are untrustworthy or do things that shake our confidence in the integrity of the scheme?

Very early LETS left things very much to individuals to do the right thing. If someone wanted to know the balance of another trader's account, they could in theory ask the treasurer for that information. In practice, no one ever did.

Individuals were trusted to back the currency they issued with future work, and one key organiser of an early LETS scheme ran up a commitment of 15,000 green dollars on that basis. This was quite legitimate in terms of accepted ways of doing things at the time, and the person who did this was acting honourably. But, it looked as though this person was taking advantage of his fellow members. What if he had reneged – skipped town? On the one hand, it doesn't matter. Everyone has been paid, and all we are losing is the renegade's work. On the other, the money that those who have been paid loses value as there are fewer people left to redeem it. If enough people leave town with debts, then confidence will be crushed.

The balance of experience is that the management of individual accounts should be regulated in some way. This can be through peer pressure; by publishing the turnover and balance of each account. This matters, since if Dave has a commitment, a debit, of 200 green dollars, but he has been a member of the network for over five years and has spent and earned over 5,000 green dollars over that time (his turnover), that is different from Jayne having a commitment of 300 green dollars when she has contributed nothing at all. We are entitled to trust Dave's commitment, but question Jayne's.

It may be that the community knows that Mavis is elderly and needs more services than she could reasonably ever be expected to provide, so no one worries. Or it may be that our local cafe is paying LETS members for a refurbishment, and we know that we will be able to buy our coffees there in the future, so again we trust the commitment of the cafe to the community. If we all know each other's balances, we can make an informed decision on whether or not to trade with them.

"We have been with Bath LETS since May 2009. We have met very kind people who offer their time to help you. We offer garden tidy-ups. On the whole we have found the scheme so easy to use and we have benefited from other people's offers, and from not paying for their time with real money. We wish more people would join as it is a fantastic way of meeting and helping your fellow neighbour." **Jeremy and Sally Cruse, Bath LETS. www.bathlets.org.uk**

Of course, knowing everyone's business like this is the opposite to the 'money is freedom' perspective, which works on the basis that I don't need to like you to trade with you, and my money is as good as yours. Here, knowing everyone's business builds community but might feel intrusive and might be seen as culturally inappropriate. For example, it has long been understood that some women need their own source of income that their husband does not control, as he will blow it down the pub. She, quite rightly, won't want her husband to know her business.

The solution to this is not to publish private details, but to have rules-based regulation by a management committee or core group. To have agreed and publicly advertised credit and debit limits, which might be extended for active traders or vulnerable people. To require people to leave their accounts at zero when they leave the scheme, and, if someone leaves with a commitment outstanding, to take them to court. It might seem draconian, but LETS money *is* money, and the courts will enforce it.

The reality is that if there are clear rules and values in place people generally follow them and self-manage their affairs. Problems come when there are no accepted rules or values in place, and people with conflicting values clash. People who take a 'money is freedom' approach and act in what they see as their own best interests and spend more than they earn, running up a large balance, clash with people who think that everyone should give and take equally. I may feel that LETS money is valueless in itself, so it doesn't matter how big my balance is – while you believe that LETS money is community credit money that is valuable because I can buy real things with it in the future. You feel that, by not giving back, I am ripping off the community.

Running a successful LETS scheme

Some LETS schemes have been going for 15-20 years, whereas some folded quickly. What are the lessons from this experience – why have some thrived, and some crashed?

Unfortunately, LETS can have a bad press because, as with the other pioneering alternative currencies discussed in Chapter 4, mistakes were made in the early days that have, in the eyes of some, unfairly labelled LETS as 'a good idea that didn't work'. That

is the case for any innovation. Experience throws up problems, and successful innovators develop solutions to them.

Avoid two fundamental mistakes

In my opinion, there were two fundamental mistakes that many advocates of LETS made in the early days, from which lessons should be drawn.

Raising unsustainable expectations

The first problem was overselling the benefits and refusing to countenance the existence of any downsides. One article about LETS was entitled 'Never knowingly undersold',[1] while for some enthusiasts LETS was the silver bullet that would solve all our problems overnight. With the 'Cheerful Disclaimer', Transition Initiatives are far more sensible and honest.

The consequence of this was that some advocates of LETS could end up looking like the latest in a long line of snake-oil salesmen selling quick fixes. Remember the old wise words in finance: 'If it looks too good to be true, it probably is.'

> ***Solution:*** don't make overblown claims for what you hope to achieve with a complementary currency. Don't set yourself up to be shot down. People who advocate and run alternative currencies should have a thoughtful, unflustered, purposeful temperament. They choose their words wisely, and do not make overblown claims.

Rigid systems thinking

The second problem was a lack of interest in research about what actually worked, and an over-emphasis on systems and design. If there were problems, LETS members often did not want to know about it ('Don't be negative'), or would say, 'Ah, it's not working because you have not followed my perfect design to the letter.'

The shame is that with more flexibility and pragmatism many of the problems that led to the demise of otherwise perfectly serviceable LETS schemes could have been fixed, and a good idea would not have got such a bad press.

> **Solution**: follow Transition Initiatives' advice to 'let it go where it wants to go'. Local context and conditions really do matter. Alternative currency models cannot be imported wholesale from elsewhere.

If these two problems are avoided – and that's not hard – then there are a number of ways in which we can ensure that we build resilient, long-lasting LETS schemes. In Bristol, Sheffield, South Powys, Brighton and a number of places in the UK, as well as elsewhere, LETS schemes are running happily, and have been since the early 1990s. What is the secret of their success?

Some of the lessons of successful LETS schemes are useful for all alternative currency schemes, and we will discuss them later, in Chapter 15. Here we limit the discussion to the distinctive elements of LETS schemes that need to be got right.

Induct people into the scheme properly

Make sure that it is easy for someone who wants to join the scheme to find out about it. If they get in contact, their phone call should be followed up. Invite them to an induction meeting and show them how the scheme works. Don't expect that if you have given them a chequebook and directory they will look after

themselves. Make sure that they are given tips about how things *actually* work from those 'in the know'. Make sure they understand the ethos: what is expected of them, and what might be a problem.

In Bristol, someone is at the cafe next to the city farm every Saturday. The Bright Exchange in Brighton holds monthly inductions at someone's flat. In South Powys, they meet new members at a farmer's market.

Run the scheme professionally

The successful LETS schemes have paid attention to the nuts and bolts of administration and account keeping. They look professional. They produce well-designed publicity materials and directories, and the directories are up to date. If a member is listed in the directory, you can have some confidence that they will deliver the services they say they will. Accounts are accurate and up to date. Subscriptions are raised from members to pay for the administration, and this subscription covers costs.

A lot of the exchanges that go on using alternative currencies happen in a private fashion, hidden from view. In our example above, Dave, Sarah and Jim phoned each other up and sorted things out privately. This assumes that Dave is confident enough to phone Sarah up, and Sarah feels confident enough to meet Dave, a stranger. What if it is dark, or Sarah does not feel safe going to Dave's house?

Things work a lot better when people know each other – know who they get on well with and might want to hang out with.

Organise social and community events to build a sense of community. This should be a core group function – to actively foster a sense of community. It also provides a good opportunity for people in small or micro-business to set up a stall to market their wares.

Forest of Dean LETS has held barbecues, didgeridoo playing, drumming and a visit around a farm. It is crucial that the sort of social and community-organising events that you arrange to encourage trading fit with local needs. NLLETS, North London LETS, holds 'taster' days for alternative therapies and other 'treats'.

Ensure that the range of skills on offer is large enough to meet people's needs

The Transition movement puts a strong emphasis on skills development. More of us need to develop our ability to grow food, fix things, make things, recycle and reuse more – all skills that are in high demand on LETS. Linking LETS to 'the great reskilling' and learning from the elders could be an effective generator of new skills and lead to the generation of vibrant new LETS schemes as part of Transition. If you haven't got one already in your area, a vibrant LETS will be a huge resource for unleashing your community's creativity.

People join LETS schemes:
- to meet like-minded people
- build feelings of community
- to share their skills
- in the longer run, to develop sustainable livelihood alternatives to our unsustainable world.

It is easier to meet the first three sets of objectives than to really develop a network wide enough to meet members' expectations of it. Unless individuals can actually share their skills and spend the alternative currency they earn, community and friendship is not enough. People will drift off, and you will never get close to realising your goal of building a low carbon local economy.

This doesn't mean that you have to build a large, extensive network. It can be 'small and perfectly formed' while meeting the needs of its members. For example, Sheffield LETS has 45 perfectly happy members.

Wellington Green Dollars Shop, Aotearoa/New Zealand.

If you do want a bigger, more extensive network, you have to actively develop the range of skills on offer through active recruiting or developing the skills of your members. Unless you have a way to grow your community's skills base it is important not to be over-optimistic about what can and cannot reasonably be expected from a LETS straight away.

If we are going to transition our local economies we need to actively help people to develop new skills – 'the great reskilling'.

Have a clear, shared ethos
You need some agreement about how the system should work. It can be a problem if half of your members feel strongly that everyone's time should be valued equally and see a LETS credit as an hour, while the other half want to pay what they think a job is 'worth', calculated in national currency. It's a recipe for conflict.

It matters less what the ethos is, so long as it is shared. If your members want a relaxed, easy-going way of interacting with everyone's time valued equally, that's OK. Similarly, if members want a professional standard of work and take the 'money as freedom' perspective (see pages 42-44), that works too – so long as the ethos is accepted and has been developed by the members themselves so they own it and reproduce it in their trades. The ethos cannot be imposed on a currency network by a well-meaning core group if the wider membership does not understand it or share it.

Make sure people know how to get the best out of LETS
New members need to have reasonable expectations about what can be achieved through participation in LETS. For example, if someone with a high-paid job and professional standards wants to find a cleaner who will turn up on the dot at the agreed time and

Intertrading

Sometimes a very local alternative currency network can be small enough to feel convivial and cosy, and local enough so everyone can meet up with each other without too many problems. But the range of services offered can be too small. If you want to stay small and cosy and be able access a wider range of services without joining a larger scheme, a solution can be 'intertrading' – trading between LETS schemes. Intertrading has taken place between LETS in Devon, between the five Bristol schemes and Glastonbury, in Wales and in New Zealand.

In Bristol, Bristol InterLETS enabled members of five small local LETS schemes, as well as members of nearby Glastonbury LETS, to trade with each other. Each LETS opened an account with each other, and when someone from Bristol wanted to trade with someone in Glastonbury, the Bristolian purchaser would pay their thanks into Glastonbury's account in Bristol, and, at the same time, Glastonbury would pay the same amount from Bristol's account with Glastonbury into the vendor's account. Through this mechanism the amount of trade that travelled between the systems was managed, so the problem of wealth moving from a poor to a rich area was not recreated.

If you don't manage the exchange, there can be problems. In the 1990s, members of the 1,000-strong Auckland Green Dollar Exchange all took the opportunity to holiday on nearby Waiheke Island. Waiheke residents all ended up with huge balances they could not spend, while Aucklanders all felt they had 'debts' they struggled to pay back.

Twenty years on, all of New Zealand's Green Dollar exchanges still successfully intertrade, as the exchange is managed. This widens the range of skills available, and fosters interdependence rather than insularity.

slave away for two hours for LETS credits, they should think again. If a job really must be done at a specific, inflexible time to a rigidly high level of quality, then perhaps LETS is not the best tool.

It's important to know, for example, that a new member can't sit back and wait for the phone to ring. It won't. It may be that you need a relaxed attitude to timekeeping, be prepared to chat with the person you are trading with, offer them a cup of tea, accept that they might be learning and perhaps accept a less-than-top-quality performance. These are all things that are more likely to be a feature of a post-carbon economy, but which for some might not compare well with our just-in-time pressurised economy, where low price, top quality and immediate delivery are expected.

LETS makes viable the exchange of skills people have and need, but for which you would probably *not* pay national currency – for example, someone to cut your lawn – or for things where the ability to pay at least a part of the cost in LETS makes the difference between a sale and no sale.

Look after your active members

If you are lucky enough to recruit someone who has skills that are in high demand (a plumber, someone good at DIY or business everyone wants to patronise), you need to look after them. Advise them to limit the number of LETS credits they earn to what they can spend, and help them to think of ways to spend. They are the engines of your LETS.

If some good earners get fed up and leave, or end up with a huge, unspendable surplus while everyone else ends up with a negative balance, the system can jam up. Those with the big balances say they are not going to provide any more services until they have spent a bit, while those with negative balances say they are not going to spend any more until they have earned a bit.

The answer is to avoid this mess by encouraging those with especially marketable skills to limit their involvement, or by training those who have negative balances to provide the necessary services.

Give clear advice about tax and State benefits

Talk to any climate campaigner or direct-action activist and one of the things they will say is that Transition Initiatives won't work as the State will close them down – one dreadlocked activist told me "the State will come for your turnips!". In the 1990s this attitude did a lot of damage and stopped many people who could have benefited from LETS from joining the schemes. Their skills and energy were lost. The fear was that the tax or Social Security offices would want to close LETS down, and the myth now is that this is what happened. The problem is, the myth is wrong. LETS were not closed down.

The situation is different for tax and benefits. Tax offices have for years been able to deal with, say, a country vet who attends a sick cow and is paid a pound of butter for his time if the farmer is going through a tough patch. The tax office knows how much a pound of butter is worth and the vet pays that amount in tax. If the same vet had been in a LETS and cut someone's lawn, i.e. provided a service that was not in his normal line of work, he would not have to pay any tax at all on what is in tax terms a 'personal favour'. So for 99 per cent of LETS trades that are not the giver's main occupation, there are no tax implications. Where tax *is* payable, then the service provider should charge part of the price in national currency, so he can meet his obligations. But the point is that the tax office does not care how we are paid, so long as we pay our taxes in sterling. The Chancellor of the Exchequer won't accept a pound of butter, or a Bobbin!

The benefits situation is more of a problem.[2] Our economic system assumes full employment, and that jobseekers' benefits are just paid for the short time it takes to get the next job, which is obviously not the case for many. Consequently, you are not allowed to work at all. (The situation is different for people on sickness benefit, and we will deal with this in the next chapter). The government in the UK formally classes participation in LETS as 'work'. Unemployed people are allowed to earn a small amount a week, but beyond that they lose benefit, pound for pound. For LETS, this is a problem, as you will lose national currency – universal money spendable everywhere – in favour of less spendable LETS money, which is not ideal to say the least.

The benefit offices want to avoid a situation where someone has quite an enjoyable time getting part of their income from benefits, and topping it up with self-provisioning and LETS. They want people off benefits and into work.

In practice, however, this is less of a real problem as the reality is that very, very few people make a large weekly income on LETS. In places where unemployment is high, in practice benefit offices turn a blind eye to low levels of LETS work, which they see as helping keep unemployed people connected to the world of work. But they won't admit to it.

If your LETS scheme has no connection to national money and cannot be exchanged for national money, and you can't spend it with businesses, then the benefit officer *might* officially disregard LETS earnings. But this is decided on a case-by-case basis and until a decision is made you won't get benefit. It's probably best not to push the authorities into making a decision on this unless you have a very active LETS scheme and an unemployed member who is regularly earning LETS credits that cannot in any way be exchanged for anything that businesses sell: i.e. it is more like time money (see Chapter 6) than a LETS currency related to sterling.

There have been no investigations of any LETS by the benefit authorities that led to LETS being 'closed down'. There was one case where a voluntary organisation was paying a cleaner in LETS for quite a lot of work each week. In that case it could be argued that the voluntary agency was exploiting the cleaner and the benefit authorities were right to put a stop to it! There are many examples of people not joining LETS or leaving a LETS scheme because they were worried about the benefits situation. Some LETS schemes have had their confidence shaken by an enquiry from a benefit officer. Possibilities have certainly been limited.

Sheffield LETS members at a trading event. Photo courtesy of Catherine Burchell, Sheffield LETS.

But for LETS the reality is generally benign neglect on the part of benefit authorities where you are actively seeking work, trading small amounts of personal favours, and live in an area with high unemployment. In this situation, very small LETS earnings from 'personal favours' work are too much bother to count – so while the official advice will always be that you must declare all of your earnings to the authorities, in reality as long as you aren't able to spend your LETS

Setting up a business on LETS

There are plenty of examples of small businesses being set up using LETS. LETS can provide the opportunity to develop businesses in areas that might be difficult on conventional terms. For example, people often find handmade and craft items too expensive compared with something less nice and unique but mass-produced, often abroad. They might like someone to give them one-to-one help, but it would be too expensive using conventional money. Paying part of the price in LETS can make the difference between someone being able to afford a handmade item and going to the local supermarket for something cheaper but inferior. Allowing people to pay with a local currency can allow someone to safely develop a hobby into a micro-business. Similarly, you might not feel that the quality of your work is good enough to charge for it, but practising on LETS can help you turn a hobby into a livelihood.

- In Nelson, New Zealand, one family has a regular and not-unsubstantial income from selling handmade jewellery for part Green Dollars, part New Zealand dollars.
- Steve in Bristol has made cards.
- In Manchester, John has helped people set up wormeries.
- Pete has given personal advice to someone wanting to use a computer for the first time.
- In Sheffield, Catherine gives music lessons for stones (Sheffield's local currency) to people who could not otherwise afford them.

credits with local businesses and are earning only a couple of credits a week you shouldn't have a problem.

For someone on benefits this is not really good enough, and it has been a barrier to people on benefits joining and benefiting from LETS. The solution is not to use LETS but to join a time bank, where time credits do not affect benefits – see the next chapter.

Either way, the reality is that the State will not 'come for' your LETS credits, and if you are able to develop a sustainable resilient livelihood for yourself using LETS and other currencies, the State will probably applaud you, so long as you are not claiming benefits. Worrying about it limits your possibilities needlessly. We should focus on our power to do what we want to do, not imagine that 'they' have some form of power over us that paralyses us.

New, more resilient LETS and Transition

Transition Initiatives provide a focus for and rationale for developing a range of alternative currencies, and the 'great reskilling' and learning from the elders, if facilitated with a LETS scheme, can go a long way towards putting into place our visions of a localised, more convivial and slower economy. LETS is a useful first step, and an easy way to manifest the energy in a community.

LETS and Transition Initiative members are often cut from the same branch. They can help each other out. LETS can provide the 'trading' arm of Transition, and a good way of publicising Transition to a wider audience. Transitioners can be new blood for a stagnant old LETS scheme. For example:

1. West Somerset LETS joined up with Transition Minehead and Alcombe and an organic gardening

group to organise a plant share. People collecting spare plants and helping out for the day were paid in Exes. West Somerset LETS has also held talks and films as part of the Transition process, and has hosted a public meeting entitled 'The Brave New Economy in West Somerset', which discussed a range of alternative currency models. *www.west-somerset-forum21.org.uk/content/transition-minehead-alcombe*

2. Rob Follett from Falmouth LETS and his colleagues were central to the establishments of Transition Falmouth. Rob helped members of Transition Truro to carry out a skills audit, which he suggested might be the basis for a LETS directory. Transition Falmouth and Falmouth LETS members regularly get together for 'green work parties'. A group of people descend on someone's house or garden and blitz some mammoth outstanding task. It works even better if the recipient provides food and the whole thing turns into a social occasion. Other Falmouth LETS work parties have involved

polytunnel construction, painting and decorating, and garden clearance. *www.falmouthlets.org.uk*

Transition Falmouth and Falmouth LETS members on a work party at Falmouth Green Centre. FGC provided food & drink and paid participants (all Falmouth LETS members) in Palms from their account. Photo courtesy of Guy Doncaster, Falmouth LETS.

South West Dorset: from LETS to Transition Town Bridport

"LETS is vibrant in Bridport – in addition to a growing and lively membership several local organisations, businesses and groups are involved and these interact with each other when there are functions on.

Bridport has many environmentally and community-aware groups, and many of these groups were already part of the LETS scheme. At the end of 2008 LETS members instigated the set-up of Transition Town Bridport, which has also joined our LETS scheme.

This means that where an individual joins a particular group they automatically have a link with LETS and through that to Transition Town Bridport – raising awareness and bringing the community together in many different ways – perfect for a Transition Town.

Trading in Nets (the local currency) is considered perfectly normal round here – we'll probably never need the Bridport Pound!" **Sue Rickard, South West Dorset LETS**

LETS online

Once it is set up and supported by one of the new online accounts packages, LETS is a really low-impact way of supporting people in their one-to-one trades, quietly, in the background – but of immense value. Rob Follett of Falmouth LETS writes:

"As a long-term LETS enthusiast who's been involved in my local group since 1994, I'd suggest that fifteen years or so experience of trading for many LETS in the UK, including Falmouth LETS, is quite an achievement and definitely something to be celebrated, comparing favourably in terms of longevity with both businesses and community groups.

My direct experience of LETS has been of a very useful person-to-person system that's built an invaluable local network of able and versatile people and has seeded several other community initiatives. Due to its informal and non-coercive nature it's been less successful for business-to-business trading, but there's no reason why different alternative currencies can't complement each other, or indeed complement new initiatives designed to tackle resource depletion and climate change, such as the Transition movement (as we're doing in Falmouth).

Much of the administrative load, cash cost, and cumbersome nature of running a traditional paper-based LETS group can be eased by putting it online, thus freeing up time and energy for organising the trading and social events that are the real lifeblood of LETS.

Whilst putting the group online initially requires some effort and expertise, particularly for an existing group, two of us on Falmouth LETS have been working with LETSlink UK to develop an existing Open Source package ('Local Exchange') that provides a directory, allows online transactions, and includes social networking features that are likely to appeal to a younger generation – see http://falmouthlets.org.uk for the new Falmouth LETS site using this package.

More details of this free Open Source software, including links to the source code and a demo site, are available via LETSlink UK at http://cxss.info – a comparative and collaborative site for LETS software."
Rob Follett, Falmouth LETS and Transition Falmouth. http://fallets.letsf.co.uk/index.php

LETS – key recommendations

- LETS are easy to set up, but do need energy to be put into making them work well. They can be an easy 'quick win' for new Transition Initiatives.
- Pay attention to running your LETS scheme well.
- Make sure everyone understands how it works, and shares the ethos.
- Put energy into making sure people get to meet each other.
- Give clear advice about tax and State benefits.
- Don't over-sell.
- Use LETS to facilitate learning from your community and 'the great reskilling'.
- Do not expect many local businesses to join. Paper currencies work better for businesses – as we discuss in Chapters 9 to 14.

The scorecard

For each of the currencies in this and the following chapters there is a 'scorecard' to see how each model scores against four criteria:

- **'Hardness'**: How easy is it to get hold of? Businesses generally favour 'hard' currencies that they can change to cash. Those without conventional money want 'soft' money that is easily available – perhaps that they can create themselves.

- **'Valuableness' or 'moneyness'**: does it look like money? Or is it a less 'valuable' means of exchange – just a way of keeping score of no intrinsic value?

- **'Localness'**: Does it circulate widely, or locally, in a small area?

- **'Effectiveness'**: How close a fit is there between the extent to which it circulates and what people want it to achieve? For example, you can't expect a wind turbine company to use a very local currency, or someone to travel too far to babysit.

THE LETS SCORECARD

Hard   Soft

Valuable   Weak

Circulates widely   Circulates locally

Effectiveness for a business (■) or community exchange (●)

High   Low

CHAPTER 6

TIME BANKING

The second option for Transition money is time money or time banking – a specific form of parallel currency that exists only as time, with one hour of everyone's time being equal. This is not to be confused with versions of LETS or paper currencies that might be denominated in time.

It may help to think of time banking as more like a system of community loyalty points. You give what you can and then get back what you need from other members of the community. Time banking's track record is strong in terms of getting people from socially excluded parts of cities, people with health problems or older people, involved in supporting each other through mutual aid. If you are concerned that your Transition Initiative looks a little too comfortably middle-class, a time bank might be a good way of helping less-well-off members of your community to make the transition to a low-carbon lifestyle.

What could be the contribution of time banking to the Transition process, to a world past peak oil and the credit crunch, and where dangerous climate change is avoided? The answer from the US time banking movement is given in the box opposite.

Time banking can be used as a tool for Transition in a number of ways, alongside a LETS and a paper currency for business. Its proven record of involving members of more socially excluded communities can expand the movement. Time banks, run by an agency that makes sure the vulnerable are supported through the transition to a low-carbon local economy, might meet some concerns that Transition pays too little attention to issues of social justice. As Transition is about building inclusive support networks rather than exclusive, xenophobic lifeboats, time banking could be a useful part of the mix.

What is time banking?

Time banking works by members of the bank helping each other out, banking and spending hours as they do so. The founder of time banking, Edgar Cahn, originally described it is being like a blood bank or baby-sitting club: "Help a neighbour and then, when you need it, a neighbour – most likely a different one – will help you."[1] Everyone's time is valued equally, no matter what is done: one hour is equal to one time credit.

How does time banking work?

- The hours do not exist in physical form – there are no chequebooks, coins or notes. Credits are kept in individual accounts in a 'bank', an account on a computer, with the time deposited and withdrawn tracked using software called 'Time-on-Line'.

- Participants 'deposit' their time in the bank by giving practical help and support to others, and are able to 'withdraw' their deposited time to pay someone else when they need something done themselves.

- An hour's work earns a credit, irrespective of what was done in that hour. Equality is insisted upon. Cleaning costs and earns an hour, as does an hour's legal advice.

- Credits and debits are tallied regularly. Some time banks provide monthly balance statements, recording the flow of time, although not all worry about people balancing the amount of time deposited and withdrawn. If you need more support from the time bank than you can give back (assuming you have a good reason for this), that's fine.

- To withdraw and deposit time credits you call a broker, who keeps a database of members, and who then calls someone on your behalf to see if they can meet your needs. The advantage of this is that you don't need to phone around to get what you need. One call does it.

- If it is unlikely that the time bank can meet your specific request, the broker will be able to tell you that straight away, and perhaps point you towards other sources of help.

- This also means that less confident people, who might not feel brave enough to phone a stranger asking for help, and then negotiate the trade, are looked after. This is why time banking works well for less confident members of our communities.

There are three kinds of time banking.

Member-to-member
Member-to-member, neighbourhood time banking puts neighbours in touch with each other so they can help each other out with whatever needs doing.

Agency-to-member
Agency-to-member time banking is run by a specific agency (a doctor's surgery, a school, a volunteer bureau, a community association), either as a member-to-member service or specifically to solve a problem: for example, to support people with mental health problems, encourage people to eat healthily, or provide alternatives to crime. The agency will integrate the time banking with its other programmes, and provide the broker.

More love, less 'stuff'

"Technological innovation alone can't save us from our lemming-like drive towards decimating the Earth's natural resources. We'll need a cultural shift to rebalance our pleasure-seeking away from global consumption lifestyles and towards less resource-intensive local lifestyles. We're going to have to substitute social capital for financial capital – more love, less stuff. We'll never get to lower levels of consumption unless we find a way to make it more fun and fulfilling than the consumptive lifestyle. This is a tall order in our competitive, consumerist Yang culture. Yet The Inconvenient Truth remains, if we don't limit our consumption we face catastrophic weather changes and ecological disasters. Only deep meaning-filled relationships within a strong local community could possibly pull us away from resource-intensive lifestyles before it is too late." From www.timebanks.org

Agency-to-agency

Agencies with unused resources can share them with other agencies. For example:

- Agency A has a minibus it doesn't use on a Friday, but needs a kitchen on a Tuesday.

- Agency B has a spare kitchen at the time Agency A needs, so . . .

- . . . Agency A pays Agency B time money for use of the kitchen.

- Agency C needs a Friday minibus, which it pays Agency A for.

- Agency A has just earned back the time money it needs to pay Agency B for the kitchen.

- Agency C lets Agency D use its crèche for a training day, earning the money it needs to pay for the minibus. And so on.

Using time banking, they can share these resources. An hour's use of the minibus is the same as an hour's use of the kitchen.

The more established time banks incorporate all three types of time banking.

Co-production

Time banking works on the ethos of 'co-production'. The solutions to our problems and the services we need can't be provided by governments alone. They are often unwilling to commit the resources, and do not always deliver services that meet local needs.

Communities can't solve their problems and meet their needs alone. They don't have all the resources they need, and might need ideas from elsewhere.

What is needed is a different way of solving problems: government agencies and citizens working together to identify and solve problems. Not communities trying to do it all themselves. Not government imposing solutions from above, thinking that 'the man from Whitehall knows best'. He doesn't. But neither do local people, alone, have all the answers.

Time banking works on the idea that people are assets with skills, ideas and resources, not problems to be solved or to have things done to them. The best way to

Garden Maintenance after the floods of 2007, Fair Shares Gloucester. Photo courtesy of Time Banks UK.

build a healthy community is to strengthen the networks through which the 'core economy' of home, family and community works. While economists and politicians will say that the best way for people to be happy and secure in their life is to get a paid job or set up a business, we also know that paid work and businesses are only one part of the economy. Children are bought up, people are fed and nurtured, clubs, churches and societies run and older people are looked after through hours and hours and hours of unpaid work that economists ignore. Helping works best when it's a two-way street. We are happiest when we both give and receive. No one wants to feel dependent or helpless.

No one wants to be isolated. Studies have shown that we humans are generally a sociable bunch. Of course we have the capacity to fall out with each other and to wipe out other communities in terrible wars and acts of genocide, but even then it is community A making war on community B; two collectives fighting. We do not live like cats, solitary, with our own individual territory; everyone fighting everyone else. We do best when we are in networks, when we have social capital.

These links might become more important as survival strategies in the future, given that we cannot realistically all go off into the woods to survive. We will do best in the future where we can support each other. LETS and time banking can help build such 'social capital'.

If you are already part of a family, club or church and can get the help you need, fine. But what if you are isolated, elderly, unwell, or live in a place where this sort of help isn't available? What if your most available options are criminality, drugs and prostitution, rather than a job? Time banking aims to provide a mutual aid network in places where it doesn't exist, and, through the network, build feelings of community and solidarity. In the 1990s it was thought that LETS could do that. In practice, LETS schemes often involve more obviously white, middle-class, green-and-alternative-minded people from the more leafy suburbs and small towns.

Denver SkillShare, Colorado, USA

"Shortly after SkillShare opened, a single mother called one night, overwhelmed by her responsibilities as parent, full-time worker and student. Three days later, on a Sunday afternoon, three SkillShare members went over to her house to clean, organise and give support. She later said that she would never have gotten through that time without their help and loving concern."

"One day, we received a call from a member who wanted to donate some of her accumulated time dollar credits to a friend who was confined to her bed unable to move. Her friend was able to access several massage and healing bodywork sessions that week from SkillShare members."

"One young woman who had dropped out of college because of health problems was able to offer housecleaning services and accumulated enough time dollar credits to receive a variety of healing services from SkillShare members, including acupuncture, which helped her regain her health."

"Two young mothers, who both worked different schedules, met at a SkillShare potluck and began to provide and earn Time Dollar credits offering childcare for each other's children. They became friends and worked out a childcare schedule for over a year."

You don't generally find LETS in the inner city or outer estates.

Poor communities trying to solve their problems completely on their own, with limited time, funding and resources, and isolated from sources of help, doesn't work. Time banking aims to fix this. It aims to mobilise the time resources of our communities, but puts the funding in to make sure that a broker is able to actively build and maintain the network. Using the ethos of co-production, agencies and community members then decide together how the resources the community has (time, local knowledge, practical skills) can be mobilised alongside the money and organisational support provided by agencies to solve problems collectively.

Because it has been shown to work well in poorer areas, cannot be spent in shops, and aims to solve problems that government wants to see solved, governments have generally been very supportive of the concept of time money. This is why time banking has found it relatively easy to get grants, and the UK government has said that time credits earned do not affect tax and social security benefits. This is why, for the most vulnerable on State benefits, time banking beats LETS as an alternative currency.

Co-producing Transition

The ethos of co-production resonates with that of Transition, and might be a way of developing new ways of involving local government and other local institutions in developing local resilience. Time banking might be a good way of making sure that major transformations of our communities happen without waiting for government to pay for them in a top-down manner (don't hold your breath), but also without waiting for volunteers or hard-pressed Transition Initiative regulars to do more. Time money can be the lubricant unleashing more community-based action, with time credits acting as a reward that can be cashed in later, perhaps even once the transformation has been undertaken and we rely more on an economy based on social capital and favours than on unsustainable 'stuff'.

The future cannot be produced by any of us alone – neither central nor local government, nor a local

Social capital

Sociologist Robert Putnam[2] and others have looked at the most successful societies, and concluded that those that work best are those that have lots of associations, clubs, welfare and mutual aid societies, business clubs and the like, at their heart. These clubs act as networks to enable people to meet up, discuss their problems, and get help – through building social capital. This is a form of capital based not on money but on relationships.

Social capital works best when we have what Mark Granovetter[3] called "the strength of weak ties". It's better to know and get on with lots of different people, who have a wide range of things that could help you, but you don't need to know them very well. A nodding acquaintance, the odd chat, but they know you are a 'good sort' and will help you out if you need it. This is called 'bridging capital'. It builds a bridge between you and other people.

The other sort of capital, 'bonding capital', works less well. This is the capital of strong, homogeneous communities, the members of which know each other very well, but who all have the same skills and needs. You do not have the diversity of skills to meet your needs. Many poorer communities have very strong bonds, but lack bridges to meet other people who can help them.

DIY Skills training project for time credits at My Time Your Time time bank, London. Photo courtesy of Time Banks UK.

Transition community alone – but must be co-produced. Co-production gives us the opportunity to transition mainstream social service, health and local government agencies, so they become part of the vibrant local economies and communities we are striving to create. It could help us to avoid the problems of the past.

How do you set up a time bank?

You will probably discuss a time bank as an option at the same time that you discuss LETS. As we will see later (Chapters 9 to 14), running a paper currency programme well is quite a task, perhaps better suited for later stages of the transition to a local, low-carbon economy where the aim is to involve businesses and develop local production. Setting up a LETS or time bank is easier.

How time banking can help

A time bank can help to:

- bring people together in a spirit of equality
- value and record contributions to community life
- build an individual's confidence and skills
- enhance the capacity of a community or voluntary organisation to make a difference
- build community networks and local knowledge
- get things done that wouldn't get done otherwise (by funding in time credits)
- encourage community participation and diversity in its participants so that there is a wide variety of skills exchanged
- embed reciprocity into the relationship between citizens and public services.

In some ways, setting up a time bank is even easier than setting up a LETS scheme, if you have a sponsoring community or voluntary organisation able and willing to host it, apply for a grant, and employ the broker. The basic elements of a time bank are defined, so there is no need to think about what to call your currency, how to value it, or how to develop a shared ethos. You can contact Time Banking UK and get all the information you need. There are only two requirements: that you stick to the 'one hour is one time credit' rule and sign up to the core values.

Time Banking UK: **www.timebanking.org**

LETS or time banking?

It is likely that when you explore local currencies as part of your Transition Initiative, you will need to decide on the advantages and disadvantages of each for your community. Time banking generally has been shown to work better in poorer communities where people might lack the confidence to take the first step to get in contact with people who might help them. They work better than LETS for agencies that want to help people to raise their confidence levels, or take the first steps back to work. And they also focus on ordinary members of the community, not businesses.

The broker

The main reason why you might plump for a time bank over LETS is the role of the broker. Remember, LETS schemes provide a directory of members who contact each other directly to get the services they need. You need to be quite confident and go-getting to pick up the phone and call a stranger; many people won't. The time broker does this for you, so less-confident members of the community are more

likely to use time banking, and vulnerable people are not left without support if the time bank can't meet their needs. On the other hand, a fairly confident and articulate member of a LETS scheme might prefer to make contact themselves, and feel patronised or constrained by the need to go through the broker.

The role of the broker also means that, if you don't have a sponsoring organisation to run the time bank for you and need to get a grant to fund your broker's salary, time banks are harder to set up and more expensive to run than a community-based LETS scheme running on volunteer time and enthusiasm, but which has little money beyond the subs it generates itself. The time bank is also dependent on the personality, skills and enthusiasm of the broker in effectively connecting people, cajoling the recalcitrant into doing something, and so on. Not everyone has those skills. Such people can be hard to find, and a time bank that loses a broker can flounder, as can one that loses its grant funding if no one steps into the breach to do the brokering. LETS is more low-key, but responsibility is more widely spread throughout the network – it can thus be more resilient to shocks than time banking.

Having said that, the very first time bank in the UK, in Stonehouse, has been run by its members without paid staff for ten years, and several other time banks have lived on after their funding from the host agency dried up – they continue to run on a mixed economy of a little cash, time credits and volunteers reaping the rewards that come from knowing that there are people around who care. On the other hand, as we see below, time banks working in areas with entrenched and multiple problems can find that without more funding they are unable to meet the very real needs of their members. Communities often can't meet their needs alone – they need support.

Elements of both LETS and time banking schemes can be combined. In practice, there is nothing to stop members of a time bank sorting things out for themselves, and some less-confident members of LETS might welcome the support of a broker. Peckham LETS and Peckham HOurBank work together, with the brokers available for LETS members, while the time bank is recommended as an alternative for less-confident applicants for LETS. Avalon Fair Shares in Glastonbury runs a time bank, trading hours, and a LETS scheme, trading Grebos.

Peckham HOurBank:
www.peckhamsettlement.org.uk/Hourbank.htm

Avalon Fair Shares:
www.isleofavalon.co.uk/community/AFS.html

Empowering excluded communities

Time banks work alongside or are run by mainstream health, social services and regeneration agencies, local authorities, Primary Health Care Trusts and even courts to strengthen the 'core economy' of family, community and neighbourhood on which the 'market economy' of paid work and businesses sits.

Time banks run by agencies can focus on solving a particular problem such as a local lack of work and social inclusion in a deprived neighbourhood, or poor health. Research by Gill Seyfang[4] for the new economics foundation shows that the ability to earn and spend time credits is way down the list of people's motives for joining a time bank – they want to help others out. Time credits are routinely not spent, but donated. People who need more help than they can give get it. You don't need to earn enough time money to meet your needs.

Time Banking and local businesses

Time banking is not seen, primarily, as a way to develop local businesses or new production. It's a way of recognising work that society often devalues, insisting that we treat every hour of work as if they are of equal value. As a result, the membership of a time bank will not generally include businesses or people who do not want to value their time so equally.

Paying in time can be a hard conception to grasp. We are used to accounting with money, but are unused to thinking of time as a currency or as a way of calculating what contribution we have made. It can cut against the common-sense understanding that some people work harder or more effectively than others. Some people might be money rich and time poor; others time rich and money poor. Consequently, not everyone's hour is worth the same to them. Businesses struggle to integrate this with the more conventional forms of value they use that are based on conventional money.

This is not to say that businesses are completely absent from time banking. Time banking does involve some local businesses by encouraging them to offer discounts and freebies as a way of rewarding people for contributing to the life of the community. Highly skilled tradespeople can use their expertise within a time bank, not as participants but as trainers. For example, plumbers train up local people in simple maintenance work. Retired professionals also keep their hand in through time banking.

Local currency expert Gill Seyfang's research[5] has been invaluable in identifying good practice in time banking. Her work makes the following points.

The broker is key

Gill's work suggests that to make time banking work effectively, a well-known and well-connected broker is crucial. The broker should be accessible and have well developed communication skills. It's not too strong to say that a good broker can 'make or break' the time bank. Given the centrality of the broker, a time bank needs adequate funding as a full-time broker is a full-time job.

The broker will have to adapt the model to local conditions, working with time bank members to make sure they get what they need from the bank, and that its development happens within an ethos of co-production. But they will also be central to dealing with the issues discussed below, which are common to all time banks. It is essential that you support your broker and do not leave them to get on with running the time bank on their own. That is not resilient – what if they leave? And you will burn them out. You can't expect them to do it all on their own. So it is important that you have a management committee or core group to share the load.

Make sure people know how to use the time bank

If new members are unsure how the system works, feel they have nothing to offer, and don't want to 'ask for help', that can sink things very quickly. Here the roles of the broker, of induction, and of social events are crucial. It can prove quite difficult to widen the range of services available, especially if the time bank is an agency-led one designed to solve a particular problem, and is working with a homogeneous community strong in bonding capital but not in bridging capital (see page 92). It can be hard to widen the range of services if the supply of new members dries up.

Actively foster community feeling

Lack of trust can be a problem in some neighbourhoods. Concerns about security need to be managed. Crucial for building cohesiveness are social and community events, through which people can get to know each other, become more confident about what skills they have, and learn all the tacit 'tricks of the trade' by which the time bank, or any alternative currency scheme, works.

Look after the active members

Make sure that those who give and receive a lot are comfortable with it. Make sure that someone building up a large nest egg of credits knows that he might struggle to spend it, and that someone who receives more than they give again feels comfortable with the situation.

Sustainable funding

It's good to get funding for a pilot project, but you need from the start to think about sustainable forms of funding, or identify an agency to run your time bank in-house. In the early days, again and again, a pilot of a time bank would be set up with short-term funding, only to be closed down when the pilot funding ran out. When the end of funding for a pilot time bank in the Elephant and Castle, London, led to the suspension of the time bank's activities while a full bid was written up, I couldn't help feeling that people in need were left dangling after all the promises the agencies had made to them.

In the USA, the experience has been that time banks found it easy to get start-up funding, when they were the latest 'big thing', but that it was much harder to get this level of support in the long term. The time banks reverted to operating with a rota of volunteers, providing a level of brokerage and support that was, despite their best intentions, not much greater in the long run that would have been provided without funding. Was the money used in setting up the time bank well spent? Could the volunteers have done it anyway?

"The most exciting thing for me about timebanking, other than its enormous power to improve people's quality of life and economic standing, is the way it creates the feeling of being in a very large extended family and improves people's understanding and compassion for others' situations. About 5 per cent of our members have disabilities, over 20 per cent earn below the poverty level, and our racial and ethnic diversity generally exceeds the diversity of our local population. Timebanking seems to bring out the best in people, encouraging generosity, reciprocity, sharing and skill-building."
Stephanie Rearick, Director, Dane County Timebank, Madison, Wisconsin, USA.
www.danecountytimebank.org

The lesson is that funding can be very useful, but if it dries up then the project can be vulnerable. There is considerable evidence that those local currency schemes that have relied primarily on the voluntary activity of their members, with funding used to get to places time-money-funded voluntary work alone could not reach, have been more sustainable than those reliant on grant funding alone for their very existence.

Having the management systems, accountability processes and documentation in place to be able to bid for and then manage a grant coming from public funds is also quite a task, which might be beyond the capacity of a new local currency scheme. There are plusses and minuses to having a grant. If it works well, you can do more. But, unfortunately, too many organisations that worked well enough on a volunteer basis have floundered when they gained more grant funding than they could manage, or began to focus less on what they were set up to do and more on accounting for the money they had and getting the next grant. It might be best to steer clear of too large a grant too soon unless you are sure you can manage it.

Build the ethos of co-production

Time banking can quickly gain a few enthusiasts – early joiners, the sort of people who are the glue of the community and who can always be relied upon to be on the touchline at children's sports days – but the wider population can be quite cynical, having seen

Car Maintenance, Fair Shares in Gloucester. Photo courtesy of Time Banks UK.

this before. Given the vast range of never-ending initiatives done *to* communities, which all claim that they will solve the community's problems, only to be replaced by the next 'big thing', this is perhaps not surprising. On the other hand, research suggests that 42 per cent of time banking participants are men, when historically neighbourliness and caring has been done by women.

Local people do not find the concept of banking time hard to grasp, as giving and receiving is the way that communities have always been built. They may feel, however, that it's not their role to solve the community's problems. They may feel that they pay their taxes and that government should sort things out.

Time banking has learned that any agency hosting a time bank needs to have a genuine resolve to change the culture away from creating the dependencies that arise from using one-way systems delivered by 'professional strangers', to a co-production approach that embraces the time banking element as an operational imperative. Time banking cannot be just a friendly add-on.

Helping the agencies to 'let go'

David Boyle of the new economics foundation has pointed to some of the problems of making co-production work in practice. Often agencies found the ethos hard to understand, and difficult to implement in practice. They were so used to providing services *for* people, and understandably thought themselves to be the experts in the field. They struggled to 'let go', to let the future of the project out of their hands. Some didn't like the unconventional hours that co-producing an initiative with members of the community entailed. Of course, the aim of co-producing services to meet local needs can fundamentally contradict the reality that many services, in the UK at least, are delivered to

meet centrally set targets. In such situations, local agencies can be no more than the local delivery arms of central government. It's important to recognise that in what you expect them to do.

Recognise and accept the limits of time banking alone

It's important to recognise – and accept – that problems can be so deep that we need government intervention to solve them. Especially in an era of public spending cuts, the pressure from government and local authorities to meet people's needs with less and less funding can be very strong, and the temptation can be there to offload problems on to communities that are just not well-equipped enough to solve them. Here, community-based programmes and projects are being set up to fail. At times, it is necessary to recognise that this is happening, and campaign for more funding or against cuts.

Integrate time banking into a comprehensive package of services

Some service delivery organisations like doctors' surgeries or social services agencies have developed a sustainable funding model by running the time bank as part of a portfolio of services to their clients, rather than as a stand-alone project requiring its own funding. Here, the brokering job is done 'in house'.

The potential of time banking in the Transition process

The potential for time banking to contribute to Transition has yet to be tapped. But a few examples of what might be possible include the following.

- Using time money to reward recycling, and allowing these credits to be used in buses as they are in Rotterdam or in Curitiba in Brazil (see pages 210-211). Using spare capacity in the transport system to clean up the city.

- Facilitating skills development and sharing knowledge through time money, especially learning from older members of the UK community who remember the war, 'digging for victory', and a world where people travelled less and life was less oil-dependent.

- Paying time credits for a neighbourhood skills survey.

- Sharing agencies' resources, getting further with less.

- Paying for environmental improvements.

- Setting up a time-bank-based Carbon Reduction Action Group (CRAG).

- Doing DIY and small repairs – especially for the elderly – and learning their skills in return.

- Carrying out environmental upgrading. We don't have the money to do this, or the government is unwilling to pay for upgrading all our homes. Grants could be used to buy the materials and the installation done using time money, perhaps as training as part of a Green New Deal. The participants could then go on to full-time work.

Watch the Rushey Green film clip at:
www.youtube.com

Elders Network, Berkeley, USA

One neighbour-to-neighbour time bank scheme run by the Elders Network in inner city Berkeley, California, felt that the social isolation felt by members without close family support was very severe. They felt that the time bank helped members get by, but that they were still very isolated and fearful. Given a lack of long-term funding, members were not getting the quality and level of support they really needed from volunteers.

Despite the ethos of time banking, when problems were severe and entrenched, and long-term support was required, the experience was that members still worried about being 'in debt'. Vulnerable members were told not to worry if they needed more support than they could give back, and if their account was negative then statements did not include a balance. The time bank encouraged people to feel that they are giving to and receiving from 'The Bank' rather than from an individual account.

The time bank tried to get people to believe that it is acceptable to give what you can and receive what you need. If there is a need, there is a need to meet it. But recipients could still react against what they saw as charity. Concern about being 'in debt' meant that some people still went without, got by, and didn't ask for help that *was* available.

"For me, the Transition process is about building relationships, about sharing skills and aspirations across artificial barriers like income, race, religion, ability and age. Time banking is a tool ready to be used to bring back to life the local social networks that have in the past made it possible for people to reflect together on issues of mutual concern and then to take collective action to improve quality of life for each other and for the wider community."
Martin Simon, Time Banking UK. www.timebanking.org

Looking after senior citizens: Walnut Creek Time Bank, USA

Rossmore Service Credits is an agency-led time bank funded through a service charge paid by the residents of a retirement community in the San Francisco Bay Area suburbs – the link below will show you what sort of community it is. Through the time bank, for example, an elderly resident can get someone to change a light bulb, rather than perhaps trying to do it themselves and having a fall. For frail elderly people a fall can be very serious indeed.

The time bank is part of an integrated programme of care provided for residents. Any given request for help might be met by the time bank, or perhaps by someone else from the management company, or by State social services. No one falls through the net.

Time bank members here feel that they are paying for the scheme from their service charges and want value for money. They don't seem to differentiate between the time bank and the rest of the services provided, but feel they've bought the package so they'll use it. The result is a scheme that meets members' needs, and mobilises their contributions in time towards helping each other out. **www.retireinrossmoor.com**

Inspiration from time banks in London, UK

Caledonian Road Time Bank runs a recycling scheme. The council does collect recycling, but there are limited facilities available to those living in flats. Street-based recycling facilities are often located away from blocks of flats. In the Westbourne Estate area, time bank members can take part in a household recycling scheme. Since August 2002, their Household Recycling Collection service has collected half a tonne of recycled material, such as paper, tin cans, glass bottles, jars and clothes. The group also organises litter picking (especially when Arsenal are playing at home), food co-op delivery, tree planting, hanging baskets, food growing and bicycle maintenance.

Hilldrop and Calle Time Bank members meet at the solar-powered Hilldrop Community Centre to exchange organic fruit and veg and enjoy a cup of coffee at the community cafe. Also in London, Mildmay Time Bank has a community garden.

'Growing Newsome', Hull, UK

Newsome Community Forum in Hull surveyed its local community to find out what local people thought about growing their own food, and what the problems and opportunities were. Local people, including members of the time bank, were trained up as interviewers. It took over 100 volunteer hours to conduct the survey, with people going door-to-door over four days with a questionnaire designed by Newsome residents.

The Forum quickly realised that the project was about far more than the food itself. People were interested in finding out how to do things together. Next stage was a 'Growing Newsome' event, where people could get together and talk. Members grew plants to give away, ran seed-planting activities, made and served the refreshments, and promoted the event.

The spirit of time banking has quickly become a key part of the food-growing project. The project provides new ways for Newsome residents to share their skills and resources, for example a garden-sharing scheme. Some members have gardens that they can't use much because of health issues, so there are plans to tackle overgrown or unused gardens so they can be adopted by other people who have nowhere to grow food, and everyone will get a share of the produce. The other plan is for a community tool bank to make it easier for the community to work together to grow their own food. http://growingnewsome.wordpress.com

Lyttelton Time Bank, Aotearoa/New Zealand

The Lyttelton Time Bank is the first established time bank in New Zealand, established by Project Lyttelton (PL), a grassroots organisation with a variety of interlinked projects focusing on creating a vibrant and sustainable community. There are three community gardens, a thriving farmers market, an education arm and a time bank.

A Community Supported Agriculture box scheme is run from two of the community gardens. People attending gardening courses are able to access the boxes, for which they pay a minimal charge and contribute their time either to the gardens themselves or to the successful running of the system (for example, creating recipe sheets for unusual vegetables included in the box). The labour is all measured by the time bank.

The local information and visitor centre is run entirely by volunteers who are paid time credits. When people accrue time credits faster than they are using them they are encouraged to donate them to the community chest, where people or community organisations can use them. For instance, Plunket (a welfare charity) uses them in its annual door-to-door fundraising to 'employ' time bankers to help with the collection.

Lyttelton West School is the first school in New Zealand to become a time bank member. 'Mr TimeBank' goes into the school to help the children work out how they are going to trade and facilitate the interaction between school and community. Already time bankers in the community are engaged in helping sew the costumes for the next school show.

The 'Welcome to Lyttelton' for those relocating into the area is helped by time bankers. Time bankers sew cloth bags (moving Lyttelton away from using plastic bags), which are filled with local bus timetables, community garden information, information on how to join the time bank, and a few other gifts of welcome together with fresh home baking.

The time bank is a wonderful tool for building strong community links. It deals with the trading of services, and future plans include a 'Genuine Wealth System' – an interest-free loan/saving scheme. Further down the track will be a swipe card, and a link between energy production and complementary currencies. www.lyttelton.net.nz

Time banks and health: Rushey Green, London, UK

Rushey Green doctor's surgery prescribes participation in the time bank for people whose confidence is low, or who might need more support in getting out and about. Some people suffer seriously from social isolation, and need help from the community to counter this rather than medication. As a result of its work, Rushey Green Surgery has won a number of awards, including one for 'Outstanding Partnership Achievement with the National Health Service'.

"Time Bank . . . has added a richness to my life, friends, a community, a feeling of being of use and all of the kindness out there." Patricia, Rushey Green Time Bank member. www.rgtb.org.uk

Time banking – key recommendations

- Consider a time bank if you want to strengthen the involvement of excluded communities in your Transition process.
- While you can run a time bank yourself, it's better to find a local agency to host it for you. The agency can get a lot of support from Time Banking UK to set the time bank up. It is not hard, and the key elements of it are set out for you. You don't have to start from scratch.
- The broker is key – find a good one, and hang on to him or her!
- Pay attention to identifying sustainable forms of funding at an early stage.
- Use time money to facilitate your Transition process.

THE TIME BANKING SCORECARD

Hard ●————————————————— Soft

Valuable ●————————————————— Weak

Circulates widely ●————————————————— Circulates locally

Effectiveness for community exchange
High ●————————————————— Low

CHAPTER 7

ITHACA AND OTHER 'HOURS'

What if you want a currency to protect and strengthen a local economy and its much-loved small, community and family owned businesses? LETS and time banking might not be appropriate. Time money does not address the needs of local businesses in any meaningful way, and has no connection to national currency. Businesses struggle to see how they could use it.

LETS schemes do try to recruit local businesses, but their success rate in this has been rather disappointing. Can a busy business that has hundreds of small transactions a day really be expected to report each one to the LETS scheme? Will a busy shopkeeper have time to wait at the till while each customer writes out a cheque, a form of money that has all but disappeared with the introduction of debit cards? If we want to involve local independent businesses in our Transition process, we need to use forms of currency that better meet their needs.

A second issue is that in practice it can be hard for a volunteer LETS accountant to keep track of what is going on. Things are manageable in a small community LETS scheme, but if hundreds or even thousands of people or businesses were involved, then the accountant would quickly be overwhelmed. Time banks solve this problem by having someone in their organisation who can manage the accounts. But what if this organisation stops doing it and you find it difficult to find volunteers? Why not forget about

accounting and just pass a paper currency from person to person?

What if you want a form of money that businesses can use but that has the egalitarian flavour of LETS and time banking rather than hard, limited conventional money? The solution might be an unbacked, time-based local paper currency – 'hours'. The best known of the US hour-based paper currencies is Ithaca Hours.

For links to a wide range of hour-based currencies in the USA see:
www.ithacahours.com/otherhours.html

Ithaca

Ithaca is a university town in upstate New York, the base for Cornell University (part of the Ivy League). Its history is as a market town for the local dairy industry. The district's dairy farmers have a long tradition of cooperation, and of trading at sprawling farmers' markets with the hippies, artists, intellectuals and environmentalists who flocked to the district in the 1960s and '70s in a quest for self-sufficiency, and in an effort to avoid the Vietnam draft. Canada was just over the border if things got too hot.

Many counter-cultural people are attracted to this geographically isolated place where radical ideas thrive. Its citizens have an independent, anti-government, anti-tax ethos, and want to make their way through life in offbeat ways. Some say bartering is in Ithaca's blood.

But Ithaca is also a 'hip' place to live that attracts many wealthy bohemians. Those tasked with promoting the town call it "smart and always unexpected. It's intense and laid-back and disdainful of convention. Ithaca is Ithaca. There's a vibe here unlike anywhere else in America." They are keen to point out that it was voted the eighth-best place to live in the USA on account of its beautiful scenery, low unemployment, low housing costs, entrepreneurial business climate, smart hotels and fine restaurants. It has also been voted the 'healthiest city', 'best mountain biking city', 'best place to retire', and the best 'emerging city'. *Utne Reader* calls it 'America's most enlightened' city'.[1] The local slogan is 'Ithaca: ten square miles surrounded by reality.'

Over 5,000 people a day visit the farmers' market's 125 stalls. All stallholders must have their products certified by a committee of their peers, to ensure quality and originality, and what they are selling must be grown or crafted within 30 miles of Ithaca. Nothing is viewed as 'waste' but everything is rather seen as a valuable resource to be managed and reused. For example, all of the organic waste produced at the market is composted and used to grow more local produce. Customers are encouraged to bring their own reusable coffee mugs and containers to further reduce waste.

If an alternative currency can thrive anywhere, it is Ithaca.

For a taste of Ithaca counterculture see:
www.ithacamarket.com

What are 'Hours'?

In the USA, anyone running a LETS-like scheme falls foul of Internal Revenue Service (IRS) regulations that govern business-to-business barter networks. The organisers are responsible for informing the IRS about the tax affairs of their members, which effectively rules out LETS.

Newspapers are not responsible for the tax affairs of their advertisers. So why not set up a local paper currency that acts a form of reward for advertisers in a local newspaper, which can then circulate between these businesses so they buy from each other? If the notes are re-circulated as change, customers can trade with each other as well. Given the countercultural ethos of the place, why not have a paper currency that assumes that everyone's time is valued equally, and print notes denominated in time – 'Hours'?

This is what Paul Glover came up with in 1991. He'd tried LETS, but it didn't take off. The first run of 1,500 Hour and 1,500 half-Hour notes led to the first real post-depression success story using local paper currencies. 'Hours' have spread to a number of US and Canadian towns and cities. Flagstaff, Arizona has its Neighbourly Notes, Tucson has Traders, Berkeley has Bread – and there are many more.

An Ithaca Hour. Photo courtesy of Lis Maurer.

Thus Hours are different from the time credits used by time banks, although both are denominated in time.

How do Hours differ from time credits?

- Hours are a paper currency; time credits do not have any physical form. They are just electronic.
- To trade using a time bank you call the broker; Hours pass from person to person and to businesses like cash.
- You find out where to spend Hours by looking at a newspaper, or seeing flyers in shop windows.
- Time banks do not seriously engage with businesses; Hours do.

How do Hours work?

Ithaca Hours work like this.

Businesses advertise in a specially created local newspaper, *Ithaca Money* (later *Hour Town*). Of course, an existing local newspaper would do just as well or even better if it was prepared to run the listings. In return, they receive two Ithaca Hours, in paper currency denominated in an eighth, quarter, half, one and two hours.

The notes are decorated with local images, and emblazoned with the slogan 'In Ithaca we trust'. They are printed on high-quality, watermarked paper with security features. The sequence of the serial numbers is secret. The notes are not backed by national currency.

If a business continues to advertise, four more Ithaca Hours flow its way as a reward. While the first businesses to advertise paid for their adverts in US dollars, once the programme was established any business that had them

could pay for its advert entirely with hours. They can also spend the notes with other local businesses and individuals, or give them out in change. Some employees take small numbers of Ithaca Hours as part of their salary, or as a bonus.

Some businesses accept 100-per-cent payment for goods and services in Ithaca Hours. Others restrict what they will take depending on how many Hours they can re-circulate locally.

The community decides collectively, at a monthly potluck meal, how much currency should be issued. The potluck recreates the Native American practice of the potlatch, which celebrated generosity. Status in the community would be afforded to the person who gave the most away, for example by feeding everyone at a ceremonial feast. Status thus goes to those who give and share, not to those who accumulate and amass.

More money is given to community groups and local businesses in the form of one year, zero-interest loans in Ithaca Hours, with decisions about eligibility made at the potluck. Decisions about who should get a loan are thus made by the community.

In 2009, 900 businesses and individuals in Ithaca accepted Ithaca Hours, which have become a familiar and accepted part of the local economy. The programme has become more formal and businesslike. The informal potluck has been replaced by a circulation committee, which makes decisions on loans and how much currency to issue. By any analysis, Ithaca Hours must be seen as a great success.

Paul Glover's site: **www.ithacahours.com**

The official Ithaca Hours site: **www.ithacahours.org**

Ithaca Money and *Bread Rising*, Ithaca and San Francisco, USA.

How do you set up an 'Hours' programme?

Setting up a paper currency of any type should not be entered into lightly. You will need to find:

- a talented designer to give the notes that intangible quality of 'moneyness'. It can be a good idea to hold a competition to design the notes, or a consultation with the community to check that people like and value the design.

- a local printer able to secure appropriate paper and engineer the security features. You will need to identify suppliers yourself – and keep both them and the nature of your serial number system secret!

- a secure place to store the notes, and places from which to issue them. A local bank, building society or credit union would be first choice, or some other secure venue for storage, and shops as issuing points.

The nature of the notes

Hours do need to have the intangible quality of 'moneyness', as discussed in Chapter 2. The notes should be of a high-quality design, on appropriate paper, and have security features designed in. They should have images and language on them that encourage potential users to associate them with value. Ithaca Hours, for example, have pictures of local landmarks, and the slogan 'in Ithaca we trust'.

The acceptability of time-based currency

To some extent, because paper time-based currency has no obvious relationship to national currency, it is less likely to engender feelings that this might be a scam, a way to 'get rich quick' by the canny organiser. Criminals are less likely to try to forge it. It's obviously emerging from and most likely to be accepted by and circulate amongst 'greens' and other 'alternative' types. It's seen as fun and enjoyable, and is a good way of raising awareness about Transition and the need for a localised economy. It is hard to see the people who use and accept Ithaca Hours as having anything other than the best intentions. If you want to get rich quick through a scam, a non-convertible time-based currency founded on equality will not appeal!

On the other hand, as they are not backed and are denominated in time, Hours are more likely to be seen as something strange, countercultural, and not serious. Businesses might struggle to value their goods and services in time. They might be resistant to a form of currency that they struggle to spend and which they then can't convert to national currency. They will have concerns about tax and sales tax implications, and bookkeeping. It might be that Hours suit local economies only in places such as Ithaca or San Francisco, where large numbers of alternative-minded people and businesses that meet their needs congregate.

So you will need to consult widely on a decision to issue time-based Hours as opposed to local money denominated in national-currency valuations, such as the currencies discussed in later chapters.

Ithaca's experiences

In working out how people and businesses are likely to react to unconventional forms of money denomi-nated in time we are not working in the dark. We can build on Ithaca's pioneering experiences.

Value

At first, Ithaca Hours had no equivalent valuation in US dollars. The suggestion was that people pay whatever they felt an Hour was worth, to show that everyone's labour is of equal value, allowing those that wanted to pay more than an Hour for an hour's work to do so.

In practice this was confusing. How many hours for a piece of pie at the farmers' market? Is everyone's hour *really* of equivalent value? What if something was hard to make, taking a lot of effort and muscle power, while everyone could easily provide an hour of less-demanding labour? How do you combine valuations in a mix of Hours and dollars and make change if there is no connection between the two?

Eventually, the compromise of an Ithaca Hour being worth $10 was arrived at ($10 being the average county wage rate in 1991). So, for example, an eighth-hour note is worth $1.25, a quarter-hour is $2.50, and so on. In other words, a form of currency valued in just time worked well enough for valuing people's time, provided everyone valued their own time equally and were happy to exchange time on that basis. (To make things easier for retailers, in 2010 a 'tenth of an hour' note, worth a dollar, has been introduced, which should make calculations easier.) But it did not work well for valuing *things* – such as a piece of pie. Scale this up, and the problem becomes clearer. How many hours to buy a cooker – or a house? You need to have a relationship between time and conventional prices.

In practice, it is debatable how effectively the relation-ship between an Hour and a dollar works. Anthro-pologist Bill Maurer's[2] research shows that there is confusion between whether an Hour *really* is worth ten *actual* dollars, or whether this is just a way of counting. If an eighth of an Hour is worth $1.25, how do I pay for something that costs $4.98? The calculations can be quite complex and confusing, and cut against Simmel's arguments, described in Chapter 2, that good forms of money make life more simple, divisible and calculable. Officially, there is no mechanism for exchanging an hour note for dollars, unless you can find someone prepared to exchange the notes in a private transaction.

A trusted issuing authority

We saw in the Introduction (page 14) that we are happy to accept our current unbacked paper money (fiat currency) if we trust the institution issuing it (the Bank of England, the Federal Reserve) not to print too much of it and if our experience is that we can exchange it for 'stuff'. Key to the success of Ithaca Hours was the character of the founder, Paul Glover, and the effectiveness with which he managed the circulation of the currency. Glover was an exceptionally well-respected, well-rooted and charismatic community organiser with an unwavering environmental ethos, who knew what he was doing. People knew him, and would trust in an initiative if he said it was OK. He was transparent in how the scheme was to be organised from the start. Glover was Ithaca's Alan Greenspan – except that he didn't crash the economy.

Managing circulation

Paul Glover also put in huge amounts of time, unpaid, cycling around the town checking to see that large numbers of unspent Hours were not getting stuck anywhere, helping businesses that were having problems to identify places to spend their Hours, or using his own (limited amount of) money to buy them back. He acted as the 'neural network' of the system, and the embodiment of trust in it.

While Glover did successfully manage his own obsolescence, passing management on to an incorporated company with an elected board, it may be that not all communities have their own Paul Glover. Those that do might find that he gets another job, moves on to another project, falls under a bus – a million things – and that the initiative fails to survive its charismatic founder. Of course, there are countless examples of committed activists staying the course. But it is dangerous to rely on it; it is far better to design a resilient system that can survive such a loss.

The (really) tough question – how much currency should you issue?

It can be really hard to know how much money to issue. Issue too much and you risk inflation and your currency dismissed as worthless paper or monopoly money. Issue too little and supplies of money run out and needs that might have been met are still unaffordable. With a paper currency it is best to be a little conservative, a little under the amount of 'just right', so you have created your own local 'Goldilocks economy' – not too hot or too cold, but 'just right'.

That is easy to say. But the really difficult issue for a local paper currency, as with conventional money, is how to judge exactly what is 'just right'. Economist Richard Douthwaite[3] pointed out that you might issue the 'right amount' of currency for a booming local economy, only for it to become 'too much' if hard times mean the economy contracts. People with stocks of local money they can no longer spend dump it, and inflation results. On the other hand, you might be too conservative and issue too little money to make a difference.

To overcome this, it might be necessary to time limit currencies in some way so they can be withdrawn from time to time. Some of Bill Maurer's informants have argued that an alternative currency like Ithaca Hours, designed to help those in need, should wither and die when the economy picks up, thus solving this problem. Others argue that the Transition process needs the creation of a multiplicity of local currency networks supporting many more localised economies, so they should be more permanent.

Unless you have your own local financial genius, the best solution to this conundrum is to have an open, democratic and inclusive process for deciding, as a community, how much currency to issue. This can range from an open community meeting with a potluck to a more technocratic decision made by a board elected from the community. What you want to avoid is the perception that the process whereby the currency is issued is either opaque or even dodgy (as was the perception in Argentina, see Chapter 8) or haphazard, lackadaisical and incontestable (see Chapter 12, page 168, on problems in Lewes). Stroud has formed a co-op to make these decisions, while Totnes has formed a community interest company. This does seem to be good practice.

Hours – key recommendations

Paper currencies can be hard to set up and manage. But because they don't look like national currency, Hours might be a good halfway house between a LETS or time bank and a paper currency denominated in relation to and backed by a national currency.

- For some people the attraction of Hours is that they are not related to national currency, and value everyone's time equally. If your community includes a large countercultural or green subcommunity who, for political or ecological reasons, are not attracted to a currency linked to national currency, then experiment with an hour-based paper currency.

- In practice, people struggle to value work and things in 'time'. It seems rather abstract. It can be hard to mix national and time money together. It is fiddly. But if you want just to trade exclusively in hours, and ignore national currency, then this is not a problem.

- Spend time on ensuring that your currency has 'moneyness' – images, paper quality and security features are key.

- Ensure that your currency is 'backed' by a trusted local person or institution.

- Manage circulation. Make sure the currency does not get 'stuck' somewhere. You need to actively manage this. It won't just happen. This can be done by working with businesses to help them to spend their local currency, or by exchanging it for national currency.

- You need to be able to fund this management process, either through subscriptions in local money, a grant, or the sweat of volunteers. If you set up a paper currency scheme without thinking this through you are likely to encounter problems down the line, and your scheme might get an unwarranted reputation as a failure.

- Don't be daunted by arguments such as 'banks don't tell you where to spend your money'. The banks issue a universal currency, spendable everywhere. You don't. You have to manage circulation.

THE ITHACA HOURS SCORECARD

Hard   Soft

Valuable   Weak

Circulates widely   Circulates locally

Effectiveness for local community-owned businesses

High   Low

CHAPTER 8

ARGENTINA'S BARTER NETWORKS

If we want to know how local currencies might perform in a really acute crisis – what the challenges might be and how to overcome them – lessons from Argentina are crucial. The Argentinian experience is also a relatively unique one, but nonetheless a useful corrective for people who dismiss local currencies as marginal and with limited potential. In Argentina, the 'Barter Networks' (*Redes de Trueque*) grew to a size where they helped literally millions of Argentines to get through an awful financial crisis from 2000-3, and became as normal a part of Argentine life as a Visa card. Nowhere else have alternative currencies grown to such a mass level of usage.

One of the objectives of Transition is to use our creativity as we move away from oil dependency, so we can avoid more unpleasant alternatives. Making a positive decision to transition to a more localised, low-carbon economy is preferable to the chaos and violence that would accompany an economy collapsing as a result of an acute peak oil crisis. But if things do get more difficult, then Argentina's experiences demonstrate the potential of communities rallying round to support each other through a crisis, even if the models they developed were flawed in the long term.

Trueque translates literally into English as 'barter'. However, the Argentinian *Redes de Trueque* did not engage in 'barter' in the sense of one-to-one exchange without use of money. Rather, they facilitated exchange using a number of paper currencies created by a range of community groups, NGOs, communities and private businesspeople. I call it 'barter' as Argentines do – but technically it is not barter.[1]

Argentina's barter networks emerged in 1997 in Bernal, part of Buenos Aires' industrial rustbelt. An environmental NGO, *Programa de Autosuficiencia Regional* (PAR – Regional Self-sufficiency Programme) wanted to explore environmental solutions to the growing poverty and unemployment that surrounded it, so that it might also provide enjoyable and resilient livelihoods for people that the conventional market economy had written off. While central Buenos Aires five or ten miles away was booming, the old industrial heartland was devastated. PAR thought about LETS, but thought it might be too small-scale, given the depth of the problems being faced. Then it hit on Ithaca Hours. The original project involved twenty neighbours, and grew to a mass movement involving millions.

Argentina in crisis

Between 1998 and 2005-6 Argentina staggered from crisis to crisis.[2] Unemployment rose inexorably. Every attempt to kick-start the economy failed. In December 2001 the IMF refused to provide any more help, and the government attempted to raid private pension funds to pay an instalment on the country's debt. Reacting against these 'unconventional' measures,

111

Sharing locally grown vegetables in Mendoza province, western Argentina.

those that could started to move their money out of the country. A bank run began to occur, to which the State responded by freezing bank accounts. People literally could not take more than a tiny weekly allowance of their money out of the ATMs. Three days of rioting followed, as aggrieved savers banged pots and pans outside the closed banks. Thirty-eight people died, and having failed to stop the riots by declaring a state of emergency the president was forced to flee the Casa Rosada in a helicopter. After five more days of chaos a new president eventually took over and promptly devalued the peso. The banking restrictions were not removed until April 2002. Argentina's economy remained shattered for months afterwards, only really recovering in 2005-6.

How did the Argentine barter networks work?

The barter networks worked through a loose network of markets where traders (called *prosumidores* – 'prosumers' – after Alvin Toffler's producing consumers) met, typically in a church hall, a disused factory, a car park or baseball court, at a set time each week to trade with each other using *creditos*, or credits – money printed at first by PAR, and later by a wide range of NGOs, community groups, neighbours or private people. These markets were seen as 'nodes' in the barter network.

A node in San Telmo, central Buenos Aires.

The credito was a unit of exchange in its own right. Some creditos were very, very roughly linked to the peso, and could be bought for pesos at a discount (say, four pesos buys you a pack of twenty creditos, with the credito supposedly being worth a peso). Other local currencies issued by other groups had no relationship of value to the peso. Buying or exchanging them for pesos was forbidden. The diversity of alternative currencies was dazzling, reflecting an outpouring of grassroots responses to a collapsed economy.

At these markets you could buy honey, *empañadas* (pasties), pancakes, pizzas, green vegetables and fruit, jams, wine, vinegar, breads, biscuits, shoes, shampoos, jumpers, nightgowns, haircuts and manicures, have a coffee at the café, watch a samba band, or peruse a noticeboard. The atmosphere always involved heated debate and haggling. Some had stalls in the tens and visitors in the hundreds, while some were in the thousands. By 2001, the organisers claimed 4,500 markets were used by half a million people spending 600 million creditos across Argentina. The real figure is unknowable.

Argentines would travel across the city, into the informal settlements in the suburbs, to the country-side, or to another city to attend as many markets as possible. No one with access to these credits would starve, which was not the case for many in the more remote and impoverished indigenous parts of Argentina. Consequently, people would queue for hours to get into the markets, and would travel some distance.

People might establish their own market with their neighbours or through their church, print their own currency, and get their neighbouring markets to accept them. Some markets were tightly run and only members could trade, while others were more open and less formal. Some markets accepted each other's credits; others didn't. But there was no central control or administration, and nothing to stop someone from the other side of what is a very large country from trading, if the individual they wanted to buy from felt their credits were good. The situation resembled depression-era America, when stamp scrip similarly became widespread.

After some time, some sort of order began to emerge from the dazzling multiplicity of parallel currencies in Argentina. Some local barter markets did their own thing completely. There were, literally, so many local markets that 'anything went'. Argentina's financial system had effectively collapsed. But three main trends can be identified, from which lessons can be learned.

The Red Global de Trueque (RGT)

PAR's Global Barter Network (*Red Global de Trueque – RGT*) operated right across Argentina, the eighth largest country in the world. PAR set up a franchising system that supplied thousands of 'start-up kits', which included a number of centrally produced credits (called *arborlitos*) that enabled people to set up their own barter markets straight away. PAR sold the kits for pesos.

Given that Argentines were physically unable to get their money out of their bank accounts and the economy had literally ground to a halt, with millions facing acute hardship, if not starvation, it's probably safe to say that the kits were central to the viral manner in which barter spread across all of Argentina so quickly. The kits saved lives. But they also provoked criticism.

The Red de Trueque Solidario (RTS)

Those who wanted to develop their own markets coalesced into the Solidarity Barter Network (*Red de Trueque Solidario – RTS*). They used their own locally produced notes, which at some times could and at others couldn't be exchanged for notes from other approved markets. Sometimes they accepted visitors from other nodes; sometimes they were closed to outsiders. They took a more militantly localist and bottom-up approach, which they vehemently contrasted with that of RGT. They wanted to develop and run their own local currency systems, not pay for PAR's 'off the shelf' kits.

RTS credito from the Mesopotamia region in the north of Argentina.

Networks organised by trusted and honest local businessmen

Zona Oueste (Western Zone) in the peri-urban informal settlements of Greater Buenos Aires was run in a robustly autocratic manner by a businessman, Fernando Sampayo, who issued his own currency backed by his own reputation for straight playing. This was not a community-based currency, but one run by a retired businessman with a conscience.

RGT's Arborlito.

Zona Ouest credito from Buenos Aires' informal settlements.

Global or solidaristic networks?

Critics in the solidarity barter networks – RTS – did not see RGT's approach as either legitimate or responsible. To put it bluntly, RTS characterised RGT's kits as a way to print and sell arborlitos for pesos, thereby making huge profits on the back of other people's suffering. RTS claimed that PAR had become a 'get rich quick' outfit.

PAR rejected this. In its view the kits were an effective way of responding to a crisis of an unforeseen magnitude. They believed that as the developers of the world's largest alternative currency system they had the right to use their innovation as they saw fit, and that critics were small-minded, interfering, jealous busybodies. The problem was that PAR could certainly be accused of being guilty of a naive lack of transparency in its dealings. Unlike RTS, where members met to collectively and openly decide how to run the network, PAR made its decisions itself, behind closed doors, and rather informally. No one else could influence PAR, and its office procedures were rather haphazard so there was no accountability; no audit trail. Some of the people PAR sold kits to were of dubious morality.

RTS argued that the best response to the crisis was the development of small, local networks from below. The market would be reinvented through money created by whoever was using it, not created for users by a benevolent or otherwise NGO or businessperson. It was concerned that PAR's actions were inflationary and opened the networks up to abuse, and that consequently the value of the currency should be maintained through community regulation to ensure limited issuance and to prevent forgery. It argued that strong community-building mechanisms should be used at the barter markets to ensure that everyone knew the ethos, cooperated with each other, did not try to put up prices or rip each other off, and were on the lookout for shysters and abusers. Everyone should produce something to sell at the market, or provide a service. You should not be able to just turn up with a fistful of arborlitos that you had bought, since if they were not backed by real 'stuff' or services in some way they were just waste paper.

RTS therefore insisted on:

- new members actively signing up to the 'prosumer' values of the network at an induction meeting

- everyone contributing produce (something they had made themselves) before receiving credits

- a management structure to ensure that markets were well and fairly run

- an active decision by all groups about whether or not to accept a new group or market into the solidarity network

- a collective decision about how much currency to print and how it should be issued.

PAR thought that this response was too small-scale and conservative, given the depth of the crisis, and that the organisers were imposing their left-wing political ideals on what should be an apolitical economic or mutual aid activity.

Zona Oueste took a middle way. Like PAR they argued for well-organised, large-scale usage of barter to meet the great need, and agreed that RTS's commitment to grassroots development and direct democracy was too slow, too political. But it also agreed that PAR's lack of transparency and aggressive promotion opened it up to the challenge that it was taking advantage. Zona Oueste ran itself as a business, insisting on full and open record keeping. There was a clear line of responsibility, formal management systems, and an audit trail.

Who was right?

In 2002 both sides of the argument were borne out. RGT was right that RTS's small, organic approach was too slow. Setting up a new market from scratch and developing the communal accountability systems RTS insisted on was too protracted a process given the speed that the crisis hit. Millions flooded to the markets in that awful year, and RTS's commitment-building mechanisms were overwhelmed. Many of the markets became wild, anarchic spaces in which impoverished people struggled with each other, often physically, to get into the market and to purchase the best goods. The embarrassed RTS organisers, unable to induct the millions flowing into the markets, felt they had created a 'monster'.

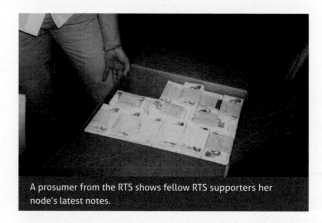

A prosumer from the RTS shows fellow RTS supporters her node's latest notes.

But RTS was also right. Printing millions of credits was inflationary, especially as there was no real relation between an arborlito and a peso, a unit of time, or anything tangible at all. Prices could shoot up from one or two arborlitos for a bag of flour to over a thousand. One person I spoke to papered his wall with the useless paper. By 2003 RGT was retiring the over-issued notes and replacing them with a more limited issuance in smaller denominations.

The Peronists strike back

The chaotic nature of PAR's central structure was also a problem, as the franchisees were not always, to put it politely, 'perfect'. Some had connections to the ruling Peronist party and would violently close down 'rival' markets to protect their political machine. At the heart of Peronism are local party bosses who provide resources like food, work, medicine and other services to 'their' clients, who reward them with votes or by turning out at a demonstration when asked to.[3] Barter allowed people to access these resources independently, thus breaking the relationship of dependency on which Peronism relied. The Peronists could not be expected to take this lying down, and they didn't.

One RGT franchisee was secretly filmed selling stolen shoes, then jailed. Others did little to maintain order at their markets, with the result that wide boys would take advantage of those who sold underpriced goods by buying up in bulk and then selling them on, often in front of the person just ripped off. People felt bruised, robbed and exploited. Rumour had it that millions of fifty-credit arborlitos had been forged by crooks and/or politicians.

The crash

In November 2002 a prime-time television show 'exposed' what it called the 'great barter scam'. Stolen goods were being sold, millions of creditos were forgeries, and the food on sale was poor quality. 'You are being taken advantage of,' the programme claimed. Overnight it seemed that the whole concept of barter catastrophically lost credibility, and over the coming months node after node closed down. A year later no more than 10 per cent of them survived.

RGT argued that the TV station concerned was a mouthpiece of the ruling Peronist party, and that the broadcast was a political attack by a Peronist government

116

concerned that barter was giving Argentina a 'bad name' internationally, and undermining the networks of dependency on which the Peronist party was based. It claimed that the Peronists also funded criminal gangs who were forging arborlitos en masse and giving them out from the back of unmarked vans. RGT's headquarters was raided, and RGT claimed one hundred thousand pesos was stolen by the Buenos Aires Police.

RTS said that this was nonsense. It argued that PAR had caused the inflation and worked with many non-ethical franchisers, and that the TV programme was right to point this out.

Why did use of barter grow to such a scale?

PAR generated a network of alternative currencies that rose to an economic level that has dwarfed all other models since the 1930s. The network kept many people alive during a devastating financial collapse. Partly this was due to the efficiency of PAR's franchising

approach. PAR provided people with a ready-made currency programme, and the nodes provided an accessible space to facilitate trading in a convivial atmosphere. People coming to the markets had to produce something, so the notes were spendable.

A weak State and multiple forms of money

In Argentina alternative currencies were readily accepted as it is a country where previous experiences of inflation and political instability meant that people were used to the form of money changing over time.

The pound sterling and the penny have a history lost in time, going back at least to Saxon times. Pounds, shillings and pence denominated as £ (L), s and d – nods to the Roman denominations of *librae*, *solidi* and *denarii*. The dollar emerges from the German *thaler*.

Argentina is different. It had suffered under irresponsible and military governments since the 1930s. It had recently experienced hyperinflation. The provinces

Sharing bread and pizzas in Mendoza province, western Argentina.

Looking good in a crisis: get your hair and nails done using local currencies in downtown Buenos Aries.

and private businesses also issued their own money, and during the 'peg' dollars and pesos circulated side by side. Thus Argentina is a country where the form of money had radically changed in response to economic crisis, and where the State's monopoly over the right to issues currency is not well established. Argentines were used to getting by during periods of hyper-inflation by unorthodox means.

Universal, community money

But there is also an issue of scale. Success was partly a result of the ability to spend arborlitos and creditos across a region, and a willingness to travel created a much larger market than would be the case for a smaller scheme. This suggests that an alternative currency that circulates at a larger scale facilitates greater levels of trade. The market was so large, and the mainstream market was in such disarray, that factories would sell goods unsellable on the open market at barter markets – which, being open to anyone, provided a significant market. Thus, at the height of the crisis the barter economy significantly accessed the realm of production for the first time in the history of alternative currencies.

Smaller RTS nodes had access to far fewer resources. Its members did little more than recycle things they no longer needed, or things they could produce at home in the kitchen or with a sewing machine. They did little more than live off the fat of the possessions that middle-class Argentines had been able to purchase during the good times. They did not produce anything significant.

Should you set up a barter network on the Argentine model?

The short answer is, at the moment: no. More regard it as an example of what *not* to do, namely set up a currency with no explicit valuation to anything, which was not local, which could easily be forged or over-produced, and which was run by an unaccountable, lackadaisical, opaque organisation managing a central-ised system that was not resilient in the face of political attack. When the inevitable crash came it blackened the name of alternative currencies for a generation. Alberto, a barter organiser in Mendoza put it like this. Asked if it helped people survive the crisis, he protested:

> *No! Not only did it not help people, it corrupted them. It hurt people a lot, and a lot of people lost a lot of things. The result is that it is hard to believe that there is anything good about barter today. Those who sold creditos and made a large amount of money out of it are responsible for this . . .*

Let's avoid these mistakes. The LETS, 'Hours' and time money models discussed in earlier chapters are better for community-based exchanges, while the paper currencies that follow in later chapters are more likely to be tools for really strengthening local resilience by involving businesses.

Of course, there is nothing wrong with a small-scale exchange network, such as a babysitting circle, exchang-ing simple tokens to keep score. But it's not a model to upscale as it's too easily subverted through forgery or inflation. It looks like monopoly money – it won't be taken seriously.

But I also think that Alberto is underestimating the benefits that many ordinary users of barter experienced. Barter, although flawed in the long run, did bounce Argentines through an awful year. As Keynes said, in the long run, we are all dead.

Voices from Argentina

"For me it was like a job . . . that year I could live off the trueque, more or less."

"I could get all I wanted."

"My freezer was always full, and there was always enough to eat for the six of us."

"I would not miss it even once."

"I don't know what I would do without it."

Lessons from Argentina's experiences

To some extent, the spectacular decline of barter in Argentina shows that those who argued for an ecological diversity of currencies, rather than one universal currency, were right. The arborlito was a universal currency, accepted all across Argentina. When the State 'took out' the issuing organisation and spread doubt about the integrity of the arbolito, confidence dropped overnight. PAR's centralised structure was not resilient.

Those RTS markets that were relatively isolated from other arborlito markets by geography or by a refusal to accept them did prove themselves better able to withstand the shock. After November 2002, attempts were made to rebuild the networks with a wider diversity of local currencies, which operated closed markets (i.e. they did not accept anyone else's currency).

Barter networks – key recommendations

- Argentina shows that it is possible for complementary currencies to become mainstream and make a real difference to people's ability to survive, literally, in an acute crisis. But . . .

- You can't just issue currency unconnected to the amount of real goods and services in circulation, or the capacity of the currency to generate new production. If you do, the result is waste paper.

- There are trade-offs to be made between providing a ready-made, transferable kit from which local people can quickly set up currency schemes (PAR-style), and slower, more organic, local action (RTS-style), which has stronger local ownership and control. Local action may be slower, but in the long run it is more resilient.

- A local currency scheme that involved millions is likely to be challenged by elites when the economy revives and those elites want to maintain control.

- It is vital that any organisation issuing a currency is beyond suspicion. PAR's associates did not meet this high standard, whereas Zona Oueste's Fernando Sampayo did.

- It is vital that a paper currency has sufficient security features to prevent forgery.

THE BARTER SCORECARD

Hard .... **Soft**

Valuable .... **Weak**

Circulation for RGT (■) or RTS (●)

Circulates widely .... **Circulates locally**

Effectiveness for RGT (■) or RTS (●)

High .... **Low**

CHAPTER 9

GERMAN REGIONAL CURRENCIES

The alternative currencies featured so far mainly involve individuals exchanging with each other. Few businesses are involved, and those that are involved are generally small, one-man-band local or family, 'mom and pop' businesses, or 'alternative and lifestyle' businesses. The regional currencies we look at in this and the next chapter are more sophisticated, larger-scale programmes that do involve significant numbers of businesses. You can buy more of the everyday things you need with these regional currencies. They take us further along the road to a resilient localised economy than anything we have examined yet.

When reading this and the next chapter it would be useful to bear the following questions in mind. They might seem a bit abstract, but are actually very important issues to think about if you are considering what sort of local currency programme to set up. You will want to avoid putting lots of work into something that does not help you get where you want to go.

- If these currencies successfully involve businesses, why is this the case – when the currencies we have looked at so far don't?

- Does a currency at a regional scale make a difference? Is it a problem that these are no longer 'local' currencies?

- Are there any downsides for businesses that use them? This matters, as the stakes are higher for businesspeople than they are for individuals: they are risking their livelihoods and perhaps a business that has been built up over years if things go wrong and they can't spend the currency they take in. Might it not be better just to build resilient local economies using the money we have?

- These currencies are not 'new money'. You have to exchange these currencies for national currencies. LETS and time money are backed by your commitment to do some work in the future, so you can create money yourself. What are the implications of this?

- Is *demurrage* – 'rusting money' – a good idea?

Regiogeld

In Germany, the introduction of the Euro is a relatively new phenomenon. Having been united from a loose confederation of principalities and city states only in 1870, Germany has a strong regional and local tradition that lasts to this day. There are concerns that a one-size-fits-all monetary policy set by the European Central Bank in Frankfurt cannot fit the diversity of local conditions from Latvia to Lisbon.

German *regiogeld* – regional money – is an attempt to

break out of community-based currencies circulating between individuals to build regional currencies that operate as a real alternative to the Euro, stimulating new regional production.

A quick disclaimer. While I have been able to directly research all the other contemporary currency chapters in this book, I have not had the chance to visit any regiogeld projects. The chapter is therefore written with the help of three German colleagues, Christian Gelleri, Rolf Schroeder and Mathias Zeeb. Given what I have said about the dangers of over-reporting local currencies and them 'never being knowingly under-sold', this is a risk for which I take responsibility.

What are regional currencies?

Building on the experiences of and limitations of the German equivalent of LETS, the first regional currency, the Roland in Bremen, was established in 2001, followed closely by the Chiemgauer in Bavaria. In 2008 there were twenty-eight regional currencies across Germany. German regional currencies aim to improve local purchasing power and to strengthen the local economy by binding money to the district and letting it flow within the community. Their aim is to establish an atmosphere of cooperation, facilitate sponsorship of local NGOs and community organisations, and build an economy that includes less monetary speculation and, in order to reduce carbon emissions, entails less transport.

The aim is for money that circulates both locally and with a greater velocity than the Euro. This is achieved by working at a geographical scale large enough to facilitate enough business circulation that the average user of the currency can buy 50 per cent of his or her requirements with it. For example, Chiemgauer regional money circulates in an area 100km around the Chiemsee lake in the centre of the Chiemgau district. Thus regiogeld circulates in an area small enough to have some coherence and be considered 'local', but big enough to include a sufficiently wide variety of businesses that enough people use it for day-to-day purchases to make a difference to the health of the local economy.

It must be said that, outside Argentina, the number of times an average user of a local currency could actually spend it in the course of their everyday life is not large. Regiogeld aimed to break out of this by creating a local currency that does make a difference.

How does regiogeld work? The case of Chiemgauer

Chiemgauer regional money started as a Steiner school project through which the school hoped to strengthen connections with and boost sponsorship from local businesses. Believing that the conventional money system does not work well for small businesses, the school students worked with local companies to develop the project over three years, until it became an independent project in 2005. Five district offices were set up, through which Chiemgauer could be issued and redeemed. By 2009 there were 50 issuing points, including a number of voluntary and community associations.

Regiogeld notes, card and card reader. Photo © Nicole Richter, Bernau, used with permission.

Value and form

The currency is linked at parity to the Euro, meaning that the complications associated with linking the currency to time are avoided.

It is issued in notes denominated 1, 2, 5, 10, 20 and 50 Chiemgauer, printed on special banknote paper and with 14 security features.

Each note costs ten cents to print, and is of a quality that gives it 'moneyness'. Local images are printed on the notes, nodding (as is the case with Ithaca Hours) to local pride.

More recently, a debit card has been introduced, funded with a regional development grant and managed in cooperation with cooperative and state banks. Thirty-five per cent of Chiemgauer transactions are electronic. A key factor is that the German cooperative and state banks are themselves regional or even local banks; for example, state banks are owned by a 'Landkreis' (district), which on average has some 170,000 inhabitants. Together, cooperatives and state savings banks have 60 per cent of the retail banking market, and dominate banking with small- and medium-sized enterprises. They are ideally suited to and interested in cooperation with regiogeld initiatives.

Issuance and circulation

Users of the currency buy them at parity from an issuing office or non-profit-making agency, spending them with the 600 participating businesses. Voluntary and community associations that act as issuing agents can buy 100 Chiemgauer for 97 Euro, keeping the balance when they issue them to others. Businesses themselves can spend them with other businesses or non-profit-makers, or redeem them for Euros at one of the district offices. If they do the latter, they get 95 Euro for every 100 Chiemgauer.

Of the 5-per-cent deduction, 2 per cent is used to fund the programme, while 3 per cent goes to fund the 3-per-cent discount available to non-profit-makers. According to the organiser, Christian Gelleri, the main advantage to businesses is "the chance to get new customers from the network. Smaller businesses depend on every single customer. Businesses have credit cards, Eurocash, cash and so on, and if the Chiemgauer brings some turnover, why not?"

Demurrage – 'rusting' money

As we saw in Chapter 2, one of the aims of a complementary currency in times of economic crisis is to speed up the circulation of the currency. In depressions, when people get scared they tend to save rather than

How successful is regiogeld?

Christian Gelleri argues that he can meet 90 per cent of his needs through Chiemgauer. The number of businesses accepting Chiemgauer suggests this is plausible. Gelleri buys all of his food and household goods in Chiemgauer, including meals in restaurants. He and his wife rent their apartment from her parents, paying in Chiemgauer: the parents in turn buy food with Chiemgauer. He can't pay for power (yet – there are plans), or pay local taxes, but he could, if he wanted, buy a car and locally produced biodiesel to run it. He prefers to bicycle, on a bike paid for with Chiemgauer. His monthly income is 200 Euro and 800 Chiemgauer.

Outside Argentina we struggle to find an example of a local currency that an average person can use to meet his or her day-to-day needs. To this extent regiogeld must be considered a success.

spend, so local businesses are hit, eventually close, and the downward spiral continues. Complementary currencies can include design features that encourage people to spend them, not hoard them.

The Chiemgauer 'ages' or 'rusts' 2 per cent a quarter; 8 per cent a year. Every quarter, those holding the notes must buy a sticker to be attached to each note, costing two cents per Chiemgauer. As no one wants to have to pay the cost of the sticker themselves, the incentive is to spend it before the due date. It is estimated that as a consequence the local currency circulates three times faster than the Euro.

Reasons for the success of regiogeld

The Chiemgauer local currency scheme is notable for its rigorous collection of data on how the currency circulates, and the way this data is made public. This, of course, builds trust. At the time of writing, in December 2009, around 2,500 consumers a month change 100,000 Euro a month into Chiemgauer, which produces 3,000 Chiemgauer for non-profit-makers. Some 98,000 Chiemgauer a month are eventually returned to the issuing offices, but only after they have circulated around the community. Seventy per cent of Chiemgauer are spent again; not redeemed. 314,516 Chiemgauer are in circulation. Based on a sample of participating businesses, the project claims that since its inception Chiemgauer has turned over the equivalent of 8.6 million Euro, of which 3.9 million was in 2008.

Strengthening regional production

Gelleri argues that one third of the trades facilitated by Chiemgauer, worth the equivalent of some 600,000 Euro, are trades that would not otherwise have happened, and which strengthen the local economy. For example, food shops prefer local apples as they can pay for them with Chiemgauer, which has stimulated local apple production. Apple juice is no longer imported from North Germany. Money stays local, and is used to facilitate more production. Given that an active user of Chiemgauer currencies can meet most of his or her needs, a local apple grower who receives 20 per cent of his income in Chiemgauer can currently spend it. Thoughtful businesses understand that the more people who accept the Chiemgauer, the greater will be the possibility that they can spend all the currency they earn, and it stays local. At the end of the day, if they do change it back to Euros, they can, with a discount of 5 per cent – which seems to be high enough to encourage businesses to try to spend the currency, but low enough that the business feels comfortable that it will not lose too much on the deal.

Strong social capital and 'embeddedness'

Perhaps the currency works so well because Chiemgau is a very wealthy part of Bavaria, itself a part of Germany with strong regional identity and one of those places characterised by strong social capital (see Chapter 6, page 92). It has built on a rich landscape of past and present alternative currencies: the Austrian town of Wörgl is just next door and Schwanenkirchen, where scrip started in the 1930s, isn't that far away. The Tauschringe movement (German LETS) had some influences on the design of models in the regiogeld. The Sterntaler, another German local currency that is now under the administrative roof of the Chiemgauer, tries to combine a time-money system with a regiogeld. Bavaria is thus close to having the rich ecosystem of currencies to which we aspire.

The Chiemgauer's success builds on (and now strengthens) a strong tradition of regional sourcing and regional cooperation of businesses, which is typical for most of southern Germany. Rural Bavaria has successfully resisted the destruction of small businesses by 'big box' and chain stores. Perhaps what Chiemgauer does best is manifest that social capital to outsiders, and not every place is so well endowed.

Social inclusion

An obvious objection to this currency is that you need be prepared to go to an issuing station to change your Euros into Chiemgauer before you go shopping. This might not be convenient. What is the incentive? Unlike BerkShares (see next chapter), you don't get a discount, so apart from an altruistic or political commitment to your community and region and the chance to endow your favourite voluntary organisation, it's not clear what the benefit for doing this is.

German observers of regiogeld such as Rolf Schroeder and Mathias Zeeb argue that in the Chiemgau, the pre-existence of strong local Bavarian culture means that it is more likely that people will be well disposed to something that strengthens that culture. A Yorkshire currency might well be welcomed in the same way. But if you are not in a region with such a strong regional identity it might not resonate so strongly.

For example, as we will see in Chapter 12, Harvey's brewery in Lewes is strongly behind the Lewes Pound, but does not source its raw materials from the town of Lewes. To do that, it would need a South East Pound. But the South East of the UK is an artificial administrative region that wraps itself around London: it has no coherence of its own. A Sussex/Kent pound might fit an economic area, but again this makes no sense in terms of local identity. Local town pride, in Lewes, does make more sense in terms of identity, but Lewes is not a credible economic area if the aim is to stimulate more local production: it's too small.

Without the instrumental attraction of a discount, it seems hard to see why someone without a political commitment to ecology or feelings of regional pride would make the extra effort to change their national currency, spendable anywhere, into money that just circulates more locally.

Rustbelt currencies – the Urstromtaler

A second obvious objection to Chiemgauer is that you need to have spare Euros that you are prepared to effectively 'lock up' in Chiemgauer until you can spend them. If you can meet at least some of your essential daily needs with Chiemgauer and can spend them easily, that may not be a problem, but the very poor are still excluded. Backing a regional currency with Euros makes the currency attractive to businesses, but relatively inaccessible to the poor unless there are other incentives, such as discounts offered by local businesses, or the ability to buy discounted Chiemgauer.

The Urstromtaler regiogeld in Magdeburg, part of de-industrialising or 'rustbelt' eastern Germany, aims to address this. Urstromtaler are also Euro backed, but as local unemployment is 20 per cent, unemployed people can earn Urstromtaler by using their skills and energy, without having to have Euros to start doing so. The programme also aims to boost local employment by providing lines of credit in Urstromtaler to premium members (mostly businesses), who pay an annual fee of 96 Euro or Urstromtaler. Through this they aim to support start-up companies and in that sense contribute to regional economic development.

'Rusting' – problems and opportunities

During economic crises the advantage of an 'ageing', demurrage currency is that it moves on quickly. It doesn't get stuck; isn't hoarded. The currency is designed in such a way as to encourage people to try to spend it. This is fine if you are actually able to spend your regiogeld without having to revalidate it, but if you cannot spend your regiogeld then you do have to either revalidate it or take a 5-per-cent discount if you redeem your regiogeld for Euros. The incentive is thus to spend, not save or redeem.

From a conventional economic perspective written for the German Bundesbank, economist Gerhard Roesl has argued that the danger that follows is Gresham's Law: 'bad money forces out good'. If customers decide to spend ('inferior', local) regiogeld and keep ('superior', universal) Euros in the bank they are effectively moving Euros out of circulation, and if this was taken too far it might lead to a drought of Euros and an 'inferior' supply of money.

In this situation a business might end up in a position whereby it has to accept a currency that is not accepted everywhere and which the business cannot itself re-circulate, instead of the universal currency it would otherwise have accepted and can spend. If this is the case and if these businesses are already operating with tight margins, then this can be hurting the very people you want to help – a perverse effect of a local currency scheme. The solution would be the business limiting the amount of regiogeld it accepts to a manageable amount, perhaps seeing it as a discount promotion bringing in some new customers. But this rather misses the wider point.

Roesl's perspective, of course, assumes that 'universal' currency is superior and a local currency is inferior just because you cannot spend it everywhere. It is a perspective wedded to globalisation, ignoring the fuel burnt and carbon emitted in the process. The arguments for making the transition away from oil dependency towards a low-carbon, more localised economy discussed throughout this book are not on that radar.

Chiemgauer seems to have broken out of this trap by circulating at a scale that means enough businesses accept it to enable them to spend on their regiogeld with their suppliers. The next step is to deepen this process by boosting the amount of local production, through regiogeld loans, to set up new businesses carrying out import substitution. Then we would see that local resilience is genuinely strengthened through a local currency. This is for the future: we will need more research to confirm whether this works out in practice.

How do you set up a regiogeld system?

On one hand, setting up a paper currency with fourteen security features and electronic payment is not cheap or easy to do. This level of complexity might well be out of the range of Transition Initiatives at an early stage of development. BerkShares, the currency discussed in the next chapter, was set up with considerable grant funding by an organisation with a strong track record. Its success went on to inspire the first Transition currency, in Totnes.

On the other hand, Chiemgauer grew out of a school student's project, and in its early days was developed using volunteer labour. Transition Stroud set up its version of regiogeld with no funding through volunteers who put their hands in their pockets and raised £800. Where there is more commitment and experience, and perhaps access to grant funding, regiogeld provides a good model for regional Transition currencies that circulate in an area larger than a small town.

It therefore makes sense for us to explore how you set up an advanced paper-based currency when we have explored all three models – regiogeld, BerkShares, and Transition currencies.

German regional currencies – key issues to consider

- Regional currencies in Germany circulate at the regional scale, which seems to be a large enough scale to enable businesses to spend the regiogeld they take in, and customers to meet 50 per cent of their needs using regiogeld. If you want to involve businesses in your local currency scheme, this seems a good model to follow.

- Chiemgauer circulate in a wealthy part of Germany with a strong regional identity, a tradition of doing things differently, and strong social capital. Is the success of regiogeld dependent on a pre-existing network of locally owned, independently minded businesspeople and local banks? Can a regional currency help *build* such a local infrastructure where it doesn't currently exist? We don't yet know the answer to this, but it is the vision. Bear this in mind when thinking about the applicability of this model to your community.

- Urstromtaler work well in a poorer, depressed part of the former GDR by paying more attention to involving those without prior access to money, and having a willingness to convert it into regional currencies. This might be a good model for other economically distressed regions.

- 'Rusting' and a 5-per-cent discount for conversion back to Euros seems to work where the currency can genuinely be spent. However, if it can't be spent yet, and if a business has tight margins, this system may be unintentionally hurting those it is aimed at helping. Think about the profitability of the businesses in your community, and discuss this with them. Don't just impose such restrictions.

THE CHIEMGAUER SCORECARD

Hard   Soft

Valuable   Weak

Circulates widely   Circulates locally

Effectiveness for a business (■) or community exchange (●)

High   Low

CHAPTER 10

BERKSHARES

The E. F. Schumacher Society, named after the author of *Small is Beautiful*, is based halfway up a mountain outside the small town of Great Barrington in Berkshire County, western Massachusetts, USA. The main aim of the society is the development of the local economy, with local currencies and other financial innovations as the vehicles, not as ends in themselves. It thus wants to go beyond facilitating exchanges between people or existing local businesses, to develop a more resilient local economy. The aim is to set standards for the sort of businesses a local community wants to see, and create a currency and other financial vehicles that empower that; for example to make loans to generate new production.

The society has more experience in developing local currencies than just about anyone else. It directly inspired the first of the UK's Transition currencies, in Totnes. It is therefore worth spending some time understanding and learning from the society's experiences in order to build on as solid a base as we can for creating local currencies. Four local currency experiments are important: SHARE, Deli Dollars, Farm Preserve Notes and BerkShares.

SHARE (1982-1990s)

An early project in the Berkshires called SHARE (Self Help Association for a Regional Economy) was, much like the local financial vehicles discussed in Chapter 14, aimed at developing local production through micro and small loans to local businesses, funded by using as collateral the money sitting idle in local people's savings accounts. Those interested in investing in socially and ecologically responsible local businesses would be teamed up with businesses seeking funds of up to $3,000, which would be loaned by a local bank at below market interest rates of 10 per cent. The aim was for citizens and businesspeople to share the responsibility for developing new local production.

SHARE members deposited between $100 and $500 into a deposit account paying a below-market rate of interest, of 6 per cent for a minimum of two years. They then allowed the bank to use up to 75 per cent of the value of these funds as collateral for businesses seeking loans, who had previously been turned down. The other 25 per cent could be withdrawn according to the usual conditions of the deposit account. Members helped shape SHARE's lending criteria, and decisions on when collateral should be extended were made using the input of a peer group of businesspeople.

When the programme began, typical market rates of interest for business loans were in the order of 17 and 18 per cent, so SHARE's loans at 10 per cent were attractive. The track record of loan repayments was good. By the mid-1990s, however, interest rates were down and the banks could see that the sort of loans SHARE had been pioneering were profitable. They moved into the market.

President Clinton also promoted the renewal of the US's Community Reinvestment Act (CRA), which requires banks to invest in inner-city areas – there is no equivalent in the UK, although the new economics foundation and others have been pushing for it. As it looked as though SHARE's work had entered the mainstream, depositors moved their support to new areas, though the model stays in place should it be required again – perhaps to support new forms of local production.

Deli Dollars (1989)

When the owner of a local delicatessen had to move his business, he found himself unable to raise the cash from the banks to refurbish the new premises. He approached SHARE for a loan. The E. F. Schumacher Society suggested that, instead of borrowing money collateralised by SHARE members, he turn to his customers for a loan by issuing his own scrip in the form of 'Deli Dollars'. Customers bought $10 worth of Deli Dollars for $8 in advance, and the money thus raised was used to pay for the refurbishment.

A Deli Dollar.

Once the deli was up and running again, the holders of Deli Dollars could use them to buy sandwiches over the coming months. The rate at which the Deli Dollars would be redeemed for sandwiches (meaning the later loss of dollar revenue) was managed by phasing their maturity date. The community thus maintained a well-loved local business, while the owner was able to move and refurbish his business interest-free. A win-win.

Farm Preserve Notes (1990)

The SHARE programme also worked with two local farmers in Great Barrington to issue 'Berkshire Farm Preserve Notes', a local scrip redeemable for produce. Customers bought the ten-dollar-valued notes for nine dollars in late autumn, providing the farmers with income in the winter months. The customers then redeemed the notes with either farmer for farm produce later in the summer and autumn of the next year. At the end of the season the farmers settled up between themselves, with SHARE acting as the clearing house.

A Farm Preserve Note.

BerkShares Summertime Promotion Programme (1991-93)

'BerkShares' began life in 1991 as a project of the Main Street Action programme of the Chamber of Commerce working with the E. F. Schumacher Society.

Main Street Action printed one-dollar denominated BerkShare notes and issued them to 70 participating merchants in downtown Great Barrington. For every ten dollars spent by a customer during a six-week summer tourist season, the customer received one BerkShare. There was no dollar backing at this stage; it was merely a summertime promotion.

During a three-day festival in the slower autumn season, the BerkShares could be redeemed for goods at any of the 70 local traders at a dollar equivalency. The percentage of acceptance was determined by the retailer. Most businesses allowed BerkShares to be used for up to 100 per cent of the cost of goods purchased. In the first year 75,000 BerkShares were issued, representing $750,000 in local trade over the six-week period. Over a three-day period 28,000 BerkShares were redeemed. Judged a success, the programme was repeated for the next two years.

BerkShares local currency (2006-present)

In 2006, the E. F. Schumacher Society won grant funding for its proposal to turn BerkShares into a local currency. Its strategy was:

- to involve as many main street businesses as possible from the start

- to partner with the strong local banking community

- to include a paper currency for its visibility and ease of use

- to use the launch of the currency as a tool for education about the importance of citizen support of the local economy.

Once the business, banking and customer communities are familiar with the tool, the planned next stage is to introduce a loan programme in BerkShares focusing on businesses producing goods that are at present imported to the region. And once there is general confidence and understanding of the loan programme, the currency would then untie from full federal dollar backing and become a tool for local economic development independent of fluctuations in the value of the dollar. This is a ten-year plan.

The society organised BerkShares Inc., a non-profit-making organisation with membership open to anyone in the region and a board of directors elected by the members. BerkShares, Inc. reflects the belief that the issuing of currency should be a service, not a for-profit business, and that the issuing organisation should be transparent in its workings and accountable to the regional community. The BerkShares board brings together the full range of skills needed to manage a local currency programme: a banker, a lawyer, an economist, an accountant, a philanthropist, a software developer, an editor of an environmental journal, a retail store owner, and a manager of a local not-for-profit organisation.

The board researched printers and sources of paper, established design features, selected local heroes and artists to honour on the currency, hired a designer, and printed $835,000 worth of BerkShare notes, in denominations of one, five, ten, twenty and fifty, at parity with the US dollar. These beautifully designed notes were printed on banknote paper, and included full security features. They reflect the values and aesthetics of the region and are a source of pride for local residents. The notes easily achieved the objective of having 'moneyness' and 'valuableness' about them.

As of February 2009, 180,000 BerkShares were in circulation amongst southern Berkshire County's population of 19,000 people. Berkshire Bank, one of the five issuing banks, issues 1-2,000 BerkShares a day in the winter, 5-6,000 a day in the busier summer, from its Main Street Great Barrington site. Over a million BerkShares have been issued since the summer of 2006, just from this one site.

A ten-BerkShares note featuring local hero and Community Supported Agriculture founder Robyn Van En.

How does the BerkShares programme work?

BerkShares are issued by, and are the responsibility of, BerkShares Inc., but the programme is run in partnership with five locally owned banks. BerkShares Inc. opened a non-interest-bearing checking account at each of the thirteen participating branches of the five banks. It then distributed all the BerkShares (total face value of $835,000) to the branch banks. Each bank verified this distribution, recording the serial numbers of notes it received. BerkShares Inc. does not hold, sell, exchange or circulate any supplies of the currency itself; all the BerkShares are held by the banks. This is essential for ensuring that the currency has integrity.

Customers go to any of the participating banks and exchange ninety-five dollars for one hundred Berk-Shares. They can spend the BerkShares at any of businesses across the south of Berkshire County that accept them – some 375 in March 2009. The dollars remain on deposit in the BerkShares account as a backing, and to facilitate converting Berkshares back into federal dollars.

That the deposit account earns no interest is an incentive and a reward for the active participation and engagement of the banks in making the scheme work. BerkShares Inc. can look online at any time and see the amount deposited in each account with each bank, and the number of BerkShares each branch holds. This enables BerkShares Inc. to ensure that each branch has enough BerkShares to meet demands, and where they might access new supplies. It also provides invaluable management information about where BerkShares are being withdrawn, and where supplies of the currency might be getting stuck.

Users of BerkShares can buy their groceries at a local whole food supermarket or the Berkshire Co-op supermarket, buy meals in local restaurants and coffee bars, buy snowshoes, cameras, the latest Manhattan fashions, bikes, get printing and advertising done, pay a lawyer, and get a website built, hosted on a solar-powered server.

The businesses can then either give the BerkShares out again in change, re-circulate them by spending them with other local businesses, or deposit them back at the bank, in which case they get 95 dollars back for every 100 BerkShares deposited. It is thus in the interest of local people to exchange their federal dollars for BerkShares, as they get a 5-per-cent advantage for shopping at local businesses. This is a clear incentive, in contrast with the Chiemgauer discussed in the previous chapter. Local businesses are also incentivised to give out the BerkShares in change or re-circulate them with other local businesses, rather than just bank them.

Explaining the success of BerkShares

As with regiogeld, we find in BerkShares a local currency programme that does seem to be involving a significant number of local businesses – a step change from LETS and time money, and perhaps a greater penetration than Hours. What factors help explain this success?

Partnership networks

BerkShares are the result of long years of research, experimentation and dedicated local work on the part of the E. F. Schumacher Society. The society has deep roots, perhaps not replicated anywhere else except, perhaps, Bavaria with its Chiemgauer regiogeld. Key thinkers and innovators of localisation and local currencies in the 1960s and '70s, including Bob Swann and Ralph Borsodi, were associated with the society. Its staff are well known

Exchanging dollars for BerkShares at Berkshire Bank, Great Barrington. Photo courtesy of Jason Houston.

and have a local track record. It has a history of experimentation behind it, such that its experiments are seen as normal parts of the local economy.

The society's strong networks of trust and partnership within the local community enabled it to pilot local currencies and, based on this track record, to win grant funding to take BerkShares to the next level. Grant funding and the time put into research means that the quality of the design, look and feel of BerkShare notes is first class and compares well with notes issued by states. Producing a local currency that looks and feels like 'money' is not something that can be done easily, quickly or cheaply. Those looking to emulate BerkShares would do well to remember this.

The partnership with the locally owned banks means that BerkShares are easy to get hold of and easy to change back to US dollars should the need arise. Users can have confidence that the banks are ensuring that the process for accounting for BerkShares, tracking circulation and maintaining the currency's integrity and security, is robust. BerkShares are thus triple-backed:

- by the reputation of the E. F. Schumacher Society, its staff and its partners

- by the validation bestowed by involvement of local banks

- physically by US dollars. Every BerkShare issued into circulation at the bank is backed by the 95 cents needed to redeem it, held on deposit.

A supportive environment

BerkShares have gripped the local imagination, involving a significant number of locally owned businesses and the local chamber of commerce. Unlike many places, Berkshire County has resisted the destruction of its small towns, main streets and local businesses by 'big box' stores and malls. There are two big box stores in Great Barrington, a Dunkin' Donuts and a Subway, but no Wal-Mart, MacDonald's or Starbucks. It is a stunning area, for snowsports in the winter, hiking in the summer, and 'leaf peeking' in the fall, and its local businesses add to the ambience and quality of life. It is a wealthy area, where people pay a premium for the ambience. Consequently there is large constituency for and a long tradition of supporting the 'local'.

There is therefore a large independent business sector to protect, and the owners can decide for themselves whether or not to join the local currency programme. They do not have to seek permission from a head office elsewhere – which, given that head office is unlikely to know the workings of the local economy in detail, is unlikely to be forthcoming. Small business owners have to multitask. They are their own sales team, logistics, marketing, accounts and warehouse. If they can see a benefit from using an alternative currency (especially to their bottom line), if the currency is easy to use, and if those promoting it respect small businesspeople and demonstrate a commitment to helping them to find ways to make it work for them, then a businessperson can make the decision to join – or to leave – the programme very quickly indeed.

But it's not just a matter of the utilitarian bottom line. Berkshire County boasts a highly educated, progressive local population with a commitment to supporting local businesses, eating locally produced healthy food, and supporting a vibrant local economy able to weather financial storms. It has a high proportion of second-home owners and weekend visitors from New York and Boston, both two to three hours away, some of whom work in the financial sector and who therefore see the full implications of what the E. F.

Schumacher Society and its partners are trying to do with BerkShares. They see the value of multiple currencies as a 'harbour in a storm'. They understood the vulnerability of the economy and the possibility of a collapse well before anyone else, and before it actually happened in 2007. Sophisticated conversations about the financial implications of BerkShares often precede a decision to convert some dollars into BerkShares at one of the local banks.

Community Supported Agriculture (CSA) was pioneered in Berkshire County at Indian Line Farm, a mile down the road from the E. F. Schumacher Library. This history of consumer support for farmers is reflected on the ten Berkshire note, which features CSA founder Robyn Van En. 'Berkshire Grown' promotes local agriculture, and expensive restaurants aimed at the weekend incomers have long stressed both sourcing local food and paying a premium for it. Local publications promote local purchasing. Even the banks are locally owned, and their managers have considerable autonomy and discretion over how they run their branches. They are encouraged to get

Buying coffee and cakes with BerkShares. Photo courtesy of Jason Houston.

involved with the community and to innovate with new products aimed at supporting local business in creative ways. So the environment is receptive to the idea of a local currency: its ethos resonates, goes with the local flow. It's seen as something unique to Great Barrington, and fosters town pride. That's why so many local businesses continue to sign up.

The early stages

Just over three years old, the BerkShares programme is still at an early stage of development. It is not fully evolved in that it isn't yet ready to function as a tool for financing local production. At this stage, the aim is to make sure that the business, banking and consumer communities are familiar with and comfortable with the concept of a new currency and, with them, to discover how to make it work as effectively as possible. In its present form it functions as a local currency note backed by dollars on deposit, a sophisticated buy-local programme, though carrying in its design the elements that would allow it to grow to a fully independent currency. BerkShares staff see it as on the way towards the final goal of a fully independent currency, but only at "stage 25 of 50 stages".

"I heard about it from local business guys and was really intrigued, based on my desires in business to be an established part of the community, exchanging with the community. It felt like a no-brainer . . . (you) just gotta figure out about how to keep them in circulation, which is the desire anyway . . . So, I think it's been great, it's sparked a lot of dialogue about supporting the local. It's fun, I think, it makes *me* feel good. And it's that supporting of local, all these notions that come together in one dollar BerkShare bill." **Lester, Route Seven Grill**

Some of the challenges in getting to the final destination, a resilient local economy, are as follows.

• A significant dependence in the Berkshire economy on goods and services sourced outside the region, limiting opportunities for re-circulation of the currency.

• The stubborn hold that globalisation has on our personal spending and financial patterns, which can make it hard for some to see the value of a local currency.

• Problems emerging from characteristics designed into BerkShares in the early stages of its evolution towards a fully fledged and independent local currency. These are discussed below.

At the current stage of the programme's development BerkShares are widely used in Berkshire County. Businesses see users of BerkShares as loyal customers with whom they have developed a relationship. By accepting BerkShares, businesses feel they get repeat trade that might otherwise have gone to the big box stores.

But the volume of BerkShares taken in and re-circulated by many individual businesses is low, no more than 1 or 2 per cent of their weekly takings. Perhaps not unexpectedly, the extent to which BerkShares has made a significant difference to the bottom line of most businesses so far is debatable.

If you want to establish a transition currency you need be prepared to offer advice and support to such businesses so that anticipated challenges do not become major problems. Some of these challenges are as follows.

The challenge of the initial discount

Remember that you need to either purchase BerkShares from a participating bank, or accept them as change. Why would you do that? You need an incentive to persuade consumers to change their ingrained spending habits and adopt a new, unfamiliar local currency. BerkShares Inc. decided to establish a 10-per-cent incentive for trading in BerkShares. The discount meant that citizens could at that time go to a participating bank and exchange 90 federal dollars for 100 BerkShares. For citizens, this was a good deal and a strong incentive.

Regiogeld and the Stroud Pound (see Chapter 13) do not incentivise consumers beyond their ability to gift 3 per cent of the value of the currency to local voluntary organisations and non-profit-makers. In Chapter 11 we will see that Totnes settled on no discount for the first issuance of the Totnes Pound, 5 per cent for the second, and none for the third. Lewes has had no discount, and attempts to introduce one were resisted.

BerkShares are cash. No billing is required, no credit card fees need to be paid, no cheques are returned unpaid. The funds are available immediately. Every credit card transaction a business accepts entails a 2-per-cent fee to the credit card company – this is seen as normal. When all of these points were taken into consideration, a conversion fee was not considered burdensome to businesses, and essential incentive to encourage take up of the currency.

The level of the discount was somewhat arbitrary in nature. It was, for instance, easier to calculate 10 per cent than 7 per cent, but coming up with the precise amount to encourage consumers without discouraging businesses from participating was a delicate balance.

> "I even tell the customers who come in and pay with BerkShares, "you're a smart customer", because there's nowhere, I don't care if you do it on the stock market, in a savings account in a bank, a money market . . . you're not going to get 10-per-cent return on your money. And [using BerkShares] you're getting a 10-per-cent return on your money." **Rick, the manager of Guidos, one of the supermarkets that accepts BerkShares**

Hurting those you want help?

As long as businesses could re-circulate the BerkShares by purchasing needed goods and services locally, perhaps as part of their personal drawings, there would be no disadvantage to trade in BerkShares. But in an economy still highly dependent on imports, this was not always possible – and exchanging BerkShares back into federal dollars meant receiving only 90 cents for each BerkShare. This cost would be borne by the business.

Some types of businesses could easily accommodate a 10-per-cent discount in exchange for the additional public visibility they received from accepting Berk-Shares. Clothes stores, for example, regularly discounted 50 per cent or even 70 per cent on end-of-range or last season's clothes. Hotel rooms are regularly heavily discounted. These stores and service providers considered it a normal, acceptable part of doing business. Snap Store, the local camera shop, happily accepted BerkShares for 100 per cent of the price of a camera that retailed for $1,000. As the cost of the camera to the shop was $930, a 10-per-cent discount translated into a loss of 30 dollars, as the camera shop could not buy the camera, or anything else it sold, locally, so was unable to re-circulate its BerkShares. Nevertheless, Snap Store remains an enthusiastic participant in the BerkShares programme. It saw BerkShares as good PR, and a way to support businesses like itself.

However, food-related businesses such as restaurants and grocery stores, and other stores selling large volumes of things people use every day with a low profit on each individual item, have very tight margins. Ten per cent was difficult for them to absorb, and some businesses consequently described it as 'taking a 10 per cent hit'. Such businesses decided to absorb this 'hit', feeling it unethical to 'pass it on', as they saw it, to another struggling business, often run by a friend in the tight-knit community.

The level of the discount was a particular issue for Guidos and the Berkshire Co-op Market, two super-markets selling organic, natural and wholefood products. Feeling that the concept of BerkShares was so closely aligned to their ethos as community-minded businesses, these locally owned businesses believed that their members and customers would expect them to accept BerkShares and they would pay a cost in reputation if they did not participate.

"Our shoppers are their (BerkShares) core support-ers. It's the fusion of the missions – believe me, if we hadn't have taken BerkShares we would have heard about it! And rightly so."
Jennifer Foley of the Berkshire Food Co-op

Guidos and the Co-op thus both accepted BerkShares with no discount from the start of the programme. As just about every other person who accepted BerkShares could find something they could readily spend their BerkShares on at these two food supermarkets, at first they were inundated. The Co-op took in some 60,000 BerkShares a month, while Guidos banked 2.2 per cent

of its total receipts in BerkShares in 2007. This was unsustainable.

Listening to, and respecting, local businesses
BerkShares Inc. recognised this problem and worked with businesses to experiment with solutions. Some businesses developed strategies to limit the extent that they would take in BerkShares they could not spend by defining tightly what could and could not be purchased for BerkShares, specifying percentages, or limiting it to certain days. Guidos decided to restrict acceptance of BerkShares to Sunday to Thursday, when the majority of their customers would be locals, not the wealthy New Yorkers and Bostonians who flocked to the town at weekends, greatly boosting Guidos' footfall. The Co-op decided to limit acceptance to 50 per cent of purchases, seven days a week. The result was that BerkShares takings dropped to a more manage-able 1.6 per cent of Guidos' receipts. In January 2009 the figure was 1.1 per cent.

However, for customers trying to understand who was accepting BerkShares, for what items and when, it could be quite difficult. Some people reacted badly to being told they could not spend their BerkShares on this item, on this day, or that only 50-per-cent payment in BerkShares would be accepted. The consumer appreciates clarity, and the differing policies dampened use by some.

Adjustments en route: reducing the discount
BerkShares Inc. spent a significant amount of time surveying both customers and businesses about their use of BerkShares and how a change in the discount (including going to 0-per-cent discount) might affect use. After two years of operation, they decided to move to a 5-per-cent discount, judging that the original deep incentive had created the familiarity of use with consumers sufficient to foster continued use.

They judged that the next priority in the development of the programme was to provide incentives for more businesses to join, so creating additional opportunities for business-to-business re-circulation of the currency.

However, to switch the rate of exchange between federal dollars and BerkShares required a carefully staged plan. New reference material would have to be printed, notices prepared for the banks, information throughout the detailed website changed, training materials altered, and signage updated. Businesses had to be informed, bank staff retrained, and public notice given in ways that reached most consumers. If notice of the rate change were known in advance it could be put to private use and create a run on the banks. Nine thousand federal dollars could be exchanged for 10,000 BerkShares before the rate adjustment, only to have the same 10,000 BerkShares returned the following week and converted to $9,500. A $500 profit.

Preparations for the change took several months, with ad space held in advance in local media venues, new materials printed outside the region, so they would not be seen in advance, and only key bank personnel informed. A three-day moratorium on BerkShare trade at the banks was announced, during which time new material was put in place. As a result of the extensive preparation the change went through unproblematically, and many of the complaints related to the 10-per-cent discount abated. New businesses regularly sign up to accept BerkShares, while citizen use of BerkShares has held steady.

The challenge of re-circulation

For BerkShares and other local currencies to act as a vigorous medium of local trade, it is preferable that the currency re-circulates frequently before returning to the bank. The number of opportunities for re-circulation will largely depend on the vitality of the local economy. The Berkshire economy is still largely dependent on goods manufactured outside the region. Nevertheless, many owners of BerkShare-participating businesses pride themselves in finding ways to re-circulate all of the BerkShares they accept.

These businesses became the biggest promoters of BerkShares. They enjoyed the challenge of spending their BerkShares and the discussions that emerged. Spending BerkShares could be fun. They saw the benefits of developing local networks and connections, local cooperation and resilience. As time went on they got more comfortable with asking those they did business with to take BerkShares, and they became more confident in explaining the benefits. They offered change in BerkShares to acquaint visitors to the area with the conception of a local currency. They offered special discounts and incentives to users of BerkShares. They took part of their personal drawings in Berk-Shares or traded their own federal dollars, one for one, with the BerkShares in the cash register and used them for family expenses.

However, businesses such as Guidos and the Co-op found that they could not re-circulate all the BerkShares they accepted. The two businesses professed themselves unwilling to break a longstanding relationship with a trusted contractor who did not accept BerkShares, and did not feel it was appropriate for them to use their buying power to make a contractor work in a certain way – something for which companies such as Wal-Mart have rightly received much criticism.

Most of the goods they sold were supplied to them through nationally owned wholesalers, who could not use a local currency. Taxes and energy bills could not yet be paid in BerkShares. The companies could not yet pay their contractors with BerkShares, as there were too few plumbers, electricians, garbage removal operators and the like who accepted them. Wages were paid electronically, and employees did not want to carry a roll of notes around in their pockets. In practice, the businesses found that their employees didn't want even a small part of their wages in BerkShares, as they could not yet pay rent or mortgages, utility bills or local taxes with BerkShares. True, they could spend BerkShares with *their* employers and on small items of personal consumption, but neither company sold everything a family would need. Generally they sold high-quality, organic and wholefoods, perceived to be expensive. Not everyone wanted to do their shopping at their workplace!

Guidos estimated that only 3 per cent of the goods it sold were produced within 100 miles of Great Barrington, their definition of 'local'. The Co-op was supplied from Chesterfield, New Hampshire, by a national supplier. Both companies sourced locally whenever they could, and were committed to doing more. But they found few local suppliers able to produce the necessary volumes for a supermarket. More local production needed to be developed.

In the long run BerkShares Inc. wishes to solve the problem of the limited number of places where BerkShares can be spent through the development of a resilient local currency system that is an accepted and unremarkable part of the local economic scene. It wants to go beyond facilitating exchange between existing local businesses and their customers, to develop more local production.

The challenge of bookkeeping
A local currency is another form of money, alongside cheques, credit cards and federal dollars, and should be handled as such. It would be fatal for a perception to grow up that there is something in anyway underhand about a local currency. It is in no way a tax dodge.

Local currencies such as BerkShares are cash. Taxes are paid on local currency income as with any federal dollar purchase, and when bills are paid with Berk-Shares, a signed receipt is required. When a business returns BerkShares to one of the banks, the bank creates a separate deposit slip for the transaction. The 5-per-cent discount is noted in the bookkeeping system as a business expense, much like the way in which a credit card fee is recorded. Thus there is an audit trail.

While this is a simple enough process on the one hand, it is an extra step for a small business owner. And while the owner of the business may like the idea of a local currency, the bookkeeper may object to the extra work.

Guidos and the Co-op reported unwillingness at first on the part of their bookkeepers to handle BerkShares, and a reluctance to use them to pay the few bills they could use the currency for, when contractors did accept BerkShares. Wanting to make the programme available at their store, the owners of Guidos worked with their accountant to be more creative in ways to spend BerkShares. Berkshire Bank developed proposals for a BerkShares cheque account, so that businesses could pay their suppliers in BerkShares with a cheque.

The challenge of established financial and spending patterns
The reluctance of some bookkeepers to add a new financial tool to their operations was also reflected in the reluctance of consumers to change financial patterns. People have established buying and spending habits. They are used to spending dollars, using credit cards, paying bills electronically, and buying over the internet. The extent to which our attitudes towards money are deeply engrained was a revelation.

Even those who philosophically supported the local currency as a way of building a more resilient local economy would whip out the credit card at a store accepting BerkShares, ignoring the fact that the credit card fee was a cost to that local business.

Experience suggests that two groups of people are most likely to use BerkShares. The first group comprises those who work in the region and live on modest salaries. They are not poor, but are perhaps three monthly pay cheques away from financial struggles. They are used to a cash economy. They cash a pay cheque and live within the means of that cheque. They intuitively know the health of the local economy, and understand its ebbs and flows. They buy from local businesses, even when the cost of goods might be more expensive than from chain stores. They know that those local businesses are providing jobs to people like them, to their friends and family. They are financially savvy, and know where discounts are to be had that enable their money to go further. Their adoption of BerkShares is quite natural and simple, without fanfare. They have BerkShares in their pockets almost all of the time and know without consulting the directory which stores trade in BerkShares.

The other significant group is the wealthy. They see the fragility of the global financial markets that they are intimately involved in and see a local currency as an insurance policy in the form of an alternative form of exchange in the event of financial collapse. They participate robustly in BerkShare trade.

The poor, of necessity, must spend a significant portion of their income on rent, utilities, transport and energy – expenditures not yet generally payable in a local currency. They require hard-won federal dollars, or unbacked currencies like LETS or time money.

Buying groceries with BerkShares at the Food Co-op.

The Berkshire region has a highly educated middle class drawn to the region by its rich cultural traditions and the beauty of the landscape. But, even though this group was theoretically inclined to the idea of supporting local economies, BerkShares organisers were surprised by how much effort it took to motivate it to participate in the BerkShares programme. More and more dependent on electronic banking, the consumer is increasingly separated from face-to-face financial transactions and the consequences and alchemy of those transactions.

BerkShares Inc. found it had to plan for more promotions, more seminars, and more community events than it had originally anticipated. It hired an executive director to be the public face of BerkShares to keep the currency in the public eye. It sent emails round to businesses saying who had joined the network. It put on seminars and made an accountant available to businesses struggling with bookkeeping. A marketing executive was recruited to extend the network. Meetings were held with businesses to monitor circulation. All this entailed expenses Berkshares Inc. had not fully anticipated.

To a large extent the role of BerkShares has been to play an educational function in the community, holding the standard for local businesses and local banks and describing how important they are to weaving together the thread of community.

The challenge of perception – what is a local currency for?

The final challenge is one of perception – how people see the currency. Is BerkShares a buy-local programme or a stage in the development of a tool for financing local production? The partnership with local banks, the structure of the non-profit-making issuer and the high quality of the paper and its security features are all part of the conscious strategy of developing an independent currency, a locally determined means of exchange which can then be used to finance the development of new local production. However, the unprecedented media attention at its early stage has tended to seal the identification of BerkShares as a buy-local programme, creating its own set of problems.

From its launch BerkShares has earned unprecedented national and media coverage, largely from the integrity of its design and concept. With the collapse of global financial markets in 2007-8, that media attention has ratcheted even higher, as local- and citizen-initiated solutions to the economic crisis are being considered. In April of 2008, for instance, the BerkShares website averaged 43,000 hits per day from all over the world, requiring a significant amount of staff time to manage – time that might have otherwise gone into further development of the local programme.

Great Barrington is a town with a strong local identity, and many locally owned businesses do consciously support each other anyway. Projects such as 'Berkshire Grown' and 'Spend in the Berkshires' encourage local trading. Some businesses consequently challenged the 'added value' of BerkShares. By all means 'shop local', they say, but why use BerkShares, which local businesses cannot yet pass down the supply chain?

The media attention has meant that the image of BerkShares has been fixed in the public's eye in its current 'buy-local' campaign phase, obscuring the larger goal of achieving an independent currency. For a local currency to become an accepted and normal part of the economy in the manner expected, many will want it to perform as a medium of local circulation, and they will judge it on that basis. The added value will only become clearer when it can be used to provide loans to develop local production, or as a means to help the local economy through a financial crisis on the Argentine model. But this is less likely to be achieved if a blanket perception emerges that local currencies do not 'work' as 'businesses can't spend them'. In this case, the project would risk being stillborn.

These are just challenges along the route to an independent, low-carbon, local economy. The time and care that has gone into designing and promoting BerkShares, and the attention paid to listening to and respecting local businesses has paid dividends. Those wishing to set up their own local currencies would do well to learn from experiences in the Berkshires.

BerkShares – key recommendations

- BerkShares have that intangible quality of 'moneyness' and 'valuableness'. This comes from the design and quality of the notes, from the reputation and track record of the E. F. Schumacher Society and its partners in the community, from the 'seal of approval' of locally owned banks, which provided convenient locations from where citizens can obtain BerkShares, and from the currency's backing in federal dollars. The BerkShares programme builds on twenty years of hard local work on the part of respected local activists and businesspeople. It is part of a long-term strategy, and is properly funded. Others following in the E. F. Schumacher Society's path might do well to ensure that their plans are as well-developed and funded.

- However, because of limited re-circulation opportunities in an economy still largely dependent on imports, businesses struggled to re-circulate BerkShares in large quantities. The programme is not yet at a stage where it can develop local production. We don't know how well a local currency will work in this context.

- As with Ithaca Hours, it has proved necessary to actively manage the currency: recruiting new businesses, helping them make the currency work for them and making suggestions about what to do when they can't spend all the BerkShares they earn. Consumers have well-entrenched spending habits. The experience is that a lot of time needs to be put into marketing and managing the currency, and this needs to be funded. This again is something to think about when planning a local currency.

- The success of BerkShares comes from the fact that it is backed. Businesses that can't re-circulate them can convert them back to federal dollars, albeit at a cost. In retrospect, although BerkShares Inc. believes that the initial 10-percent incentive was an essential part of the strategy for getting people to break from their old financial habits and use a new currency, it may have been too high a discount for businesses that operate on low profits for high volumes of goods and that could not re-circulate as many BerkShares as they accepted. Five per cent may provide a balance between incentivising customers and encouraging businesses to find ways to re-circulate, rather than bank the currency.

- Issuers of local currencies are viewed as leaders in a citizen movement to take responsibility for shaping their own local economies. As such, organisers should expect their programmes to be in the media spotlight; that spotlight becomes a player in defining the currency and its role in the local community. The businesses, banks, community officials and citizen users of the currency should all be prepared for this public role and welcome it as an opportunity to share the values and aspirations of a more decentralised and democratised economy.

THE BERKSHARES SCORECARD

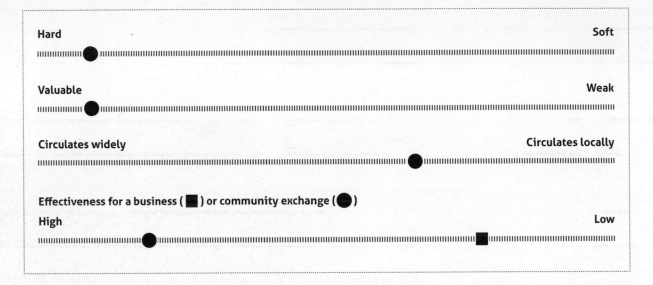

Hard   Soft

Valuable   Weak

Circulates widely   Circulates locally

Effectiveness for a business (■) or community exchange (●)

High   Low

B£
10

**Ten
Brixton
Pounds**

Money that sticks to Brixton

0001259

B£10

B£
5

2 for £1.99 each

The Brixton Pound:

Supports local independent traders
Keeps circulating within Brixton
Builds community connections
Helps cut carbon emissions

For a list of participating traders and issuing points go to www.brixtonpound.org

FIVE

Supported by: Lambeth Council, nef (the new economics foundation), Mode's, Transition Town Brixton

PART THREE:
TRANSITION CURRENCIES

"[Localisation] does not mean walling off the outside world. It means nurturing locally owned businesses which use local resources sustainably, employ local workers at decent wages and serve primarily local consumers. It means becoming more self sufficient, and less dependent on exports. Control moves from the boardrooms of distant corporations, and back to the community where it belongs."
Michael Shuman, *Going Local*

"There's a kind of thrill about it, it seems to me. You hold those notes and you say, Can you do this? Can we just print it then? It seems too simple. Aren't there laws against it? . . . no, it IS legal to print your own. You can use what you like as money after all, if someone will accept it."
David Boyle, at the launch of the Brixton Pound

"Another world is not only possible, she is on her way. On a quiet day, I can hear her breathing." **Arundhati Roy**

CHAPTER 11

THE FIRST TRANSITION CURRENCY: THE TOTNES POUND

by Noel Longhurst

Totnes should need no introduction as the home of the Transition movement. It was here that the story of BerkShares crossed the Atlantic and took root in the Devon countryside. In turn, Totnes inspired Lewes, which then inspired Brixton – while Stroud decided to try an alternative path inspired by regiogeld. Like many places, Totnes once had its own local banks – and local pounds – until, during the nineteenth century, State- and banks-issued currencies controlled by elites consolidated their hold over our economy and our lives.

This chapter is written by Noel Longhurst, a founder member of the Transition Town Totnes Economics and Livelihoods group. He helped to launch the Totnes Pound and became a key member of the Totnes Currency group for the first 18 months of its existence. His PhD examined why Totnes seems to be the cradle for so many interesting experiments in localisation.

For more on the Totnes Pound see: **http://totnes. transitionnetwork.org/totnespound/home**

Totnes

The small market town of Totnes sits perched above the river Dart in the bucolic South Devon countryside. The aesthetic beauty of the town and its rural surrounds has attracted a steady stream of writers and artists, and also inspired many people to think that another world might just be possible. Not least Leonard and Dorothy Elmhirst, who started an experiment in rural regeneration at the nearby Dartington Hall estate in the 1920s. Dartington's experiments in the arts, agriculture, education and commerce were not only in many ways pioneering but also drew in to the area a steady stream of liberal and progressive thinkers over the following decades. Someone once described it as a bit like Bloomsbury-by-the-sea.

Totnes Pounds being spent in Greenfibres.

By the 1970s some elements of the Dartington milieu were experimenting with the ideas that emerged from the counterculture, and their growing numbers (partly because of Dartington's school and Art College) meant that they began to have an impact on the town itself. During the 1980s Totnes developed a reputation as a 'bohemian', 'alternative' or 'new age' centre.

147

Although such terms are sometimes used in a derogatory or dismissive sense, the area has continued to be a site of 'alternative' activity, with pioneering work in permaculture, organic farming and anti-GM campaigning in recent years, not to mention the emergence of the Transition movement.

Many longer-term residents observe that the town has got busier over the last twenty years. Certainly the area has increased in popularity, both as a place to visit and to live. This has had an effect both on the cost of living and on the mixture of shops. However, the historic nature of the town centre has prevented redevelopment and preserved a retail centre that consists predominately of independent retailers. The food writer Matthew Fort once described the local food culture as akin to Naples, with a range of local organic and biodynamic growers. And those factors, along with the continuing existence of a number of different countercultural traditions, makes Totnes an interesting and unusual place.

The Totnes Pound: how it works

The Totnes Pound is, at the time of writing, a locally produced paper currency backed by sterling on deposit. At present it exists in only a one-pound note denomination, although there are plans both for higher-value notes and for an electronic version of the currency. People exchange sterling into Totnes Pounds and then spend them with participating businesses. These businesses are listed on the Totnes Pound website, and display 'Totnes Pounds accepted here' signs. The intention is that the businesses then spend them with other participating businesses, either directly with their own suppliers or by paying their staff partly in Totnes Pounds.

The decision to call the currency 'Pounds' was an explicit attempt to make a statement that this currency was comparable to sterling – that it has 'moneyness'. As we saw in Chapter 6, the sometimes whimsical names given to LETS currencies ('Acorns' in Totnes) can undermine their credibility and perhaps prevent a wider constituency from using the alternative currency. The use of the term 'Pounds' in Totnes was intended to normalise the currency and encourage people to accept that it was money they could use.

The Totnes Pound is fully backed. People receive Totnes Pounds in exchange for sterling, which is banked. This means that if there was a 'run' on the currency all Totnes Pounds in circulation could be converted back into sterling. This has proved to be an important factor in building up trust in the currency.

> "The biggest impact has been to raise the profile of Totnes, make it a 'go to' place, which has a not insignificant impact. It has also got people thinking and talking about what happens to the money and how it leaves the area. It is only a start but an important start. It is also a tangible link for businesses to become interested in Transition more generally." **Paul Wesley, Harlequin Books**

Developing the Totnes Pound

As described by Rob Hopkins in the Foreword, the original inspiration for the Totnes Pound came from a short course on the 'Future of Money' at Schumacher College outside Totnes in January 2006. One of the teachers on the course was Bernard Lietaer, a former Central Bank executive in Belgium who was involved in the design and implementation of the ECU currency convergence mechanism that preceded the launch of Euro. Following a distinguished career in the financial industries, Lietaer is now an active advocate for local currencies and monetary reform.[1] It was a common convention that guest teachers deliver a public lecture during their time at Schumacher, normally on a Wednesday evening. Lietaer's lecture on complementary currencies included some references to BerkShares.

It was that lecture that convinced Rob Hopkins of the wider potential of local currencies to contribute to the Transition process and raise the media profile of climate change and peak oil as issues. The apparent strengths of the BerkShares model were very attractive. Two of the group that eventually launched the currency were also in at the lecture and familiar with the model.

Therefore when later discussing the currency at the Transition Town Totnes (TTT) Economics and Livelihoods group, we did not spend a great deal of time looking at other currency models. We were attracted by ways BerkShares and other 'backed' currency models such as the Salt Spring Dollar seemed to be able to engage with the business community in a way that currencies such as LETS had not. We were also aware of the similarity between our model and the regiogeld currencies, but apart from the Eko currency at Findhorn in Scotland we could not find any other contemporary examples of a backed local currency in the UK.

For information on the Salt Spring Island Dollar, British Columbia, Canada, see:
http://saltspringdollars.com

We have always seen the Totnes Pound, like BerkShares, as a serious, long-term project that would inevitably encounter problems on the way. But we saw experimentation with a model that did not have a strong record in the UK as healthy, and as a way to inspire similar projects in other communities. The sense of embarking on a pioneering experiment, very much in keeping with the Transition ethic, was very appealing.

The Totnes Pound has evolved through three specific phases, each with its own banknote.

Phase one: March–May 2007

The first incarnation of the Totnes Pound was issued at the official launch of the Transition Town Totnes (TTT) Economics and Livelihoods group on 7 March 2007. Because of cost constraints the first phase notes were very simple, compliment-slip-sized notes, printed on

The Findhorn Eko

Since 2002 the Ekopia Resource Exchange at Findhorn has issued a local currency called the Eko, in denominations of one, five, ten and twenty Ekos, at parity with sterling. The Eko circulates within the Findhorn Foundation and at the Findhorn holiday park and a local cafe. Since the successful trial, 15-20,000 Ekos have been in permanent circulation and Ekos are now into a third issue. As a result of the surpluses created, grants of £400 each have been made to a community festivals group, a wind farm, an ecological guest facility and a youth project.

Noel Longhurst and Robert Vint with the first Totnes Pound.

durable paper, but with no discernible security features. On the front was an image of an original Totnes Pound from 1810. The reverse contained background information about the currency. There were also boxes that accepting shops and users could sign so TTT could track the circulation of the currency.

Three hundred Totnes Pound notes were given away at the meeting, or 'gifted' into circulation. We explained to the audience that this was an experiment and that they should go and spend them with the eighteen participating businesses and, to spread use, ask to spend the Totnes Pounds at other businesses and to receive the Pounds in change.

Findings from phase one
At the end of the trial the team visited all the participating businesses to collect feedback and find out whether the notes had circulated as planned. The feedback was as follows.

- The project was very popular and both businesses and the community would like to see it developed further.

- Although most of the businesses had seen some notes, there were not enough of them in circulation to make a real difference.

- Their scarcity meant that they had a certain novelty value, which was seen as a good thing. For example, tourists bought them as mementos.

- There was not enough information provided, so shops had to spend time explaining the idea to customers.

- The notes were too big for wallets and tills.

Phase one of the Totnes Pound received considerable media attention locally, nationally and internationally. At the end of the pilot phase the project team met to consider the feedback received and to decide whether to continue the experiment or whether to stop and spend some time planning and resourcing a longer-term model. The decision was made to build on the existing momentum, and plans for the issuing of a phase two note were quickly developed and implemented.

A phase two Totnes Pound note.

Phase two: July–December 2007
Phase two was conceived as a bigger experiment to build on the momentum and to test the system further. The intention was to put up to 10,000 one-Totnes-Pound notes into circulation for a period of six months – July to December 2007.

The scaling-up of the project brought a number of important considerations into play. Whereas the first phase had been a playful experiment, with the notes effectively 'backed' by trust in Rob Hopkins and TTT, the planned expansion of circulation meant that we had to ensure that there was confidence in the currency.

Building confidence
One way that we did this was by introducing some security features for the note. Working with our

A reflection

Should we have spent a little more time developing our ideas and getting funding? Personally, I am glad that we cracked on with the project because experimentation and practical 'learning-by-doing' can be more fun and productive than having lots of meetings and writing funding bids that might come to nothing. We very much thought of ourselves as pioneers.

On the other hand, if you compare what we did with the amount of planning, preparation and funding that has gone into BerkShares, perhaps we did move a bit too quickly. We might have reflected a little more on the full range of tasks necessary to manage a currency and how these were going to be accomplished.

Had we raised a bit more money we might have been able to provide a higher-quality note. We didn't know it at the time, but experiences in Lewes and Brixton (see Chapters 12 and 14) seem to suggest that spending time and money getting the 'moneyness' of your local currency right pays dividends.

printer we decided to use a plasticised paper that is difficult to source unless you are within the printing industry. We also added a thermal mark (which didn't work very well) and some ultraviolet ink (but then found that most businesses didn't have UV scanners). Finally we also 'overprinted' each note with a unique serial number.

Other currency projects had advised us that low-denomination notes are not normally forged, and we were confident that the level of security we were using was more than sufficient. In fact we jokingly suspected that it was probably the most secure one-pound note in existence! The phase two note was designed quickly by one of the project team. The front had well-known images of Totnes whilst again the reverse had background information on the currency.

The second way in which we ensured confidence in the currency was by backing it with sterling. It was at this point that the Totnes Pound began more closely to resemble the BerkShare model. Because of the need to change sterling into Totnes Pounds, three businesses and the Totnes Museum were recruited to act as

exchange points to enable the phase two Totnes Pounds to be 'purchased' at a rate of £9.50 for ten Totnes Pounds. This 5-per-cent discount proved to be a very good incentive for those purchasing the Pounds.

Building momentum

For phase two we produced a 'Users' Guide' leaflet, which explained the rationale of the project and how it worked. These were distributed to all the businesses that were participating, as well as other places around the town. We issued a press release and also put some pages on the TTT website about the currency.

A launch event was held, which, because of the rush to get the currency out, was fairly low key but did give people the first opportunity to get their hands on the new note. Some of those who turned up helped recruit new businesses. Businesses were formally 'signed up' for phase two, signing some terms and conditions that ensured they understood how the currency operated. We also set up an email list for receiving a (roughly) monthly update of how the project was proceeding. We also made efforts to hand-deliver this to the businesses that did not have email.

"It is about moving it on from something that's a bit twee to something that works. It doesn't work on big-ticket items, it works on small-ticket items or services. We need to get a window cleaner to take it, to pay for a service that is ten to twenty quid every week. I want it to succeed. I give a 10-per-cent discount [for payment in Totnes Pounds] and am quite happy about that. It makes business sense for it to work." **Andy Garner, Totnes TV and Electrical**

"It has been intermittent and sporadic, quite active recently but very quiet before that. I get other traders bringing them in and spending them. It's created a huge talking point and I have been on TV all over the world. When people are reminded about it circulation goes up noticeably and then gradually drops down. What would I do to make it work better? If it looked more like a banknote, with maybe a five- and ten-pound note. Not sure how to keep awareness high after the launch though."
Dave Lacey, Sacks Wholefoods Ltd, Totnes

We aimed to recruit 50 local businesses to participate – a target that we managed to exceed. Businesses were able to circulate the notes by giving them back out as change, or, we hoped, by spending them with suppliers and other participating businesses. Otherwise they could exchange surplus Totnes Pounds back for sterling at the same 5-per-cent rate of exchange, i.e. ten Totnes Pounds for £9.50. This, it was hoped, would encourage businesses to move the currency on, rather than simply exchange it back. Businesses were able to set their own level of participation. Some took five Totnes Pounds per transaction, whereas others took just the one. By the end of phase two just over 6,000 notes had gone into circulation.

Management and accountability

In the short term 'Totnes Currency' was established as an unincorporated community organisation in order to open a bank account. However, the upscaling of the project meant that we needed to develop more formal management and accountability structures for the currency, particularly as we were now backing it with sterling. We took some legal advice from a local Community Enterprise Unit, who are specialist business advisers for 'not-for-private-profit' businesses. They suggested that an Industrial and Provident Society would be the best form of legal structure as it would enable us to have two tiers of membership, one for business and one for the general public, and provide a mechanism for raising money from the local community to finance future developments. We hoped that this structure would engender greater local ownership and management of the currency in the longer term.

A phase three Totnes pound note.

Phase three: January 2008 onwards

The decision to issue a third note was based on a number of factors.

- Firstly, we had publicised phase two as a six-month experiment and felt that we needed to honour this.

- Secondly, some of the phase two notes were getting quite tatty through usage and we also discovered that in certain circumstances the ink could run.

- Finally, we were also interested in trying to calculate the leakage that had occurred, i.e. the notes that had disappeared from the area.

In January 2008 we began to replace the phase two notes in circulation with a new phase three note, designed by a local artist. The phase three note no longer had any information about the currency on it and looked the most 'money-like' of the three notes to date. We also designed a new leaflet, which had a map of where the Pounds could be spent, rather than the basic information we had previously concentrated on. We no longer formally 'signed up' new businesses but we did give out an information pack that explained how the currency worked, and included stickers and leaflets.

The other substantive change for phase three was that the exchange rate was adjusted to parity with sterling. The decision to do this was thoroughly debated by the group but was based on perceived circulation problems that began to occur later in the autumn of 2007 (detailed on page 156). This shifted the benefits of the scheme away from consumers and towards businesses, as consumers lost the 5-per-cent incentive that was gained by exchanging sterling into Totnes Pounds, whereas businesses could now exchange excess notes back for sterling without penalty. Not surprisingly, several businesses were quick to increase the number of Totnes Pounds that they were willing to accept and hold.

Phase three was planned to last for at least a year, not least because there is a time and resource implication involved in introducing a new note. Owing to the loss of the customer incentive we began to encourage businesses to use the Totnes Pound creatively and come up with their own discounts and incentives. Slowly, throughout the year more and more began to do this.

In July 2009 the Totnes Pound Group decided that a proportion of the sterling on deposit should be put to work. The group offers interest-free loans to projects within the community that are following through on the Transition ideals of rebuilding local resilience and reducing carbon emissions. The loans are between £300 and £500 and for terms of six months or twelve months.

Business use of the Totnes Pound

By the middle of 2009 around 70 businesses were actively signed up to the Totnes Pound. This entitled them to listings on the TTT website and on publicity literature. They also received updates on news from the project. However, anecdotally we know that other businesses have also accepted Totnes Pounds from customers. Participating businesses are mainly retail outlets based in Totnes town centre, but there are also some from further afield, as well as some service-based businesses.

"The idea of the Totnes Pound is to try to keep trade local within the town. We joined because we agreed to the spirit of the idea. Councils for reasons best known unto themselves have allowed out-of-town trading centres to flourish and expand." **Jim Pilkington, Salago, Totnes**[2]

Not surprisingly, the turnover of Totnes Pounds varies from business to business. The businesses that seem to have the highest turnover of Totnes Pounds are food outlets, perhaps because of the small denomination of the note and the fact that people often make small regular purchases in these shops.

Unfortunately we do not have detailed statistics on how many businesses have accepted the currency. We have not asked businesses to keep records, because of our reluctance to impose any additional burden on them, conscious that having to deal with two currencies adds to their overall workload. We do, however, have records of the excess notes that have been cashed in, which gives us some idea of the places that have received greater numbers of notes.

How businesses were recruited

Businesses were recruited by a number of different volunteers who each had their own ways of promoting participation in the scheme. The important thing was to have a conversation with the business about it and about how their business could practically benefit from the Totnes Pound, and there was a general consensus that we should keep it as simple as possible. Therefore we did not regularly get into detailed discussions with the businesses about monetary systems or about peak oil. We were also conscious of the fact that businesspeople are generally very busy and concerned with the welfare of their businesses. Therefore we were aware of the need to highlight the benefits of the currency to them, if only to justify the additional work that participation entailed.

Despite the fact we did not specify a common approach our conversations all contained similar threads, along the following lines.

- The currency operated as a form of local loyalty scheme and would therefore retain wealth locally, sometimes invoking the idea of the 'local multiplier' (see Chapter 1, page 33). The businesses that have provided the most support for the Totnes Pound are those that are generally sympathetic to what it is trying to achieve in terms of localising the economy, especially in the early days.

- It is good publicity for the business and the chance to earn some kudos by being associated with a progressive project.

- As the media profile of the currency grew, we also would point to the publicity that it was generating for the town and for the Transition Towns model.

- During phase three, when Totnes Pounds were at parity with sterling, we would sometimes challenge the business with the question 'Why not?' There was no risk of financial loss, as excess Totnes Pounds could be exchanged back for sterling, so as far as we were concerned there was no risk to participation, only benefits.

- By phase three, by highlighting how many other businesses had joined and maintaining a steady growth of participants, we hoped that businesses would be motivated to join by a sense of not wanting to miss out.

- We did not, however, stress the long-term plan: building more local production and local resilience. With hindsight we have wondered whether we should have been more explicit about the longer-term ambitions of the project, and whether this would have had an impact on recruitment. We wonder if the Totnes Pound is just seen as a way to promote the town or as a local loyalty scheme, rather than as a tool for building local resilience. This omission might have been a mistake.

"It encapsulates a lot of what I like about building resilient and sustainable local communities, so for me it was absolutely obvious and as long as it exists we will participate in it and speak positively and optimistically of it. For me it's not about how many come through the door necessarily; at this stage in the game this is really early days.

We don't talk to our businesses . . . possibly because they are all WHSmith and Boots, you know many high streets have been decimated . . . so the reason why I immediately said yes to the Totnes Pound was because I think it's an absolutely vital part of an overall package of solutions which will get us to a better place."
William Lana, Greenfibres, Totnes

"It just felt like a good community thing to lend our support to . . . keeping the economy in the one place. I feel that it's something that we're doing to support the local . . . that feels good and that feels unusual and makes an interesting point and makes customers think." **Jamie Sermon, Greenlife, Totnes**

Successes

The Totnes Pound has had a number of positive impacts. Perhaps most significantly, it has generated a significant amount of national and international publicity for Totnes and the Transition Towns concept. It has promoted a wider debate around both peak oil and the economic role of complementary currencies – something we hoped that it would do when the currency was started. Politicians such as Claire Short and commentators such as George Monbiot have both since written about the possibilities that local currencies could offer. It has also inspired other communities to undertake their own experiments, most notably Lewes and Brixton, who have taken the model to new levels.

Closer to home we have, at a basic level, proved that a local currency can function, however imperfectly. We also know that it could function much more effectively, and how, given time and resources, we could increase its economic impact. The extent to which businesses and individuals have engaged with currency is also encouraging. Although we lack data on the detailed webs of transactions that take place in Totnes Pounds, we know from the fact that the currency is constantly going in and out of active usage in the economy that it does circulate. The challenge is to increase the depth and breadth of that circulation.

Challenges

As a project that was initiated with an explicitly experimental ethic it is not surprising that the currency has experienced some challenges in the early days of its existence. These are mainly in the areas of recruitment, circulation and resources.

The challenge of recruitment

Some businesses have been more sceptical about the wider aspirations of the project but most acknowledge the positive publicity that it has generated for Totnes. For some, however, there is a concern that the Pound is exceptionally well presented, but that the perceptions exceed the reality. As noted in earlier chapters, this is a major, but sadly recurring, problem with alternative currencies that are 'never knowingly undersold'. Of

155

course, while you cannot control what reporters will write about you, you can make sure you don't over-claim too soon.

In a similar vein, and as was the case with BerkShares, some were supportive of the concept of supporting local small businesses but in practice did not understand why this needed a local currency. Why not use pounds sterling? Perhaps here one of the problems is that the wider picture – especially the long-term aim of developing local production – was not explained. We concentrated on keeping it simple, rather than on building commitment.

Perceptions have run ahead of reality as some Totnes businesses have refused to participate. This is for a number of reasons. For example, some conduct the majority of their transactions electronically and therefore see no point in engaging with a new form of paper-based currency.

We have generally struggled to recruit businesses that are parts of chains because the decision as to whether to do so was not within the authority of the local manager. Similarly, some businesses did not wish to participate because the owner or their staff did not live in Totnes and they were worried about their ability to spend their Pounds. This was a particular issue when we tried to recruit market stalls, many of whom are not locally based.

Some businesses were reluctant to participate because their accountants were concerned about whether there would be tax or legal implications. Finally, one business did agree to participate but saw worrying parallels between the Totnes Pound and the restrictive currencies that used to be issued by employers in the nineteenth century and which were widely regarded as being unjust (see Chapter 2, page 43).

The challenge of circulation

We have no systematic understanding of how ordinary people use the currency between themselves. But the comments we have received suggest that they use it in the same way that they use conventional currency, which is good to hear as this is just what we hoped would happen. We have always tried to encourage people to carry a mixture of both currencies at any one time.

However, there are two problems with circulation that have hindered the development of the currency. The first is that businesses have reported that customers have a general reluctance to accept the Totnes Pounds as change. We suspect there might a couple of root causes of this.

• One possibility is that the early adopters who embraced the Totnes Pound were keen to take advantage of the 5-per-cent discount. This meant that they wanted to spend notes and then exchange further sterling into new Totnes Pounds. Therefore there was no economic benefit to them in accepting Totnes Pounds back as part of other transactions. This meant that businesses were then trying to encourage other people to accept them back as change, people who may not have been familiar with the currency or indeed even suspicious of it.

• Another possibility is that people believed that, because of the exchange rate, the notes were actually worth only 95p. The net effect of this was that over a period of months several businesses stopped trying to offer Totnes Pounds as change and instead waited for them to be requested.

This obviously hindered the currency's circulation. Furthermore, towards the end of 2007 some businesses began to put a limit on how many Totnes Pounds they were willing to hold at any given time. Some were reluctant to cash them in and take the 5-per-cent loss because they perceived that some of the early adopters were regular customers who would have come in anyway. This is when the circulation began to get 'sticky' and prompted the decision by the Totnes Pound Group to move to parity with sterling.

The second major issue with circulation was that businesses generally found them difficult to spend. This was primarily due to the medium of the currency as a one-pound paper note. Obviously many businesses do not pay their suppliers in cash, preferring to pay either electronically or by cheque. This therefore limits the circulation of the pound. Furthermore, it hinders the development of a local economic multiplier that is based on businesses transacting with other local businesses.

"It's a brilliant idea in theory, but only works if the majority of traders take it up – to be an active currency. Fantastic publicity for the town, and initially very popular, but as time has gone on it has dwindled. It's very difficult for traders to push it. It needs another publicity boost."
Mike Sealey, Totnes Pet and Garden

Where businesses were able to spend the pounds it tended to be in one of two ways. Small-scale owner-occupier businesses were able to take the Pounds out of the till and then spend them, for example on their lunch. Some businesses also experimented with paying some of the Totnes Pounds to their staff. However, this was not easy as again many salaries these days are paid electronically directly into a bank account.

The challenge of resources

To date, Totnes Currency, the organisation that has managed and developed the Totnes Pound, has primarily been resourced with voluntary labour. It has raised some income through donations, events and through the 'leakage' of the currency between phases (i.e. currency that disappeared out of the locality but for which the backing asset remains). However, the day-to-day operation of the currency has been reliant on volunteers. Attempts have been made to secure some development funding in order to get the currency to a point where it is economically self-sustaining. Unfortunately, perhaps because of the radical nature of the project, no substantial funding has yet been secured.

The reliance on volunteer labour has a number of implications. Firstly, the project has developed more slowly than we would have liked it to. Furthermore, most of the resources have been focused on managing the systemic elements of the currency system, such as looking after the exchange points, recruiting and talking to businesses, and managing the exchange between sterling and Totnes Pounds. During the first two years a considerable amount of time was also spent on talking to the media about the project, which was useful for promoting local currencies, the Transition idea and Totnes itself, but did little to develop the currency on the ground.

The concentration of resources on the maintenance of the systemic aspects meant that there was less time to work proactively on the 'community development' side of the currency. We did provide information in the form of leaflets, posters and a website, but there is no doubt that we could have done more to raise the profile of the currency locally and to explain the rationale behind it. This would have almost certainly increased its circulation.

Furthermore, the limited resources meant that we were not able to communicate with the community as effectively as we would have liked to. For example, during phase three, despite the press coverage and publicity, some people did not realise that the Totnes Pounds were now at parity with sterling. Finally, the other problem with a reliance on volunteers is the turnover of people involved and the disruption that this can create – problems that any voluntary-based organisation faces.

Other issues
In addition to the main challenges there were also a number of other issues.

Denomination
One factor that hindered the development of the currency is that we have only a one-pound note – a small denomination compared with a fiver or a tenner. One the one hand this is beneficial because it encourages business participation, owing to the fact that the risks to the business are low and their 'exposure' to Totnes Pounds can be kept at a low level. However, it also limits the practical usage of the currency and therefore limits the total amount in circulation. Do people want to carry round a large wad of one pound notes? No. There are plans to introduce larger denomination notes in 2010.

How large a circulation area?
The denomination factor links to another issue: the appropriate scale of the currency. To date it has focused primarily on Totnes and Dartington, partly owing to resource issues and partly to align with the wider Transition Town Totnes process. However, questions about the longer-term business model and about the ability of businesses to spend Totnes Pounds within their own supply chains mean that we need to think more deeply about what is the most appropriate geographical scale for a local currency such as the Totnes Pound.

Legal doubts
Although it is perfectly legal to issue your own currency as long as it obviously doesn't look like sterling, there is a perception that the legal framework for issuing paper-based currency in the UK is not clear. As reported in Chapter 10, some businesses in the Berkshires declined to participate because of their accountants' concerns with regards to tax and accounting procedures. These concerns also delayed the registration of the Industrial and Provident Society by the Financial Services Association: it asked for more detailed information on the operations of the currency before it approved the establishment of the cooperative.

Local culture
The local cultural context also affects the development of any given currency. Totnes, with its widespread reputation for 'alternative' ideas and lifestyles, is a great place to experiment with ideas that might seem too outlandish in more conservative places.

However, there is also a danger that some people will automatically reject such ideas if they are perceived to have come from the 'alternative' community. One example is a comment that appeared on a BBC internet discussion board about the Totnes Pound, stating that "the 'Totnes Pound' is the latest incarnation of alternative trading schemes got up by the soya beans and wigwams brigade, whose economic nous could be written on the back of a fag packet."

Forging alliances with 'respectable' organisations such as the Chamber of Commerce and the local council may help to counter such perceptions and build wider trust in the currency.

Make sure that businesses do benefit
Finally, it seems that the issue of economic need is pretty fundamental to the successful functioning of a local currency such as the Totnes Pound. When it was in its most vibrant phase it was being driven by consumers who were keen to benefit from the 5-percent discount. Since we went to parity with sterling,

consumer demand for the currency has not driven the circulation in the same way.

Although we have tried to build a new set of discounts this has been a slow process, and it is difficult to raise awareness of the changes amongst the wider community of users. Similarly, we have yet to really meet the needs of the local businesses with the currency. Although it has been good for raising the profile of Totnes, the direct economic impact to date has been minimal. Again, to really get businesses to use and promote the currency in the longer term it needs to meet a tangible economic need.

> "We are committed to a sustainable future, so by joining the scheme we are keeping money in the community, encouraging yet more people to buy locally, building trust and contacts. We welcome the Totnes Pound and hope that locals use our service not only for pleasure but for commuting as well."
> **Andrew Pooley, General Manager, Riverlink Cruises, which offers a 10-per-cent discount to local residents paying with Totnes Pounds.**[3]

Plans for the future

At the time of writing, the Totnes Pound Group has a number of key priorities for the immediate future.

- Complete the registration of the Industrial and Provident Society, Totnes Currency, and launch it. It is hoped that this will increase wider local involvement in the currency, provide mechanisms for investment and put the currency on a solid foundation for the future.

- Explore an electronic currency. It is a broad consensus within the group that to really flourish there needs to be an electronic version of the Totnes Pound. It is likely that this would run in parallel with the paper-based money, which has an important symbolic value. The legal structures for electronic currencies are already in place, as are several mechanisms of exchange such as mobile phones or smart cards. The possibility of a small transaction fee also provides not only an income stream for Totnes Currency but also an incentive for business involvement, if it is less than the fee for conventional credit or debit card transactions. Research is being done (in 2010) into how this side of the currency could be best developed.

- Introduce a higher-denomination note. Totnes Currency would like to introduce a higher denomination note in the near future. As discussed, the one-pound note limits usage and circulation. A higher-denomination note demands that security is properly attended to but would also influence the number of notes in circulation.

- Pilot how the 'asset', the sterling on deposit that backs the currency, could be 'diversified' or invested. When explaining the Totnes Pound we often expound the ideas of localisation and local multipliers. We have rarely got on to the longer-term aspiration of using the asset to support local economic development. The group that runs the currency is now piloting small loans to Transition-related activities, which should raise awareness of this function of the currency.

- Continue to seek development funding and refine the business model. To be a sustainable entity in the longer term and have a significant economic impact it seems likely that Totnes Currency needs to be able to employ staff and be an economically self-sustaining social enterprise. There are a number of ways in which it could generate income, which have already been mentioned, including electronic transaction fees and income from the currency asset base. Work on developing the business plan is continuing, as is the search for funding, which would 'pump prime' the organisation.

"The Totnes pound has been a positive story for the town, bringing a lot of enthusiastic attention. It has been a key stepping stone in putting complementary currency theory into practice, stimulating new projects to be launched. The transition to a more local and equitable money system is going to be a long one, but as with all aspects of Transition, it is about making a start on that journey. We have learnt a lot and can now put that to good use in taking the next steps for the Totnes Pound." **Mark Burton, organiser, Totnes Pound**

THE TOTNES POUND SCORECARD

Hard   Soft

Valuable   Weak

Circulates widely   Circulates locally

Effectiveness for a business (■) or community exchange (●)

High   Low

CHAPTER 12

BUILD THE WORLD ANEW: THE LEWES POUND

The Lewes Pound was the second Transition currency in the UK. Launched at the height of the financial crash of 2008, it received worldwide publicity and has become an accepted and well-loved facet of this small Sussex town. Inspired by work in Totnes, the Lewes Pound comes in higher denominations, including a twenty-one-pound note. Again, high-quality design, providing those intangible qualities of 'moneyness' and 'valuableness', are key to its success.

Tom Paine adorns a Lewes one-pound note.

Lewes

Lewes is a small town in East Sussex nestling in the South Downs just north of Brighton. Home of the eighteenth-century radical republican Thomas Paine, the author of *The Rights of Man*, which inspired the American and French revolutions, it maintains a strong alternative culture amongst what townies call the 'Lewes Lentils'. It is close enough to London and Brighton to entice high-profile international speakers to talk in the city, and the turnout is always good. It holds famously rowdy bonfire nights on Guy Fawkes Night in November. Like Ithaca, it's a university town – Sussex University is one stop away on the train. While Sussex students gravitate towards trendy Brighton, staff will often be tempted to settle in the more genteel Lewes. House prices have risen as a result.

Not one of the UK's homogeneous clone towns, Lewes has maintained much of its local distinctiveness, with a long high street supporting a wide variety of similarly sized, small locally owned stops. Many of the shops feel they probably would not be viable anywhere else, Brighton's Lanes perhaps excepted. Like Great Barrington, Berkshire County, USA, Lewes is a 'foodie' place: many local delicatessens, pubs and restaurants specialise in selling locally grown food. Like Totnes, it is surrounded by a hinterland of agriculture, and locally grown fruit and vegetables, and even wine, is sold in the town's delis and farmers' markets.

In short, it's the sort of place a local currency should flourish, perhaps to help the town to recreate the local resilience it had until so recently.

Lewes past

Lewes used to host far more local production. Mr Caitlin, the local tobacconist, a Lewes resident for over 60 years, told me:

"It was more a working class town, really, until Sussex University came. So 40 years ago we had two cinemas, the quarry, the iron foundry, two breweries, and Baxters print works, the first colour printers. There was work, 600 people worked at Baxters. We had the cattle market until 1994 . . . we had agricultural fairs, we had two or three agricultural dealers, a wholesaler, but over time that has played a far less important role in the town. That is a shame, because paying your dairyman in Lewes Pounds who could have paid the feedman and so on, the need for all that has gone."

For more on the Lewes Pound see:
www.thelewespound.org

Developing the Lewes Pound

The Lewes Pound is an initiative of Transition Town Lewes's business group. The group had surveyed local business's preparedness for peak oil and climate change and discovered that very few businesses had even begun to think about these issues. What the survey did uncover was concern amongst the business community about the credit crunch, about the amount of money leaving the town through the big Waitrose and Tesco supermarkets, and the long-term loss of local production. The idea of local currency emerged as an obvious possible solution to these issues. Could a local currency encourage more local circulation, keep local businesses going, and build a sense of community?

Inspired by Totnes, the business group informally decided to give it a go. Ideas were still just being batted about when the local paper contacted Adrienne Campbell, one of the founders of Transition Town Lewes, to find out what was planned. Told that there were as yet no firm plans, the journalist persisted: "What, in a nutshell, are your ideas?" The next thing the group knew was an article in the Brighton *Argus*, which went on the wires and was picked up by the BBC, CNN and the like. The world was told that Lewes would soon have its own currency!

The business group decided that it should step up to the mark. This was May 2008. It settled on a tight deadline of a launch of 10,000 one-Lewes-Pound notes in September, and set itself two targets: fifteen traders prepared to accept them, and enough sponsorship from local businesses to make it happen.

The 100 Club

The first step was to set up a network of Transition Town Lewes members, called 'The 100 Club', who agreed to use the new currency and give feedback on how it could and did work. Members of the 100 Club could buy 22 Lewes Pounds for £20. In the context of the emerging credit crunch and the press profile, the 100 Club caught the imagination, signing up 350 members.

Six local businesses agreed to sponsor the pound for £250 to £750 a go, in return for their logos on publicity materials. Seventy businesses were signed up to accept the Lewes Pound. The criteria for launch being met, the club was closed.

Design issues

A local designer and member of the business group created the notes, working very hard to make sure that they looked like money: he would not put his name and reputation to anything that was not up to scratch! It soon became clear that to 'look and feel' like money, rather than like a voucher, the paper needed to be of banknote quality. The designer was clear about this, but it would not be cheap.

Specialist security printers were found with the help of the Totnes Pound Group, and the printers helped identify the right security features, which needed to be complex enough that any would-be forger would need to be good enough to forge sterling, in which case they would probably spend their time on the bigger prize. Again, this was an unexpected cost.

The sponsoring businesses were approached again, and the funds secured to print 10,000 notes at 30p a note for paper and 10p for printing: with the addition of funds for publicity, the cost of the project was £5,000 in all.

The notes could be bought and redeemed for a pound sterling at a number of issuing points around the high street, with no discount, with the money backing them always on deposit. Traders who accepted them could always be sure they could get their money back. The notes would circulate until September 2009, by which time they would need to be redeemed for sterling. After that date, they could not be redeemed: the incentive was therefore to spend, not save.

The Pound nearly becomes another victim of the credit crunch

A hiccup at this stage nearly caused the Lewes Pound to be another casualty of the credit crunch. The banking group that we now know as Barclays actually started in Lewes High Street, and in the early days the local manager was interested in supporting the Pound, perhaps acting as an issuing point. Some local businesses speculated about the advantages of having Lewes Pound accounts. But literally a week or so

before the launch Barclays pulled out, citing regulation issues. Given the central role of local banks in Great Barrington (see page 130) this was a major blow, and the contrast between the role of banks in the UK and the USA couldn't be stronger.

September 2008: Unleashing the Lewes pound

The Pound was unveiled in Lewes Town Hall in September 2008. Tom Paine adorned 10,000 one-pound notes, declaring that "we have it in our power to build the world anew". In that, the currency sums up the ethos of the Transition movement.

The mayor, the *Guardian*'s Polly Toynbee, the Transition Network's Rob Hopkins, and the director of the new economics foundation, Stewart Wallis, all spoke, and it quickly became clear that given the fevered atmosphere in the town 10,000 notes were not enough. The 350 100-Club members bought at least 7,700 notes, and the rest quickly disappeared as residents and collectors alike snapped them up, some selling them on at a profit on eBay. Four factors perhaps explain the exceptional success of the launch.

Timing

As it coincided with the onset of the credit crunch and the collapse of major banks and investment houses, media attention consolidated the business group and made it set a deadline for itself. The key elements of the project were in place at the right time to catch the wave, and the launch consequently caught the imagination. It received worldwide media attention, from the BBC to *Time* magazine to CNN. If the aim was to raise awareness about the possibility of a small town printing its own money, then timing could not have been better.

The quality of the notes

The notes had 'moneyness'. This was the first launch of a new local paper currency for one hundred years that looked like real money. Interest from collectors, and from local people bright enough to capitalise on this, was strong. Feeling themselves to be in the spotlight, the organisers made sure they got the notes right. Like BerkShares, Lewes Pounds look and, importantly, feel, like money. The paper is not just of a high quality, it is banknote paper. A creditable number of businesses had agreed to accept the note before it was launched. Convenient issuing points had been agreed, and in particular having an issuing point at the town hall implicitly gave a measure of gravitas to the Pound. In short, the Lewes Pound, from the start, had 'moneyness' and 'valuableness' and looked like a serious project. It was not 'work in progress'.

The Tom Paine connection

The third factor was the iconic status of Tom Paine. 2009 was the bicentennial of his death, and interest in the notes from the United States, as Tom Paine memorabilia, was intense. Notes were mounted in display cases, stuck to fridges, and sold on eBay at £30 a shot to collectors.

The nature of the place

Finally, as with Great Barrington, Ithaca and Totnes, the nature of Lewes matters. Lewes had a large number of local shops worth defending, and a large enough population interested in shopping locally. The town's fierce independence was shown when a local pub was taken over by a multinational that decided not to take the local beer, Harveys. It was subjected to a four-month boycott, and beer consumption dropped from 28 barrels a week to one before the brewery relented. Transition Town Lewes was well embedded in the town, and many of its key movers and shakers well known and respected. They shopped regularly in local businesses, so the proprietors knew and trusted them. Transition Town Lewes had over 600 people on its mailing list, in a town of 17,000. It was thus a trusted and embedded local institution.

The overwhelming media interest also meant that early faltering steps were undertaken in the full glare of publicity. The organisers were hard pressed on launch day, running round town to supply the issuing points with new supplies of currency. By the third day, supplies had been exhausted. Notes began to emerge again at the weekend, but an exhausted organising committee was somewhat overwhelmed by the experience.

After the launch

After the frenzied launch, things in Lewes quietened down significantly. The organisers had rather under-estimated how much a local currency scheme, once launched, needs to be nurtured and developed. They had no funding, beyond the commitment of about twenty enthusiasts making sure that the notes continued to circulate. To promote the scheme a traders' group was formed to think of ways to spread the development of the Pound, but without funding progress was slower than hoped. But by August 2009, 130 businesses and four societies accepted them, and the notes seemed to be circulating well enough, if at low levels.

July 2009: the second issuance

In its first incarnation the Lewes Pound existed only in the form of one-pound notes, so its utility for large purchases was limited. In practice, given the small scale of its circulation in the early days, this was not a problem for most purchases, but in July 2009 notes in the denominations of one, five, ten and twenty-one pounds were issued into circulation.

These notes continued with the Tom Paine theme on one side, but for the other side of the note themes were suggested by local schools and artists. The pound note featured a planned new environmental centre, while bonfire night adorned the twenty-one-pound note (an old guinea was twenty-one shillings). The twenty-one-

Launching the Lewes Pound second issuance.

pound note symbolises the fact that 5 per cent of all Lewes Pounds issued – i.e. one pound out of every twenty – would be donated to a community fund, the Live Lewes Fund, to support local projects. This was proposed after feedback from users who wanted to see tangible evidence of wider community benefit. The new notes were launched with some fanfare at a community street party, at which films were shown, bands played, and a hog was roasted.

This time, the emphasis was on security and quality of design rather than expensive banknote paper. Old one-pound notes would need to be exchanged for new notes by September 2009, after which they could not

be redeemed or exchanged. The new notes will remain valid until 2014, showing the founders' long-term, Transition-led ambitions. The Lewes Pound Group is now officially incorporated as The Lewes Pound CIC (Community Interest Company).

The reward – the Lewes Pound one year on

The Lewes Pound has succeeded admirably in promoting the possibility of a town creating its own currency. The initial aim of raising awareness has been more than achieved, and the organisers have been blown away by its success, far beyond their expectations. There is a consensus that the Pound has been effective in raising the profile of the town. I carried out 'vox pop' conversations with 50 people on Lewes High Street and found both near-universal awareness of the Pound and positive thoughts about it.

The threat to local businesses represented by two ever-expanding and predatory large supermarkets, the existence of a large number of locally owned businesses worth defending, and the fact that businesses are accepting it without any real problems, means that the idea of a local currency has caught on in Lewes. Arguments for strengthening local circulation in a small, geographically well-defined town made sense.

The businesses that use the Pound are, for the most part, all spread out along quite a long high street, so they can easily talk to each other and solve problems. Customers can easily walk from shop to shop. Issuing and exchange points are close by.

The businesses are generally a similar size, and consequently take in similar, quite low numbers of notes, so circulation never gets stuck and the businesses can quite easily re-circulate the notes they take in as change. For example, a fruiterer readily took Lewes Pounds and paid customers in Lewes Pounds for excess supplies of vegetables from allotments. He re-circulated most of his notes, but if he got stuck he could easily pop next door to the butchers, which was an issuing point. The butcher gave Lewes Pounds out in change, to people who then went next door to the fruiterers. The butcher bought chickens from a local supplier, who gave them out at the farmers' market, and so on. You can even enjoy a convivial pint of local ale at the end of a hard day, for Lewes Pounds.

Business owners who were enthusiasts called using Lewes Pounds 'amusing', 'enjoyable', 'fun', 'interesting' and 'intriguing'. They enjoyed getting to know their customers. The currency was not world-shattering at this stage, and not contributing significantly to the development of a localised, resilient economy, but it was working. And from little acorns, oaks may grow. Given this, the Lewes Pound must be considered a success.

Challenges

Despite the success of the Lewes Pound, there have nevertheless also been challenges.

The challenge of boosting circulation

The Lewes Pound does seem to be circulating amongst local businesses, but, as yet, at fairly low volumes. Masters research by Jeppe Graugaard of the London School of Economics suggests that between November 2008 and June 2009 3,831 Lewes Pounds were issued at the town hall, and 3,522 redeemed for sterling. Two other issuing points issued 500-600 a week in 2008, dropping to 250 a week by May 2009, with more being redeemed than issued. I spoke to twenty businesses in the late summer of 2009. They mostly said that they took no more than 30 Lewes Pounds a week over the till, although a prominent enthusiast – a butcher specialising in local produce – took in 2-300 Lewes Pounds a week, a quarter of his income.

The positive side to this is that the Pound is an accepted part of the Lewes scene, and, unlike in Great Barrington, circulation does not seem to be getting 'stuck' anywhere in a town with lots of small, similarly sized businesses. Forty-five per cent of the businesses surveyed by Jeppe Graugaard said that there was no downside whatsoever to the Lewes Pound.

Research by the Lewes Pound Group suggests that 52 per cent of people using the currency say they use local stores more than before, with 44 per cent saying that they spend more locally. Jeppe Graugaard's research found that 10 per cent of Lewes Pound users

This is what a few shoppers in Lewes High Street said about the Lewes Pound:

"It's given me something that I like, and have a sense of, and when I've got friends that say 'I've heard about the Lewes Pound in the paper'... Whether that affects other people in Lewes in the same way I don't know. It has certainly given me a sense that this is an unusual and special place."

"When I hand my money in Lewes Pounds to somebody it is like I am creating... I'm building my relationship with them. It means that I value them, and I'm responsible for them, just like they're responsible for feeding me."

"There is a kind of feeling that goes with spending and receiving Lewes Pounds... it is like a signal to people, and a signal from them to you, that they are concerned about [the community]."

Hamish Elder, Joint Managing Director, Harvey & Son (Lewes) Ltd, said:

"Harveys has been at the heart of the Lewes community for 230 years. We source our raw materials (hops and malt) as locally as we can, and use water from our own well. We endeavour to sell our beers within 50 miles of Lewes. So Lewes Pounds make complete sense for us. A local currency for a local beer certainly helps cut down the beer miles.

The profile of the town has been raised since its introduction. Many visitors have heard of the currency; some make a special trip to acquire the note. And when local traders give out a Lewes Pound in change and explain what it is, it starts a conversation and tourists will go and spend that pound with another Lewes trader."

spend 30 per cent or more of their weekly shopping budget in Lewes Pounds. Most Lewes Pounds spent by consumers stay in circulation; only 5 per cent are redeemed.

Graugaard's research also suggests that 15 per cent reported problems with accountancy issues, and 10 per cent felt that re-circulating or redeeming Pounds was 'a hassle'. The extent that this is really that much of a hassle can be doubted, given that there are enough issuing points close enough to the businesses that take them, so exchanging small numbers of notes is not really problematic. But it is one more thing to do in a busy day for a local businessperson struggling to keep afloat in a recession, perhaps with the bank breathing down his or her neck.

Research for the Lewes Pound Group of 62 of the 130 businesses that accept Lewes Pounds shows that only two businesses pay staff or suppliers in pounds. Six per cent of the owners of businesses accepting Pounds use them for their personal drawings, but business owners who did not live in Lewes struggled to do this. Interestingly, young people were particularly resistant, believing that the sort of shops they went to didn't accept them – the chains, perhaps. You can't generally get famous-name-branded clothing with Lewes Pounds, although White Stuff, a clothing chain, does take the Lewes Pound even though this isn't endorsed or supported by the organisers.

Only 10 per cent of the businesses surveyed used discounts. Half of the businesses that accept the

Pounds do not redeem them: they re-circulate them as change. But 46 per cent redeem over half their Pounds, and 30 per cent redeem 90 per cent of them. Some businesses became adroit at predicting who would be likely to respond positively to the suggestion that they take Lewes Pounds in change and who would not, especially as awareness of the Lewes Pound was near-universal in the town. Others gave up asking quite quickly, especially when they were busy or did not come across Pounds very often.

Unsurprisingly, at this stage 72 per cent of businesses suggest that the Pound has had no discernible impact on their business. Given that many businesses are reporting that the number of customers using Pounds is declining, there is a danger that its usage may wither given the challenge of overcoming people's ingrained habits around money and the advantages of 'universal money'. Unless you proactively ask for Lewes Pounds in your change, going to an exchange point is one more transaction to perform in a perhaps already busy day, no matter how conveniently located they are – and it seems difficult to conceive of a way of making Lewes Pounds more accessible than they are now.

By the summer of 2009 many businesses felt that the level of energy and enthusiasm in the Pound was dissipating. They were offered Lewes Pounds by customers less and less often, and no longer proactively offered them as change. The result was that Lewes Pounds had a small number of enthusiasts, both businesses and consumers, who used them regularly, but the wider public and local business community rarely used Lewes Pounds in their day-to-day life.

Many businesses expected that they would see more Lewes Pounds when the second issuance came out, but this was not the case. The Lewes Pound group

estimates that 5 per cent of the local population uses Lewes Pounds in some way, and that given pressures to participate in our oil-fuelled and consumption-based economy that's not bad, and it means that no business has problems handling those levels of currency. But it also means that we still are a long way from moving our economy on to a resilient basis.

The challenge of the redemption fee

For the second issue, the Lewes Pound CIC aimed to levy a 5-per-cent redemption fee, which would have the dual purpose of funding the Live Lewes Fund and act as a barrier to redemption. As in Great Barrington, the 5-per-cent redemption fee for reconverting a Lewes Pound back to sterling has been particularly controversial. Citing difficulties with the credit crunch, businesses revolted when the second tranche of notes was issued. If the redemption fee was imposed, they said, they would leave the scheme. There was a widespread feeling around town that setting up a business was a brave thing to do, that times were hard, and that anything that made it more difficult was to be avoided.

Things came to a head at a meeting of the traders' group, where it was decided that the 5-per-cent contribution would be put on hold. But not all of the businesses that accepted the Lewes Pound heard about the meeting or participated in the decision. There was some criticism that the decision had been made in a rush, by an ad hoc, unconstituted group, and that there were no minutes or formal structures of accountability. The process had been 'lackadaisical', one businessperson told me. This points to the need for things to be done in formal, accountable ways. The contribution to the Live Lewes Fund would remain, but would now be financed by the 'leakage' of notes out of the community as a result of collectors buying notes they would never spend.

The challenge of nurturing local business leadership and ownership

To be sustainable, a local currency needs an income stream to pay for someone to help develop its usage and local production. Working on a voluntary basis meant that the Lewes Pound Group felt that they were fire fighting, rather than being on top of developments. They are seeking funding to employ someone to develop the scheme and ensure that its momentum keeps on growing. In Lewes, businesses failed to understand this, and refused to accept what some called a local 'council tax'.

The business community, it was felt, was fighting amongst itself, not speaking with the same voice. Business enthusiasts of the Lewes Pound found it much, much harder to recruit new businesses or persuade their suppliers to accept them after the redemption fee was proposed. They felt that too many of their fellow businesspeople were being negative, failing to try to re-circulate the currency in change or to their suppliers, and were looking for things to moan about or reasons not to participate. They had closed minds, it was felt.

Others could not believe that a business was struggling so much that its profitability would be imperilled by a five-pence contribution to the local community that in the long run would benefit it, especially given low levels of circulation: it was being stingy. If things were so tight, they thought, perhaps the business did not have a future.

From the point of view of the Lewes Pound Group and business enthusiasts, local business had been handed a valuable tool on a plate, for free, developed by the hard work of volunteers. Many local loyalty schemes charged businesses for membership, they argued. There needed to be some buy-in from businesses: they needed to take control and develop this tool, especially by developing local supply networks. The needs of businesses should be balanced with the wider needs of the community.

This is a sensitive issue. There is a need to ensure that in promoting the long-term agenda – building resilient local economies – we do not inadvertently make things harder for struggling local businesses if they are the sort of businesses we want to see in our community. We need to understand and respect the needs of local businesspeople.

On the other hand, we do not want to just promote local businesses for their own sake. Transition is not about boosting town pride. We need to keep the long-term agenda in mind, and build sustainable local currencies that promote it. This might mean insisting on a funding stream. As we see in the next chapter, this was the approach adopted in Stroud.

> "We keep a really positive attitude towards it. I have heard people being very negative about it, and what I've hated is getting into negative discussions with traders, or people who are anti it. I think that's a shame. Give it a positive slant and hope it's successful. I hope it encourages goodwill and communication in a small town." **Peta King, Kings Framers, Lewes**

The challenge of speculation and leakage

The Lewes Pound launch was in many ways another victim of financial speculation, as collectors and Tom Paine enthusiasts bought up notes on eBay. In one sense, this is a problem: the local currency is acting just as a global currency, subject to the whim of speculators. Notes fly out of the local economy in the same way as sterling, and no longer provide a local multiplier.

To manage the problem and provide a revenue stream, the Lewes Pound Group put together commemorative packs that included a Lewes Pound note and a letter of verification signed by the mayor. These were sold to collectors for £10, raising over £1,000.

But this also had unintended benefits. Speculators who purchase the notes directly from an issuing point, as opposed to on eBay, leave their sterling on deposit. This money, which will probably never be reclaimed, could be used for community benefit. Leakage funded the second currency issuance, and could be used quite legitimately for loans to deepen local production or donated to the Live Lewes Fund. After 30 September 2009 it was no longer possible to redeem the first issuance of Lewes Pounds. As a significant amount of the sterling that backed the first issue was still on deposit, it was decided that there would be a consultation with the community about what would be done with it.

The challenge of localisation – how 'local' is local?

Fifteen per cent of businesses surveyed by the Lewes Pound Group have considered substituting imports for local production. But they often found that they did not source their supplies from Lewes and its surrounds. They felt that a currency that circulated at a larger scale, perhaps a Sussex Pound, would enable them to do more.

As we found in the Berkshires (Chapter 10), some felt that the idea of getting people to spend more money locally was a good one, but they could not see how a local currency specifically helped in this regard. They believed that many of the enthusiasts of the Lewes Pound shopped locally anyway. They wanted as many people as possible to shop locally, but to do so spending pounds sterling that they could then use more easily to buy supplies and pay bills with.

> "When it first came in, I got the Lewes Pounds and used them. Now that I've got into the habit [of using local shops] I don't necessarily use [Lewes Pounds] as much. But I've got into the habit of using those small shops, and that's the key."
> **Lewes Pound consumer**

Lewes is also a tourist town. Tourism-focused businesses reported that tourists were often interested in the Pound and had heard about Lewes as a result of publicity related to it. Some tourists would buy Lewes Pounds or keep them as souvenirs. But generally tourists didn't seriously consider using them for everyday purchases during their visit. They were concerned that once they left the town they would not be able to spend any notes that were left over. Why should they bother exchanging pounds and Lewes Pounds at the beginning and end of a visit, they asked?

Deeper Transition

The Lewes Pound group responded to these concerns by explaining that building a low-carbon economy is a long-term endeavour. The Lewes Pound is but one of many tools to support the transition to a low-carbon economy, not a means to change the economic system overnight. Relocalisation using sterling is a perfectly rational approach. But there does seem to be something about a local currency that seems to put the issue of relocalisation and resilience into the public domain with an effectiveness that simple 'buy local' schemes using sterling alone can't match.

A local currency is, in any case, more than a tool for getting people to buy more from local businesses; to keep consuming, but just consuming locally. Growth, but local growth.

A local currency, as part of a Transition process, is a tool to change perspectives and spending habits, as a step along the way to a low-carbon economy in which people make their livelihoods in more resilient, sustainable and convivial ways. Relocalisation using sterling alone is unlikely to achieve this deeper transformation. We want more than a more local version of the economy we have now.

Without a local currency we would also not have a useful tool for increasing local resilience that could act as a way to help a community in the event of an Argentine-style financial crash – a crash we narrowly avoided when the economy was refloated by a huge issuance of new sterling in the wake of the Lehman Brothers collapse in September 2008. Imagine what the benefit to the lives of Lewes residents the Lewes Pound

"We don't see the Lewes Pound as an exclusive local currency. It is complementary, and will work to support local trade, while sterling will be used for national and international trade. It is all about finding the right balance between global and local economies . . . It's the start of a conversation about the importance of the local." **Oliver Dudok van Heel, Lewes Pound Group**

"The Lewes Pound has been successful in getting a conversation going across all social and age groups here in town. It's accepted at the small shops on the estates, as well as the organic shops. It's still small fry compared to Tesco, who takes two-thirds of all retail spend – £33 million per annum. But it's a tool that's now embedded in our culture, ready to scale up, along with other Transition ideas, when the world wakes up." **Adrienne Campbell, Lewes Pound Group**

Phase two Lewes Pound notes. Photo courtesy of Oliver Dudok van Heel.

would be in a world where politicians had not undertaken a Keynesian reflation, and a deep, long-lasting depression was the result. The Lewes Pound and the other Transition currencies could have been as important as depression-era scrip or the Argentine local currencies were in their time.

As confidence in the Lewes Pound deepens it is hoped that the direct backing of each Lewes Pound with a pound sterling can be broken, and loans can be given to develop more local production. It is hoped that more local food and power can then be developed, really

contributing to a deeper local resilience. This would be the prize of a well-established, embedded local currency for towns like Lewes.

The Lewes Pound, then, is a small acorn in need of watering, care and attention, but it does seem to have taken root. A well-designed currency, fully backed, with no discount, is established in the town, albeit at low levels of circulation. It has got off to a good start, and other communities would do well to learn from its successes and its mistakes.

THE LEWES POUND SCORECARD

Hard   Soft

Valuable   Weak

Circulates widely   Circulates locally

Effectiveness for a business (■) or community exchange (●)

High   Low

CHAPTER 13

THE STROUD POUND CO-OP: A LOCAL CURRENCY FOR THE FIVE VALLEYS

with Molly Scott Cato

The Stroud and Brixton Pounds were launched at the same time, in September 2009. Stroud is a place with a strong eco-socialist tradition, much like Ithaca (see Chapter 7). Members of Transition Stroud wanted to set up a currency that they controlled democratically through a co-op – the Stroud Pound Co-op. They were also inspired more by Christian Gelleri's experiences with Chiemgauer (see Chapter 9) than with BerkShares or the Totnes Pound. Their story therefore has a slightly more radical tinge to it than those that precede and follow it.

The chapter was written with Molly Scott Cato. Molly is a Reader in Green Economics at Cardiff School of Management, Director of Cardiff Institute for Co-operative Studies, and author of *Green Economics: An Introduction to Theory, Policy and Practice*. She is a member of the core group of Transition Stroud and co-ordinates its Lifestyles and Livelihoods working group, with whom she developed the Stroud Pound. She is also on the core group of Stroud Community Agriculture and is a Director of Stroud Common Wealth.

Stroud

Stroud has a heritage of local currency activism. In the 1980s and 1990s it had one of the country's most successful LETS schemes, with hundreds of members including shops, wholesalers and cafes. You could get anything from legal services to plumbing for Strouds.

The national Time Banking UK office is based in Stroud, and there are two Fairshares time banks within the Five Valleys. The local MP is a member of the Cooperative Party, with a long track record of supporting alternative currencies and credit unions. It's one of the few towns where the Green Party forms the majority on the council. On the train line to London, it hosts a vibrant alternative culture and many local businesses and agricultural producers.

The Stroud valleys, whose busy watercourses provided power in the early years of the industrial revolution, also have a long history of manufacture whose signs are still visible in the valleys, parts of which retain an industrial feel. The industrial heritage

Exchanging sterling for Stroud Pounds.

also created a radical tradition, which has survived industrial decline: the five river valleys have been described as 'a red hand in the middle of Tory-blue Gloucestershire'. Stroud has a vibrant farmers' market, much local food is sold in eateries, and it is noted for its co-housing and Community Supported Agriculture projects. For all these reasons, then, it's the sort of place a local currency should thrive in – particularly given the quite significant levels of local agricultural production and the opportunity this offers to have money making several loops before it is switched back for sterling.

For more on the Stroud Pound see:
www.stroudpound.org.uk

Community-owned, democratic money

It is unsurprising, then, that the Lifestyles and Livelihoods working group of Transition Stroud should turn its attention to the possibility of setting up a local currency to support the move to a low-carbon and locally provisioned economy for the district. Stroudies are serious people: from the beginning discussions revolved around how to design a currency that would actually stimulate more local production and exchange. They were not prepared to put a lot of time and effort into a currency that just became a substitute for sterling, going round one circulation loop and then being exchanged straight back again.

They wanted to ensure that local people, as well as businesses, benefited from a local currency. In a town with a strong red-green ethos, if supporting local businesses just led to a more local version of unsustainable economic growth and more consumption, that would be counterproductive. Supporting local

businesses for its own sake was not good enough: local people should also be partners in the economic health of the town. What was needed, it was felt, was clear understanding of what was wrong with our present financial system and the sort of growth it has led to, and a currency that would help nurture the low-carbon economy of the future. In discussions aimed at recruiting businesses, Stroud took a more explicitly politically aware line than some Transition currencies, stressing the practical importance of building the local economy over more political discussions about growth, exploitation and the nature of the economy.

What Transition Stroud wanted was a partnership between local consumers and businesses so each would contribute and benefit. They wanted users of the pound to 'buy into' the ethos of the project, and have democratic oversight of it. They consequently set up the Stroud Pound Co-op Ltd as a non-profit-making company to run the scheme. Unless they are given Stroud Pounds in change, consumers can't just buy Stroud Pounds (or teasels, as they are familiarly known). They have to join the Co-op for a one-off payment of five pounds sterling, which gives them the right to participate in the management of the currency, elect the core group and the like. Participating businesses must join the Co-op for a fee of £60 per year, and are listed in a directory and on a website. Thus steps are taken to build in democratic control from the beginning, and to discourage the forms of eBay currency speculation that characterised the launch of the Lewes Pound.

The Stroud Pound – a British regiogeld?

One of the members of Transition Stroud's Lifestyles and Livelihoods working group had a keen interest in the biodynamic movement, and had met Christian Gelleri, designer of the Chiemgauer regiogeld (see

Chapter 9) at a conference. Another member was Molly Scott Cato, a prominent Green economist. The group thus wanted to set up a form of currency that was explicitly ecological. Impressed by the planning that had gone into the Chiemgauer, and its connection with Steiner education, members of Transition Stroud invited Christian Gelleri to give a presentation and run a day-long workshop about the Chiemgauer in January 2009. This sealed the decision to develop a currency modelled on the Chiemgauer, with demurrage ('rusting') and co-operative forms of management built into the design from the start.

The key feature of this design is that the money has a form of negative interest rate (called demurrage), which means that, like many aspects of nature, it decomposes, gently losing value over time. The theory is that there is an incentive to spend it quickly, so it should out-compete the national currency. To encourage the money to remain in circulation, Stroud Pounds lose 3 per cent of their value every six months – on 31 March and 31 September. At the end of the six-month period, the value of vouchers may be restored only by purchasing and affixing stamps amounting to

The Stroud Pound is unveiled, September 2009.

3 per cent of the face value of the note. Vouchers can then be used for a further six months. After two years the notes are replaced, subject to a further demurrage charge being paid. New notes will be printed as required to fulfil demand, but all notes in circulation will be backed by an equivalent amount of pounds sterling, which will be held in reserve.

Consumers buy their Stroud Pounds at parity with sterling, but are not able to exchange Stroud Pounds back into pounds sterling, as they are for spending, not saving. Traders can reconvert them, but at a discount of 5 per cent. As with regiogeld, 3 per cent of this discount goes to support the local projects nominated by purchasers, and 2 per cent to run the project. The latter 2 per cent is crucial for generating an income that will create a livelihood for someone to manage and develop the currency. Volunteer sweat equity works during the first flush of enthusiasm, but one thing that the people of Stroud learned from the experience of LETS was that a money scheme can very soon become a victim of its own success if volunteers become overwhelmed by administrative work.

A particular attraction is that a proportion of the value of converting pounds to Stroud pounds will be sent to local good causes – another model taken from Chiemgauer. When joining the scheme, individuals can nominate a local charity or social enterprise of their choice to support. Thereafter, for every currency unit purchased by that individual, 3 per cent is allocated to the chosen local charity. This is important because it creates an incentive for people with no particular interest in the local economy or Transition Stroud to join the scheme. For example, Cotswold Care Hospice has been nominated by several members. If it joins the scheme and receives donated money, then people whose relatives may be suffering from cancer might join up to the Co-op and start spending more of their money locally. Stroud Valleys

Project, whose office in Threadneedle Street is being loaned as the outlet for the exchange of money, is the default good cause if none is indicated.

Raising awareness and developing ideas

Setting up a local currency represents a daunting investment of time and energy. To publicise the advent of the currency a series of consciousness-raising events was held, including film screenings and bartering events using temporary currencies – first the bean and later the teasel. These felt like playing but were actually deeply educational, helping to reveal the economic strategies people work with under capitalism and how changing the nature of money challenges these.

Designing the currency

The Co-op had a working group of eight people absolutely committed to this project and well versed in the subject. There has been considerable support from Christian Gelleri, including his advice on tweaking the Chiemgauer design and an offer to sell the special security paper that their currency is printed on, to save on the expense. Steve Charlwood, a local collector of currencies, provided invaluable advice and numerous examples of designs of currency that seemed to suggest that they had 'valuableness' and 'moneyness', as well as advice on security features, watermarks, papers and inks. Steve and local architect/designer/artist Ronan Schoemaker spent many hours discussing options with the team, getting the design right. Particularly important was colour and design, what local images suggested local heritage and thus had value, and how to combine images, colour and writing in an aesthetic way that also conveyed valuableness and moneyness.

Ensuring local buy-in

Meeting after meeting thrashed out what might or might not work, and ensured that local people felt part of the process. The local paper held a vote about the name for the currency, which again had the added benefits of helping the local community to become aware that Stroud would soon have its own currency, and feel part of it from the beginning. The 'teasel' (a local plant used as part of the finishing process for the felted cloth – Stroud scarlet – for which Stroud is famous) tied with 'Stroud Pound': the decision was to call it the latter and hope it will casually become known as the teasel, much as a pound is also a 'quid'. Much envy was expressed about Lewes's 'ownership' of Tom Paine; Stroud discussed fighting back in the

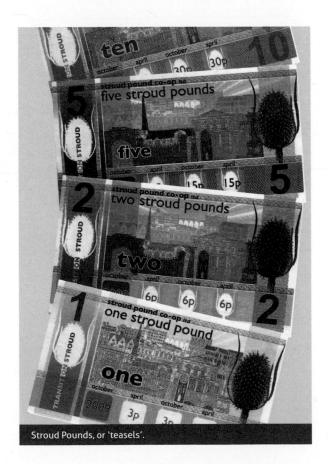

Stroud Pounds, or 'teasels'.

battle of icons with local varieties of pig (the Gloucester old spot), cattle and apples. Local businesses were a key partner in these discussions.

"Get a design together as early as possible and go through as many iterations as you can, with lots of consultation on design. Even now it's printed, if I had known then what I know now, we might have made different kind of decisions." **Ronan Schoemaker, designer, Stroud Pound**

In the end the team hit on local author Laurie Lee (of *Cider with Rosie* fame) for the ten-pound note in honour of his devotion to the Five Valleys and his socialist commitment (he fought the fascists in Spain) set against a backdrop of his home – Slad Valley. This followed the agreement of Laurie's widow Kathy and daughter Jessy. "Laurie absolutely loved Stroud," said his wife Kathy. "I think he would have liked the idea of being on the currency." The fiver features a rare local butterfly and a local tradition called the 'dog tree', where grieving owners can leave mementoes to their departed pooches. The two-pound note features the lawnmower, a Stroud invention, and the teasel adorns the one-pound note. All notes have spaces for the stickers needed to revalidate the note to be attached.

Balancing 'moneyness' and 'valuableness' with cost

Believing that the project needed to be independent and self-financing from the outset, the Co-op decided it would avoid grants or sponsorship and raise the money for the printing of the notes from its own resources.

The implication of this decision was that cloth-based banknote paper was prohibitively expensive. Tamper-proof cheque paper was used as an alternative, with security provided through an ultraviolet layer, a watermark, and microprinted security features. This paper, and good design, would be of high enough quality to communicate valuableness and moneyness and avoid the problem of early designs of notes looking more like vouchers than notes, while staying within cost limitations.

A range of notes was produced from the beginning, in large enough denominations, it was hoped, for circulation to really take off. It took some time to find a printer able to do a run of 20,000 notes within the budget: most currency printers deal in runs in the millions. In the end 20,000 notes cost around £800: fifteen pence a note.

Launching the Stroud Pound

The Stroud Pound (S£) was launched at the Stroud Festival in September 2009 in Threadneedle Street, Stroud. S£1,500 was issued by Co-op members dressed as bankers. By the launch fifteen businesses and seven agencies had signed up to accept the money, including Star Anise cafe, Stroud Bookshop, Stroud Brewery, a record shop, a butcher and a baker, and – interestingly – two sub post offices. This, it must be said, is less than the 70 achieved by Totnes or the 130 in Lewes, but creditable for an unfunded grassroots effort.

"The design brings all the energy together. It asks for a bit of a commitment from everybody, but at the end there will be a better local economy for us all. We've set this up cooperatively: it's your Co-op, it's your money, and we hope that next year you will help make decisions about the money, because we've got control of the money so it works for us. Use it creatively: think of creative ways to change the economy. You have to believe that we can do this." **Molly Scott Cato, Stroud Pound Co-op**

Timing is obviously a factor in explaining the more low-key launch. Lewes in particular caught the imagination with its launch at the height of the credit crunch. A year later, when Stroud launched, some felt the recovery was under way. Media interest was, as a result, less intense. A second factor might be the launch of the Brixton Pound (see Chapter 14) later the same week so the metropolitan press did not have far to go to cover something happening just over the Thames. There has also been less interest from collectors.

> "I think it's fantastic: I love the idea that it feels like *anarchy*, it feels like a real sort of, two fingers up in the air to big business, to Tesco's, to a system that, not through choice, I am part of. It feels resilient, exciting and brave. It feels like a step out in a different direction, it feels very brave . . . It's a real act of positive defiance . . . I love it!"
> **Jane Rose, Transition Stroud**

Challenges and opportunities

As with other local currencies, there were strengths and weaknesses of Stroud's approach in the early days.

The challenge of a more political approach

The more political style of presentation for the rationale for the Stroud Pound, in contrast to the Totnes or Lewes Pounds, may be an issue. To get your first Pounds you have to join the Stroud Pound Co-op for five pounds sterling, thereby joining a club and in some way buying into its ethos. Not everyone is a 'joiner', and not everyone may share the club's ethos. I observed some people being put off by this at the launch. Remember that the Simmellian 'universal money' approach (see Chapter 2, pages 42-44) would be that money liberates you from such obligations. The Stroud Pound wants you to join the collective.

Asking people and businesses to 'join' the Co-op meant that at the launch the number of opportunities for purchasing Stroud Pounds was limited: they can be bought only from 10am till 1pm every Saturday from the Stroud Valleys Project, in contrast to the larger number of issuing points in Great Barrington, Totnes or Lewes.

On the other hand, limiting places where the Pound could be bought at the launch also deters collectors and speculators, who would then take the money out of the local economy, and ensures that from the beginning the currency is managed by a transparent, democratic and accountable organisation.

The more political approach might affect relations with businesses. For the political reasons discussed above, the Stroud Pound Co-op has insisted on preventing customers from redeeming them, on a discount of 5 per cent for businesses that redeem them, and on demurrage.

A wider network of exchange points is also planned. And, of course, there is nothing to stop you getting your first Stroud Pounds in change, and nothing formally to stop a business that wanted to from exchanging Stroud Pounds for sterling for individuals. How much control the Co-op has in practice over a paper currency that travels from hand to hand is an open question.

The discount and demurrage are more significant questions.

The challenge of the discount

Given the severity of the recession at the time of the launch in September 2009, many local businesses struggled with the 5-per-cent redemption. They argued that it was not appropriate in the current harsh economic climate. A walk around Stroud town centre identified a number of barometers for a struggling local economy that were completely absent in Lewes: empty units and pound shops. Stroud is a poorer place than either Lewes or Totnes. It is not a 'latte town'.

The Stroud Pound Co-op was critical of this reaction. Given that the object of the Stroud Pound is something that all benefit from – local consumers *and* traders – it was decided that while it was possible to make an introductory offer of just a 3-per-cent redemption fee, the principle of participation in a collective endeavour should remain. Businesses *should* put something back if they are to benefit from the loyalty of customers who could easily go to the supermarkets, thus saving money. The 'deal' was clear in the joining documents, and the expected commitment was made explicit from the start.

This debate has focused explicitly around a prominent local business that refused to take part. Sunshine is a relatively large and long-established health and whole-food products store, with four sites in the town. The owner of the stores, a member of a long-standing Stroud family, said that while he knows everyone involved in the Stroud Pound and thinks it a good idea, it would not work for his business. With over 600 customers a day, many of whom can reasonably be expected to want to spend Stroud Pounds, he could see no way in which he could re-circulate the notes. Staff did not want them, and he could not envisage his suppliers accepting them. It added another layer of complexity to accounting and handling VAT, and he had little enough time for this anyway. Business, he said, was hard enough as it is without the prospect of a 5-per-cent deduction which was, he said, "not exactly attractive, is it?". Consequently, he was "not interested". His customers shop locally anyway, he felt.

In a way, he has a point. His business *is* big enough and central enough in the shopping habits of likely Stroud Pound spenders that he would take in a large number of notes. He would be in the same position as Guidos and the BerkShare Co-op (see Chapter 10, page 136). These two businesses felt consumer pressure to join, and they said that they would "quite rightly" be penalised for non-participation. They saw the redemption fee as a community donation. Sunshine resisted this pressure at the beginning, while the Stroud Pound Co-op felt it was time for the business, which the people of Stroud had supported for many years, to 'put something back'. It was necessary, the Co-op felt, to get the balance right between listening to local businesspeople and developing a local currency model that could maintain itself over time with an income source from the 2 per cent of the redemption fee allocated to run the programme. How this tension, about which there is no clear answer, works out in the long run will be interesting.

The challenge of demurrage

Given the relatively limited number of places that the Stroud Pound can be purchased from and then spent, we don't know to what extent demurrage might be a disincentive. 'Rusting' money, subject to demurrage, was accepted in the Great Depression since scrip was often the only form of money people had. The economy had jammed, and desperate measures were needed to get people spending. In contrast, in the leading economies today we saw 'quantitative easing', a massive injection of national currency to fight the recession that broke out in 2007-8 so that money is not as bone-crunchingly scarce (or even absent) as it was in the Great Depression. Regiogeld uses demurrage, but it can be spent in far more places, and taps into deep-seated feelings of regional pride. As we see in Chapter 16, as a result of having adopted the Euro, Ireland was not able to carry out quantitative easing. As the recession dragged on into 2010 and public sector workers saw real wage cuts, Ireland's Liquidity Network experimented with a currency that rewarded spenders and penalised hoarders.

Early evidence suggests demurrage does not seem to have been a disincentive in Stroud. Three months after the launch 3,500 Stroud Pounds were still in circulation and only 150 had been redeemed. Twenty-seven businesses accepted them. On the other hand, we don't know to what extent ordinary users of Stroud Pounds understood the implications of something quite technical such as demurrage, and we don't know what will happen when the first stickers need to be purchased. Might some people get a nasty shock? We will need to monitor this.

The challenge of deepening local production

The Co-op has concerns that the town of Stroud itself may be too small and may, at the time of writing, contain too few businesses to achieve the critical mass necessary for sufficient business-to-business circulation through which to build an independent currency that can delink from sterling. To boost levels of local production, once the Stroud Pound has gained local acceptance the Co-op plans to create Stroud Pound loans to fund the development of new forms of local production, much as a bank does with conventional currency (see Chapter 2, page 41).

The potential of local currencies for deepening local resilience by funding new production is an interesting one. What we don't yet know is whether local currencies need to circulate in a large enough area to include sufficient *existing* locally owned businesses, such that circulation between them is possible – or whether a local currency can actually *rebuild* a local economy by funding new businesses, producing things that were previously imported. Here the 'Cheerful Disclaimer' comes to mind – this is an experiment. We don't know if it will work, and can only find out. But there are real concerns that compared with the geographical coverage of Chiemgauer, Stroud is too small an area within which to develop a resilient independent local currency that does deepen local resilience.

On the positive side, the Five Valleys boasts considerable rural production that should be brought into the scheme: a difference when compared with Great Barrington, Totnes or Lewes, where this production has largely declined. The Co-op can build on this, and on the weekly farmers' market. Now that the Stroud Pound is in circulation it may be possible to use it as a base for other developments, such as Transition markets, which will enable local producers to exchange surpluses, or Transition gigs or fairs where only teasels will be accepted for admission and trade.

The challenge of concerns about growth and commodification

The well-developed nature of the local counterculture brings mixed blessings. The local council's Greens, for example, have been a little resistant to the Stroud Pound, which they see as a way of boosting consumption. They don't want to grow the local economy or encourage consumption at all, and this includes local consumption. Why use money at all, they ask? They have struggled to grasp the longer term nature of the project or the more cooperative, ecological approach being taken by the Stroud Pound Co-op. They see the Stroud Pound as just a tool for local businesses. Arguments for boosting footfall and town pride fall flat.

The second issue is that the residual memory of the town's defunct LETS scheme has lingered. While Stroud LETS was pioneering in its day and notched up ten years of successful trading, it ended in a rather unsatisfactory way as key members moved away or had health problems and LETS rather fizzled out. Some of the businesses who accepted the currency ended up with large balances of Strouds that they could not spend. At least one business that was active in LETS has consequently been wary about the Stroud Pound. It may be possible to turn the problem into an advantage. There are plans to relaunch Stroud LETS and link it to the Pound, which may lead to a more diverse ecosystem of currencies in the Valleys, capitalising on the heritage of LETS.

> "The notes look beautiful. It's amazing what can be done when a group of people get together and try to do something different, not more of the same . . . In this country we've created a warehouse economy where we are all dependent on crap jobs, insufficient work and moving stuff around instead of making it . . . I think there are a few people around thinking, well, perhaps the last thirty years has been a mistake and we need to fundamentally rethink where we are going as a country, as strength lies in making stuff, not shifting it around."
> **Charley Butcher, Stroud Pound Co-op**

> "It's nice, clean money . . . I feel elated that there is another way." **Graham Patefield-Smith, Stroud Pound Co-op**

The reward: towards more cooperatively managed currencies?

The Stroud Pound Co-op is experimenting with a more explicitly political approach to establishing a local currency on cooperative principles. In a town with a strong Green and Socialist heritage, boosting small businesses and the local economy for its own sake isn't good enough if it just leads to more growth and does not benefit the wider community. What is needed, the Co-op argues, is the germ of a new cooperative, democratically managed economy. It has interest from major national cooperatives who would like to help to develop the model.

Taking a more explicitly political approach means that those businesses that do buy into the project know what they are signing up to, and are more likely to understand the project's broader aims of stimulating more local production and eventually delinking from sterling. This will have benefits later.

But the more political approach might have scared off some businesses who, in the Berkshires, Totnes or Lewes, might have been attracted to something with no downsides and which, focusing on boosting town pride and the local economy, had an obvious economic benefit to them.

Either way, the Stroud Pound Co-op's more political approach will add to our understanding of the possibilities of local currencies as the experiment develops over the next couple of years, especially if the Stroud Pound breaks its links to sterling in favour of a link to local commodities.

> "Starting a local currency is a deep learning experience. Clutching our own notes for the first time last night generated a mixture of hilarity and awe. As the past year has proved, money is right at the centre of our lives. It really does make the capitalist world go around. Just try to imagine what would have happened to your life if the high-street banks had seized up and your credit card had ceased to function last September. No cashpoints, no ability to pay in shops, very soon nothing in the shops. This is the vital role that money plays in a complex modern economy, and the money we are using has inequality designed into it. It is controlled by the very forces that are wreaking havoc on our planet. Making your own money gives you a chance to really change the economic system that is so all-pervasive as to be invisible and unquestioned."
> **Molly Scott Cato, Stroud Pound Co-op**[1]

THE STROUD POUND SCORECARD

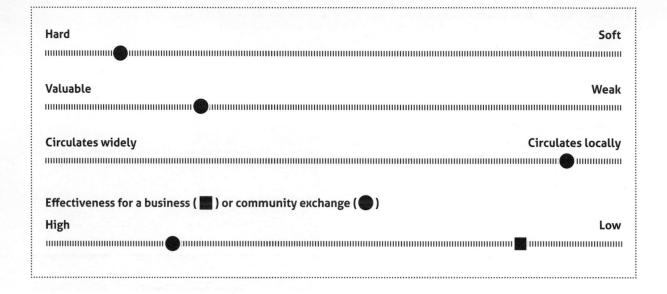

Hard   Soft

Valuable   Weak

Circulates widely   Circulates locally

Effectiveness for a business (■) or community exchange (●)

High   Low

CHAPTER 14

LOCAL MONEY IN A GLOBAL CITY: THE BRIXTON POUND

Anyone labouring under the misconception that the Transition movement looks back rather wistfully to a simpler world where everyone lived in small towns surrounded by market gardens, and wants to create a closed-off world where no one travels – which may, to some, seem faintly xenophobic – should go to Brixton and see what a Transition Initiative in the heart of a global city looks like.

Brixton

Just south of the River Thames, in South Central London, Brixton was once a place that seemed to epitomise inner-city problems. It was notorious for the riots of 1981, when the district exploded in open rebellion in response to heavy-handed – some would say repressive – policing. It remains a place characterised by the press as a haven for drug dealers and gangs, a place where the police should openly carry machine guns.

But there is another side to Brixton, which now hosts a vibrant multicultural community, a high street that retains some big-name shops (the legacy of government intervention after the riots) and large numbers of locally owned shops and cafes centred on the famous Electric Avenue market. Many of these shops and cafes are focused on Brixton's multicultural communities. There is a lively artistic and music community. There is, in Brixton, something worth celebrating and protecting.

Brixton's famous Electric Avenue market.

Building local resilience in a global world

London is, of course, the world's greatest city, the centre of global connections, the powerhouse of the financial colossus[1] that almost brought the global economy crashing down in 2007-8. This deeply unsustainable model of global finance capitalism is now fundamentally incompatible with the need to cut crude oil and carbon out of the way we run our economies.

But London is also famously a city of villages, where car journeys through the city centre are taxed and people are encouraged to cycle or use public transport – or even walk. It's a melting pot. Where some communities might not fully accept people born just a few miles away, London has always welcomed incomers.

Walk along a London street and see the newsagent, an immigrant from Pakistan, selling every newspaper under the sun. Walk past the Irish, Somali or Vietnamese community centre. Buy some fish and chips (in East London Polish Jews meet Catholic Irish, and invent the national dish). Have an Italian ice cream or a Colombian coffee in an Greek cafe. You'll hear every accent and language on the planet as you walk about. That's why I personally love it.

London is a place characterised by a welcome to immigrants hoping to escape an awful life often caused by the actions and decisions of those in the square mile; immigrants who often have to live and work next door to those who have more wealth than they could dream of. Dealing with the consequences of such inequality, which can manifest itself in incredibly resilient and entrepreneurial community groups and local businesses, but also in gangs, drugs and shootings, is a key issue for the city.

London is a global place, but also made up of localities such as Brixton within which people live, work, enjoy themselves and do business. We can combine a vibrant, diverse, resilient local economy with multiculturalism and connection, the good and low-carbon parts of globalisation. We are not all destined to retreat to inward-looking villages and towns. Another world is possible, and Brixton shows us how it might be constructed.

For more information on the Brixton Pound and to sign up to use it, see: **www.brixtonpound.org**

Developing the Brixton Pound

Like Stroud, Brixton had an active LETS scheme in the 1990s. Transition Brixton was an early joiner, coming

in at number 12 on the list of official Transition sites. The Economy and Business group considered reviving Brixton LETS until the success of the Lewes Pound suggested that they follow a paper currency route. One of Transition Brixton's early events was a 'Local Economy Day', in June 2008, to explore ways of deepening the local economy. At this event, a pilot local currency was sold to participants who could then use it to buy their lunch at four local eateries – some went to all four. The idea caught on, and as news filtered through the networks of the events down the road in Lewes, the Economy and Business group decided to explore things further.

Brixton Pounds.

Mobilising finance and support

The group was aided in this by staff at the new economics foundation, a local 'think and do tank' that has for many years supported the development of complementary currencies as a means of creating a more sustainable and socially just financial system. Two of the members of Transition Brixton also work for the new economics foundation and advise the project in terms of strategy and communications. Eventually nef seconded three people to work on the Brixton Pound, providing invaluable advice and £1,000 funding. Discussions with Lambeth council provided more funding and advice. Four local businesses provided more support and sponsorship, with their names on the notes and in publicity. Other supporters and businesses donated small amounts on a PayPal account.

An early stage, following the lead of Lewes, was to set up a 1000 club of people prepared to buy and use a currency. It recruited 800 members, including some businesses and councillors. Even Facebook was used to provide a way of supporters getting in touch – the relatively youthful team behind the Brixton Pound was doing things its way.

Mobilising community buy-in

As with other local currencies, a key aim of the Brixton Pound was to support small businesses as they face the challenge of the credit crunch and competition from large chains, build closer relations between Brixton residents and businesses, and reduce supply chains and hence carbon emissions and fossil-fuel dependency.

But a key new theme also emerged: pride in Brixton, in its diversity and locally owned businesses, and a perception that while outsiders thought Brixton was characterised by poverty and crime, local people knew differently. They had something they wanted to nurture and defend.

This brought in the council's Town Centre Director as a key ally, along with a senior councillor, the cabinet member with a remit for culture and social inclusion. They brought the council's support alongside, providing £6,000 funding and help with publicity and printing.

Designing the currency

Designers worked on the new notes, and a web-based poll discussed who should be on the notes. Paper and security features were discussed with a security printer referred to the group by its colleagues in Lewes. The notes cost £6,000 to produce on banknote-quality paper.

The Pounds are backed by sterling and can be bought and sold at a 1:1 exchange rate. Discussions with businesses indicated that any redemption fee would not be welcome. Issuing and redemption points were set up at a local supermarket, a money exchange shop, and a coffee shop.

Managing the project

"The business engagement was really the most time consuming. That's something I would recommend to others – start that really early, along with the design process with the notes. Involve them in the early decisions. We should have done more of that early on, and kept discussions open longer, but it's learning lessons . . .

It's important to discuss things as you go along, and be prepared to meet each other halfway, not just do things the way you want to without involving others. Designers need to be free to do their job, but other people have ideas too. You need a good design brief – perhaps our design brief was not good enough as we were volunteers and learning as we went along as well, and needed to get the notes in on time."

Tim Nichols, Brixton Pound Project Manager

The launch

After a year of hard work, including weekly meetings sometimes lasting three hours, giving out flyers, talking to people on the street, endless presentations to businesses, stalls at local events and lots of media work, things came together at the spectacular launch at Lambeth Town Hall in September 2009 – recalled by Rob Hopkins in the Foreword to this book. The council donated the room, and the warm-up was provided by local musicians. The 70 businesses signed up by the launch advertised their acceptance on a display on the wall, in a leaflet, and online.

> You can find which businesses accept the Brixton Pound using a facility provided by googlemap: see **http://brixtonpound.org/where/spend/**

The mayor, the Transition Network's Rob Hopkins and nef's David Boyle launched one, five, ten and twenty-pound notes emblazoned with the local heroes who shaped the area's diversity:

- Olive Morris, founder of Brixton Black Women's Group, brandishing her megaphone on the one B£

- Gaia scientist James Lovelock on the fiver

- Jamaican Trotskyist, historian, author of *The Black Jacobins* (the seminal book on the eighteenth-century slave revolt in Haiti) and cricket fan C. L. R. James on the tenner

- Dutch immigrant, the painter Vincent van Gogh on the twenty.

B£6,500 of the 40,000 notes printed was issued before supporters and organisers danced the night away to dub reggae at a local pub – they bought their beer with Brixton Pounds.

Local heroes

Interestingly, apart from the very much alive James Lovelock, the heroes are mostly all dead. Two contemporary local heroes, David Bowie and Linton Kwesi Johnson, declined the honour. Would you like to see yourself on money? Probably not. Also interestingly, one famous resident of Brixton was not a front runner:

Former Prime Minister John Major. I can't think why the only man to run away from a circus to be an accountant was not considered.

Olive Morris's family were pleased to have her remembered but pointed out that she was a very radical person: to have her on the notes communicates a message. The Pound team responded that that was a part of Brixton that they want to honour. They wanted to show that local currencies are not just for small, country towns full of middle-class white people. They can work in a diverse global community too.

The important issue is to be sure that you have permission to use anyone's image on your notes, especially if they are alive and likely to object!

Customers queue to get their first Brixton Pounds.

The first day

The next day, queues formed at Morley's, the locally owned department store, as more proud Brixtonians bought their Pounds. Media interest was intense. By lunchtime Morleys had sold out of its first allowance of B£1,000 and was replenished with another B£750: the organisers had learned from problems in Lewes.

Issuing Brixton Pounds in Morley's department store, Brixton.

The notes celebrate – they actually scream out – the multicultural and vibrant nature of a convivial place worth defending from the blandness of clone towns and from climate catastrophe. They also put a lie to those who mix up localisation and protectionism. No one sees Brixton becoming a 'quaint', backward-looking island cut off in the middle of London, something out of 'The League of Gentleman', as one business sceptic put it – "this is a local shop for local people: there's nothing for you here . . .".

"I really like to use the Brixton Pound because I think it's really important to support and invest in your own community. Having a Brixton currency encourages people who live locally to spend more money locally, and the more good businesses that are independent that you have in a community, the happier it is." **Rosie Lovell, Rosie's Deli Cafe, Brixton**

Explaining the Brixton Pound's success

As with the all the currencies discussed so far, there are a number of reasons why the Brixton Pound's launch and early days seemed so successful. Some are factors that can be replicated, while some refer more to the nature of the place the Brixton Pound was born in, and the people responsible for its birth.

"It's changing Brixton from being infamous to famous." **Blacker Dread, Blacker Dread Music Store**

Building on strong foundations

After much hard work and persuasion of sometimes hard-to-convince local business owners, the Brixton Pound has got off to a flying start. The organisers were able to put together a skilled and committed young team drawn from Transition Brixton, nef and the council. The legacy of LETS means that many Brixtonians are open to the idea of an alternative currency. The team was able to raise enough finance and in-kind support from these networks to develop what are, in my opinion, the highest-quality and best-promoted notes to date.

Hitting the ground running

With 70 businesses signed up, there was somewhere to spend the notes from day one. The businesses can see the pound as being something unique to Brixton that it is hoped will raise the profile of the area and draw in more visitors to patronise its locally owned businesses.

If a business decides to redeem its Pounds, with no deduction, sterling available on deposit to back it and a wide range of issuing and redemption points within walking distance, there is no downside to the pound at all for businesses. It is an initiative that promotes local businesses and adds to positive perceptions of Brixton's strong community and diverse economy. It runs alongside other initiatives designed to promote the area, such as a farmers' market and the Brixton bazaar, a street market. The town centre manager's agenda was certainly addressed by the Brixton Pound, and it helps local businesses to weather a recession that has seen a 30-per-cent decline in takings.

A supportive council interested in exploring ways for stall owners to pay their pitch fees and residents to pay council tax in Brixton Pounds (large numbers of people pay this in cash at the moment) is a really important element in the story. Lambeth council is supporting the scheme and encouraging its 2,000-strong staff to use the B£, and one of Lambeth's credit crunch taskforce commitments is to support local exchange schemes. Finally, the link with the credit union is very innovative. The pound shows that a viable currency can be developed in an inner-city area.

Money is life

"There's still a moment of breathlessness when you hold a Brixton Pound in your hand. As if you were somehow touching the stuff of life. And in a way you are. Because money is like blood. It circulates around us, and when it disappears somewhere – because of some squall on Wall Street – our lives seize up a little.

So money is life, and we can make our own. That's why I say those Brixton Pound notes are alive. It is a small liberation to use one. A bit like the moment Gandhi made salt for the first time: a symbolic moment of revolt, using the stuff of life. So every time we use one of these notes, it seems to me – and we are going to have to use them if this is going to work – it is a moment of liberation." David Boyle, the new economics foundation's local currency expert

Timing
Launching in September, after the summer holidays, was a conscious choice. Many products are launched in September, and the situation could be monitored in the run-up to Christmas with the possibility of a second

issuance. One idea to maintain the momentum is a programme to get Brixtonians to commit to doing their Christmas shopping in Brixton Pounds.

Challenges and opportunities

But there are some challenges ahead.

The challenge of maintaining momentum
We saw in Chapters 11 and 12 that one year on Totnes and Lewes found reduced enthusiasm for and declining circulation of their pound. Working on advice from Christian Gelleri and the experiences of regiogeld, Stroud wanted to use the deduction for redeeming the Stroud Pounds to fund someone to develop the scheme; however Brixton, like the other Transition currencies, does not have this. There are two options: a grant could be won (and given the support of the council and nef the odds are good), or LSCU could undertake this role. But as yet this is a potential vulnerability of the project's future viability, given that experience shows that businesses need continued support if they are going to continue to use what is not a 'universal' currency.

The challenge of geography
Brixton is in the middle of a global city, at the end of a tube line. People, goods and services, and money, flow in and out of Brixton every day, like a beating heart. The flows in and out are immeasurably greater than in the other, more contained and geographically distinct Transition towns.

The political boundaries make no economic sense: two miles from Brixton in either direction is another London borough, while Lambeth is a long, thin borough. How far away from the heart of Brixton can members and businesses be for the currency to still represent and support 'Brixton'? Where exactly does

'Brixton' start and stop? Brixton LETS struggled with making sense of these boundaries: might the Brixton Pound have the same issue to grapple with?

How widely the Pound circulates of course will determine what resources are available with it, what supplies businesses can obtain, and what production can be generated. A broad conception of 'Brixton' is likely to maximise the usefulness of the note.

After the enthusiasm of the launch, stores that accept the Pound have found that shoppers who do not live in Brixton are less likely to accept it in change, and again we have the problem of businesses struggling to find suppliers locally. As with other local currencies, there is a perception that those who spend the Brixton Pound would have shopped locally anyway.

Local currencies and chain stores

At the end of the day, how tightly or widely the circulation of any paper currency evolves through the decisions of individual businesses and consumers to use it. You can't stop people using a paper currency in the same way you can refuse membership of a LETS scheme or time bank. One new issue is that, noticing how popular the Pound seemed to be with Brixtonians, the local branches of some national chains asked if they could accept the Pound. If the objective is to support locally owned businesses this makes no sense.

"It is a good position to be in. Getting large chain stores on board with the concept of investing in the local community has huge benefits. We don't believe in excluding people from the conversation, as long as the integrity of the project is maintained and the community members and local shop owners continue to benefit." **Tim Nichols, Brixton Pound Project Manager**

On the other hand, if the ability to spend money locally in chains means that more people use the Pound, and it circulates more widely within the local economy as a result, rather than being redeemed straight away, then that makes sense. In any case – can you stop people using a paper currency in whatever way they please? The Brixton Pound group decided on a permissive approach.

The challenge of local production – or the lack of it

Next to nothing is produced in Brixton. Food comes from the wholesale market at Nine Elms. None of the businesses I spoke to either sourced anything locally, or had given much thought to how they might spend the money they took in, beyond giving it back out in change. As part of a global city, Brixton is particularly strongly integrated in global economic and migration chains. Beyond the usual scepticism about what some will always see as 'monopoly money', a lack of opportunities to spend the Brixton Pound does seem to be the main objection advanced by those that refused to take the Pound – and, at present, they do have a point. While it is undoubtedly a good news story for Brixton, which may increase footfall in Brixton businesses, the extent that it does develop local resilience and cut carbon out of our economies will be doubtful until more of the things sold in shops in Brixton are made locally.

Tim Nichols, the Brixton Pound manager, recognises that the Pound is likely to hit a wall in the short term, especially with food retail. But the long-term plan is to set a target to seriously boost the amount of food produced locally, fuelled with the Brixton Pound. Blacker Dread, local Music Store proprietor, wants to explore ways to use the Brixton Pound to fuel the already-vibrant local music scene: locally produced CDs for Brixton Pounds, anyone? Local currencies have the capacity to make conventionally more expensive local artisan production competitive with globally mass-produced cheaper products (which are cheap only because labour, health and safety and environmental standards are lower, and transport costs are cheap). As the effects of peak oil and climate change really start to be felt, the economics will change – and Brixton with its Pound is well placed to capitalise on the fact.

What matters, for Tim, is the presence of a strong sense of local identity, local culture and local businesses from which to build, and a group with a vision who wanted to do something about it. We cannot expect much to be produced locally in an area like Brixton, given the intensity of globalisation. Making change by building a more resilient future is the long-term agenda. There are many good elements of globalisation, but there are also many downsides, and the Brixton Pound is attempting to fix those by putting the heart back into the local economy.

Blacker Dread Music Store accepts Brixton Pounds.

The challenge of circulation getting stuck

On a more practical note, given the participation of a locally owned department store where clothes, make-up, shoes and other everyday items can be bought for Brixton Pounds but are not produced locally, the Brixton Pound might be mindful of the problem first identified in Great Barrington (see Chapter 10) of circulation getting 'stuck' in large businesses that take in much more than they can give out if circulation levels are high. They might find transferring large numbers of Pounds back to sterling burdensome.

Interestingly, this is not a problem that the department store has encountered during the early days of the Brixton Pound. The department store is by far the most popular exchange point in Brixton. By January 2010 Morleys had issued almost 18,000 Brixton Pounds, averaging around a thousand a week, ten times more than are spent in the store. This may be because the store has not promoted its acceptance of the Pound that well, or because, unlike the food stores in Great Barrington, people do not spend money at a department store very often.

> "When we were wanting to take this on there were more people wanting to help than we really realised, than we reached out to. And as things went on we realised that these people were out there."
> **Tim Nichols, Brixton Pound Project Manager**

The reward?

The Brixton Pound will be worth watching as it develops. It has already shown itself to be a powerful reflection of the pride many Brixtonians feel in their oft-maligned borough. But will it be a powerful enough tool to actually help to maintain the area's quite vibrant local economy and small businesses in the face of hard times? And can the Pound, as it strengthens, act as a tool to strengthen local production in the heart of a globalised city? Time will tell.

THE BRIXTON POUND SCORECARD

Hard   **Soft**

Valuable   **Weak**

Circulates widely   **Circulates locally**

Effectiveness for a business (■) or community exchange (●)

High   **Low**

CHAPTER 15

HOW TO DO IT: STARTING AND BUILDING A LOCAL CURRENCY

In this chapter I suggest a process through which you might, as part of a Transition Initiative, decide on what sort of community currency you want to set up, and how you might do it. Unless you want to go for a particularly well-designed paper currency, on special paper, with the banks signed up and all the state-of-the-art security measures, complementary currencies can be easy to set up. A number of accountancy packages are available online to help you run your accounts.

Setting up and maintaining a vibrant network is a bit harder. Some complementary currency networks around the world grew to quite a size, while others stayed small. Some lasted fifteen to twenty years and are still going strong, while others ran out of steam. What are the lessons to be learned? 'Forewarned is forearmed': you can avoid problems in the future if you are aware from the start how things can go pear-shaped.

Decide why you want to set up a complementary currency

Don't assume that a complementary currency is right for you. You might be able to achieve your goals using national currency. Think about what you want to achieve with your currency, who is likely to use it, what resources you have to develop and manage the currency, and what your area is like. Remember to consider the full range of currency models discussed

in this book, not just the existing Transition currencies – remember the need to avoid path dependency, discussed on page 23. For example:

- You might have a large number of green-minded, quite self-starting and alternative people in your community, but not many locally owned businesses. LETS might be the best option.

- You might feel that people in your area need more support, are currently excluded from the economy, and involving businesses is not a priority at all. Time banking might be best.

- You live in a community with a radical local culture and lots of alternative-minded folk who have their own lifestyle businesses. They are concerned that a local currency would just be another form of growth, commodifying what is currently shared. A paper hour-based currency might fit.

- You are in a small town set in an agricultural hinterland, with a vibrant, locally owned high street. You can envisage a high level of local resilience, with food and power generated locally, but local business owners are quite conservative. You want to deepen your local economy. A backed paper currency would fit.

- You have good relations with councils, regional development agencies and chambers of commerce.

You live in a region with a strong local identity. A regional currency, like regiogeld, might make sense.

- Money in your community is moving too slowly as a result of the recession. Banks continue not to lend. Demurrage, or rusting money, might be best.

The important thing is to think through the options and be clear about what you want to do.

Don't launch too quickly – develop your local network and skills base

The Transition movement places a lot of emphasis on laying the foundations and building up to a great unleashing. It's the same for successful currency networks.

Whatever form of currency you use, make sure that you have a large enough network of people who do actually have the time and skills to trade with each other, rather than politically or community-minded 'hangers on' who are interested in the ideas but can't see how they would use an alternative currency themselves.

Many people *do* have useful skills they can offer straight away, but not everyone has. Many skills that are highly valued in the money economy (say, geography lecturing) will have few takers in the Transition economy, where plumbing or growing food – some of the real skills in the Transition movement – are in demand. It may be that you need to be a little further down the 'great reskilling' road than you are now before you have the range of skills you need to run a more complicated local currency scheme. Start with a LETS or time money scheme and concentrate on reskilling.

Unless you have a respectable number of locally owned businesses in your community that you want to protect, it would perhaps make sense to hold back a paper currency for when you feel your Transition process has enough local credibility for businesses to take it seriously, and you have enough committed people, and your Transition Initiative is resilient enough, to manage the after-care that businesses need if they are to use a paper currency in the long term. This might mean that your community is further along in the Transition process than one that is developing its skills with LETS and time money.

Consider a pilot

Sort out the glitches and learn how to work your currency through experimentation. Putting a time limit on how long your scheme will last enables you to recall a currency that hasn't worked, relaunch it, or discard it if it doesn't fit.

Build the currency scheme through people and businesses, not systems

The temptation can be to get a grant, set up a currency scheme, employ a worker and then start to recruit members. But it's always a mistake to put the machine, the money system you are setting up, before the ghost in the machine – people – and expect the people to fit your plan. You might end up with an expensive project that does not meet local needs, because you are being design-led, rather than working with what you have locally in terms of people, resources, ways of working and culture.

Far better is to find out from people what they would like a currency scheme to do, then decide which form of currency system is best from the options. You can design the most appropriate systems for operating the scheme effectively once it is up and running. While systems and management are important and have their place, people should always come first.

Think about how people can find out where to spend the currency

Once you have a network big enough for actual trading to take place, it's time to produce your first directory or newspaper – either in printed form or online. What the directory looks like and the skills in it add to the sense of 'valuableness' of your currency, so it matters. A well-presented directory full of useful skills manifests the valuableness of the currency, and helps make the potential of a local currency real. 'I can get all this with that funny money? Wow!'

So make sure the directory or web pages are well designed, have enough useful skills from people who you think will deliver, and are up to date. A web-based directory is obviously easier to keep up to date than a printed version, but then not everyone is online – there are social equity issues here. It is much easier to design and maintain good-looking directories on computers these days than it was in the past, when too many early LETS directories were shoddy and contained next to nothing useful, so people thought 'this doesn't work' before it had been given a chance.

If you are using a paper currency, think about stickers for shops to put in their windows. Collect emails from businesses and people who have agreed to use the currency, and use an email list to tell people of new places to spend the currency. Have a website that makes the vibrancy of your local network visible. Transition Brixton spent a lot of money on promotional materials and web pages that show where you can spend your money. BerkShares Inc. has an email list.

Ceremony matters – make a song and dance as you unleash or launch

Manchester LETS made sure that it had signed up about a hundred members before it launched. It then got them together in a hall, with many having stalls offering things like food, cards, clothing and the like. A bell was rung (to start trading), and the scheme was launched.

The new Lewes Pound notes were unveiled at a community event at Harveys Brewery. Harveys produced a special commemorative beer, the Quid, a local beer available for local money. There was live music, film, kids' entertainment, stalls, a bar by Harveys and local food (including a hog roast). If that wasn't enough, there were circus skills workshops, a clothes swap, a poetry cafe, live performance, Wimbledon coverage (with strawberries and cream!) and stalls ranging from local food producers to bonfire societies. Lewes Organic Allotment gave advice on growing vegetables, and Lewes Residents Landshare helped find land to grow it on. The Brixton Pound launch was a vibrant occasion, as described by Rob Hopkins in the Foreword to this book.

Given that many of the things offered through local currency are personal services between two people, often at their homes, it can be difficult to manifest all the energy that is exchanged: it's hidden away, and can be hard to see. A formal launch brings it all together. (Transition Initiatives use the technique of 'the great unleashing' for the same reason.) If you have a paper currency, perhaps have a launch at one of your key trading sites, in the high street. Cut a ribbon or ring a bell to start trading. Invite the press along.

Have regular inductions

Whatever model of currency scheme you adopt, it's very important that new people with new skills and needs and new businesses are helped to join the network; otherwise it can seem like a cosy hidden club for those in the know, which can quite quickly run out of steam. Have regular 'drop in' sessions where people can come to find out more and join. Members of Bristol LETS spent an hour every Saturday morning at the cafe at the local city farm for this purpose. Have leaflets and newsletters on display in libraries and information centres; have a good website. The Bright Exchange in Brighton holds early evening induction and get-to-know-you sessions for all new members once a month.

It might be that using a local currency is just not right for some people or businesses in the early days, and it's worth telling them there and then rather than them getting disappointed later. Some people might not have a skill that anyone is likely to want, and no time or interest in learning a sellable skill. They might have unreasonable expectations about how much their skills are worth. They may not have the time, be on the phone, or live too far away. They might be too old or ill, and in need of more comprehensive support.

Some businesses might not, and might never be able to, source their inputs locally or sell locally. If so, don't waste their time. Wait until your currency is more accepted and work with them to boost local production and local sales, or just help them to cut the carbon emissions generated by their activities and to trade fairly. Don't make a fetish out of using a local currency when it will probably always be complementary, and the real goal is to boost local production and consumption in order to cut carbon emissions and global resource consumption.

The core group

A typical local currency core group will include the following.

- A core group facilitator.
- A treasurer/accountant. In LETS or time banking he or she will be responsible for keeping individual accounts up to date and producing statements. Paper-based currencies need someone responsible for deciding how much currency should be issued, safeguarding its integrity, and managing the national currency on deposit. Members of the community need to know that someone is in charge, that they trust them, and that this person is accountable to the community – if they mess up, they can be replaced. This role may be a team job in a large local currency scheme with many weekly transactions to be recorded.
- A treasurer in charge of sterling income (subs, grants) and expenses.
- A directory producer or webmaster. If you have a printed directory, you will need a team to deliver directories and statements, or charge enough sterling to members to post them.
- Someone in charge of induction and marketing – making sure people know about the scheme, how to join, and where to spend the local currency.
- A newsletter editor/publicity person.
- A social secretary/trading events/markets coordinator.
- A secretary.
- In a larger local currency scheme, brokers to liaise with businesses to ensure that they can spend their local currency.

Encourage users to participate straight away – spend money!

It is really important to make people feel useful by getting them involved right away. Alternative currencies operate on the basis that everyone has something to give, something they enjoy doing and makes them feel valued and worthwhile. Developing effective ways of enlisting people's passions and skills (skills audits, parties, gardening sessions, etc.) takes practice. Many members have a great deal to offer, but they don't always realise what skills they have and often need time and encouragement before they feel ready to use an alternative currency in their day-to-day to lives. You need to encourage people to be creative, think of new ways to spend and earn the currency, and to act as ambassadors for the scheme encouraging others to use it. Businesses need help and support in making it work for them in the same way.

It's not good enough to assume that once people have joined they will know how to make the scheme work. They need to understand the tricks of the trade, how to set prices and negotiate what needs to be done, what skills are likely to be in demand, and what to do if they are too much in demand. Some schemes 'buddy' experienced members with new people to help them get the best out of the scheme. This support needs to be ongoing. Someone has to be responsible for making sure this happens.

For time banks, this is one of the main tasks of the broker, requiring special listening and people-skills. LETS schemes have given this responsibility to core group members, or buddied new members up with more experienced ones. Paper-based currencies need a broker or problem-solver, checking that the money isn't getting stuck anywhere.

Make people feel safe and confident

It is important that members of the network feel safe, especially when they are going into other members' homes. For time banks, the time bank broker needs to be aware of any health problems or behaviour that might put members at risk. These can include severe mental health problems, a tendency to be abusive, alcohol misuse or other health issues. To make sure time bank members feel safe, references can be taken up for all new members. However, this can pose a problem for marginal people such as refugees, or people who are very isolated. Others might object to what they see as prying.

An alternative is to build trust through group activities, such as gardening or shared meals, to give a new member, the broker, and other members time get to know each other. These group activities also provide opportunities to share information and enable new people to get a feel for how the currency works.

This is less of an issue for the other forms of currency, but even then you have a duty of care to be sure that you are not putting people using your currency in harm's way.

Establish management and community-building mechanisms

Despite the hopes surrounding early alternative currencies that once launched they would run themselves, it has proved necessary to manage the complementary currency economy – just as the Bank of England's monetary policy committee manages the mainstream money economy. Someone needs to keep a weather eye on the health of the local economy and the flows of money through it.

Are there some people who do not seem to be trading, earning amounts of local money that they might not able to spend, or running up a large debt and giving nothing back? Is an income being generated to pay people to do the jobs needed to run the currency network, such as talking to new and existing members, problem solving, or doing publicity? Avoid getting into a situation where you are fire-fighting or the word on the street becomes 'it doesn't work'.

The most successful schemes have also worked hard to build a sense of community between members, so they won't rip each other off, provide a quality service to each other, and support each other. They hold regular social events and markets, and perhaps have a newsletter or sidelines such as a local currency dating service, walks, sports events and the like. Wellington Green Dollars had a shop. Linking a local currency to Transition culture makes this a bit easier – people are meeting socially anyway, so this will be less of a job. But schemes that did not put energy into building a sense of community often found that the volume of trades was not large enough to keep people interested, and they drifted off.

Look after your core group – avoid burnout

Managing a local currency scheme is quite a big undertaking, not unlike running a small business (or a successful Transition Initiative). You need to be prepared for when activists get burned out, lose interest, get a job, have children, fall under the No.55 bus, etc. – a million and one things.

Make sure that you have fun running your scheme. Pay each other compliments. Give each other rewards for all your hard work. Perhaps have a system of 'duvet days' – let core group members who have been working hard say that for a few days or weeks they aren't going to do anything, without having to justify themselves. This is again a management issue, common to Transition Initiatives and myriad voluntary and community-based organisations.

Towards a more diverse financial ecosystem?

Once a currency network is up and running and you have an active core group you have two choices. You can be happy with what you have: a network of like-minded convivial souls exchanging services with each other, which is fine. Or you can decide that you want to develop a bigger network covering a wider area, or a deeper one providing more services.

You might want to expressly link your currency scheme to 'the great reskilling', with those with skills training those without, and being paid for their time through local currencies. Local currencies can be a good way for people to practise their skills. They might not feel ready to charge sterling for their services, but prepared to work in a more supportive environment. You might want to target specific skills or services that you want to be offered: food or power generation, or trades such as carpentry or plumbing.

It might be that at this point you build in the other forms of currency that you didn't start with, or build links to other financial vehicles. You then have a vibrant and robust local money network, contributing greatly to a resilient, local, post-carbon economy. Given what we know about the 'strength of weak ties' (see page 92), the success of alternative currency schemes rests on the ability to mix people up and engage them on the basis of what they can do, rather than segregate them and confine them to activities organised around their particular needs, or with people like them – which reinforces bonding, not bridging.

How to set up a paper-based currency

- Get together a committed group of people and involve the wider community in discussions – decide on the form of currency you want to develop.
- Set up a club for people to pledge to use the currency, and donate time and money to set it up.
- Talk to local businesses and the council about your plans; get their feedback – and hopefully sponsorship.
- Identify a designer or a design team, and research paper and security features. The other Transition currencies can provide pointers, but you need to do the leg work to make this happen yourself. If I were to reveal all the security features and sources of paper that are out there it would make life easier for forgers.
- Look at other forms of currency: what looks like money, and what doesn't. Look closely at design, printing, use of images, the grouping of images and words, which all convey 'moneyness' and 'valuableness'.
- Consult the community on design and the name of the currency. Produce many early designs and work over them again and again until they are right. You can't do this too early, or go through too many iterations.
- Consider a limited pilot launch at, say, a festival, to raise awareness and iron out the glitches.
- Formalise the organisation behind the currency, if you haven't already.
- Identify ways to communicate with users to tell them about your plans and get feedback.
- Identify ways to involve the community about decisions about their currency, so they feel they have ownership.
- Identify your criteria for the launch – how many businesses do you want to accept your currency? How much conventional money do you need in order to print enough local currency of suitable quality that it looks serious and makes a tangible impact on the local economy?
- Talk, talk and talk to local businesspeople. Listen to their concerns and meet their objections. Help them think of ways to make the currency work for them.
- Identify a launch date, and make sure you hit it.
- Launch with sufficient vigour and flair to make it an event to remember.
- Be ready to manage a chaotic few early days. Avoid Lewes's problems (running out of money, speculation, more press interest than you can handle – perhaps pressuring you to go faster than you are ready to).
- Review and manage circulation.
- Issue new notes and recall old ones as necessary.

Setting up a Transition currency – key recommendations

- Transition currencies are not 'new money' like LETS or time money – they have to be exchanged for national currency, so some purists might object. But when backed by sterling they do have a good track record of involving local businesses, and it seems hard to imagine how a local economy might undergo Transition without their involvement.

- It's important to build a strong team of volunteers who are committed to making the project work and have the time available to help before you make plans to launch the currency. Don't underestimate the amount of day-to-day work and consultation that is required to develop and maintain it.

- Get the balance right. Do you want to spend time building links with local organisations, business associations and the council and get a grant to build a fairly sophisticated local currency scheme (as in Brixton), or do you prefer a more organic approach (as in Totnes or Stroud)? If you are too 'grassroots' the risk is of your currency looking second rate and too few businesses using it; if you want to get it all perfect from the beginning the risk is of ending up with lots of meetings and failed grant bids but no currency. Don't be a latter-day Proudhon (see pages 61-62). Lewes seems to have charted a good middle course.

- Spend time and resources on getting the look, name and 'feel' of your currency right, and ensuring that it has 'moneyness' and 'valuableness'.

- Make sure that the organisation behind the currency has credibility – the good name or one key founder with a strong, local track record might be enough.

- In time, a more sustainable organisation is necessary to build and maintain trust and integrity in the currency.

- Links with local business associations, local banks or other local financial vehicles are necessary to ensure that the currency maintains its integrity.

- Try to ensure that you focus on both sides of the currency: both the technical side of circulation management and the 'softer' side of promotion and community development. Both are essential to grow the usage of your currency.

- Research the model that you are planning to use and try to stick to it. It can be hard to communicate changes in the way that it operates once it is under way. That said, don't be afraid to change things if they aren't working.

- You can never do enough awareness-raising to encourage usage. This needs to be an ongoing task using a variety of media and approaches.

- Remember the importance of maintaining belief in the currency for users, businesses and volunteers.

- Don't plan to change the notes too regularly, as this creates a lot of extra work for the project team.

- Think about how to make circulation work – do you have a diverse enough ecosystem of local businesses that could reasonably be expected, in time, to trade with each other more? How much does your town produce itself, or could be reasonably expected to produce itself? This might mean that you go for a regional currency, rather than one trading in a small town and its hinterland, unless your intention is to get individuals trading with each other and local small businesses, at a small scale, rather than developing local production.

- Remember your objective: your aim, long term, is to build a resilient, low-carbon, localised economy. It is not to increase footfall in local businesses if that just means more growth. You need to balance respecting and listening to local businesspeople with your long-term agenda.

- Remember too that the long-term aim is to delink from national currency so you have an independent local currency that you can use to deepen local resilience. Don't allow yourself to be labelled as just a 'buy local' scheme.

TRUEQUE ZONA OESTE
Red Global del Trueque

VIO 31-12-03

UN CREDITO

1

0039050 A

1 CREDITO

Valor Humano Energético

ekopia resource exchange ltd. the park, findhorn bay, moray, scotland, IV36 3TZ

www.ekopia.findhorn.com

£E 1

Moya — The windmill at Findhorn
photo: Dave Till

£E 1

DATE OF ISSUE 1 May 2003
DATE OF EXPIRY 31 Jan 2006

£E 1

ONE EKO

issued by ekopia resource exchange to support our local economy, promote local enterprise and publicise local initiatives.

ECO VILLAGE ISSUE # 2

ekopia is a partner in the findhorn ecovillage project

PROMISE TO
HONOUR HERE TO
BEARER

chairperson ekopia

SERIAL NUMBER: FF22354

PART FOUR:
TOWARDS RESILIENT LOCAL ECONOMIES

"I sympathise with those who would minimize, rather than with those who would maximize, economic entanglements among nations. Ideas, knowledge, science, hospitality, travel – these are things that of their nature should be international. But let goods be homespun whenever it is reasonably and conveniently possible and, above all, let finance be predominantly national." **J. M. Keynes, *National Self-Sufficiency***

"If we command our wealth, we shall be rich and free; if our wealth commands us, we are poor indeed." **Edmund Burke**

"Traveller, there are no roads. Paths are made by walking."
Chinese proverb

CHAPTER 16

TOWARDS A DEEPER ECOSYSTEM OF CURRENCIES AND LOCAL FINANCE

We now have some track record of local currency development, and have learned some lessons. We are no longer working in the dark. Some local currency schemes have twenty years' experience of trading under their belts; there are time banks that are really meeting previously unmet needs for those the money economy has written off; and Ithaca Hours, Transition currencies and BerkShares are circulating amongst a creditable number of local businesses and becoming an accepted part of the local scene, not considered to be something strange.

BerkShares, regiogeld and the Transition currencies are pioneering the next stage in the move to a low-carbon economy, moving from being a means of circulation between existing local businesses to tools for building greater local resilience by stimulating new local production. The experience of Argentina shows that millions of people can be bounced through the most acute financial crisis with an alternative currency that was flawed, but met short-term emergency needs.

Some mistakes have been made, and we can learn from them and avoid them in the future – many of the pioneers were charting a new course, without maps. They did not, could not know what problems might be encountered. It's worth remembering that our local currency models are still in their infancy, more like Wright's biplane than a Boeing 747. But we do have designs, and experience to work from as we create better models and learn about how they perform in the real world and are operated by fallible and illogical human beings who don't always do what the model says they should do.

Financial 'Garfinkeling'

Talking about money does raise unconscious fears and anxieties and can challenge accepted, taken-for-granted, common-sense behaviour. Some people react very badly to this.

The American sociologist Harold Garfinkel used to get his students to disrupt the 'taken for granted', everyday rules of social interaction to see what would happen. For example, at a dinner party they would take a guest's drink out of his or her hand and put it on the side, or blatantly drop litter. A famous experiment was conducted on the New York City subway in the 1970s, when experimenters boarded crowded trains and asked able-bodied but seated riders, with no explanation, to give up their seats. Reportedly, the experimenters themselves were deeply troubled by being involved in such a seemingly minor violation of a social norm. Being 'Garfinkeled' was, to put it mildly, unsettling.

Proposing local money can seem like 'Garfinkeling'. Of course, common sense tells us that ordinary people can't make their own money. If they do it will be 'monopoly' money, or just 'cause inflation'. 'The bad guys will take advantage, and forge them'.

Lessons from existing models

We probably now have enough evidence to be confident that:

- LETS schemes seem to work well for 'alternative-minded' members of our communities.
- Time banks seem to work well amongst socially excluded communities.
- Paper time-based currencies work well amongst 'green' and 'lifestyle' businesses, where alternative-minded or 'BoBo' ('Bourgeois Bohemian')[1] customers are happy to accept them as change.
- Even flawed alternative currencies developed by communities can bounce people though a crisis and out the other side. At times, we need to put creating enough money to solve a crisis before other considerations, even if we have to deal with the mess afterwards.
- The Transition currencies have been accepted by many locally owned small businesses. Provided the business does not feel it will be overwhelmed and can easily exchange back to conventional currency the local currency it can't re-circulate, with no or only a small discount, even the sceptical accept that they have no serious downsides. But it might be that trying to get exchange going in a small town is drawing the boundaries too tight – regional money might be better. They are also not 'new money', so may not contribute well to the objectives of social justice and inclusion.
- BerkShares and German regional currencies seem to show that a currency circulating at a county or regional level is more likely to attract enough business participation to facilitate business-to-business exchange (rather than a business just redeeming unspendable local currency after one loop).

However:

- Given that we are dealing with a highly globalised economy, few businesses at present trade with other local businesses to any meaningful extent, and consequently it is not surprising that they struggle to spend the local currency they earn. This is something that needs to change if we are to construct the resilient, low-carbon local economies of the future.
- The extent that we can create new forms of money that we can then use to develop the range of goods and services we produce locally, especially food, power and the other things we use every day, is untested. Local currencies have yet to demonstrate their capacity to actively localise a globally connected economy.

As the economist J. K. Galbraith famously said, conventional wisdom says that money should be limited, 'hard': "Anyone who says otherwise is a crank, a crook or a fool." Enron, WorldCom and Bernie Madoff show us that scams happen in the real, mainstream economy. For this reason, most people will be more comfortable with backed currencies than with personal credit or time-based currencies, especially where their livelihoods or businesses are involved. We need to be clear that we are experimenting with one of the bedrocks of society – money – and realise this is a long-term process, not a quick and easy project.

Deepening the local financial infrastructure

But we also do not have that much time. We need to build resilient communities in preparation for the inevitable energy descent, and to facilitate the major cuts in carbon emissions necessary to avoid dangerous climate change. A vibrant diversity of alternative currencies is more likely to protect us than a reliance on a single monetary monoculture that may fail. This means we need to keep innovating with alternative currencies until we develop more resilient models that do work better than the early experiments we have today, which are perhaps mere glimpses of what could be.

The fact is that nowhere have we yet pulled all of the different financial models together into a supportive network on which to build a more localised economy where we *produce* more of what we need locally – not just exchange that which we already have, or stop it leaving our economy. This ecosystem could include a broader range of complementary currencies and financial vehicles than those we have today. We can see how this ecology of money could be further developed with new forms of currency, meeting different needs.

In what follows we explore a few more inspired ideas to take things further and give you some more pointers. This is not comprehensive – all we can hope to do is light a few imaginations and set you off in a new direction. We explore commodity currencies, special-purpose currencies for measuring the carbon we are emitting and for developing local energy production, and electronic currencies. We then look at a range of alternative financial institutions: local banks, community development financial institutions, credit unions, microcredit, and local bonds.

Commodity-backed currencies

If the quantitative easing – 'printing money' – practised in response to financial crises is excessive, then it may be that the result is a return of inflation. People would see their money's purchasing power decline rapidly. Anyone on a wage, a pension, or living off fixed savings suffers, as they did in the 1970s. Any alternative currency linked to national currency will see inflation transmitted between the two: both will lose their purchasing power.

The alternative might be a return to money *directly* linked to commodities. Given that gold and silver are

commodities that have the qualities we look for in money (see Chapter 2, page 38), many people buy gold sovereigns, krugerands and the like as a way to maintain their wealth in periods of high inflation. Libertarian groups concerned about the devaluation of the US currency have created silver and gold 'liberty dollars' as an alternative.

> For information on liberty dollars see:
> **www.libertydollar.org**

It might be that for ecological reasons a community would prefer to link its currency to a basket of locally produced, valuable commodities such as wood, food products or other forms of local production. This money is backed by commodities that, it is hoped, will keep their value in ways that 'fiat', paper currencies fail to.

Of course, if the price of the commodities that commodity-backed currencies are based on changes, so will the value of commodity-backed currencies. As discussed in Chapter 2, we saw this in the sixteenth century when the huge new supplies of American silver and gold led to the great inflation of that century. To avoid this the proposal is that any new commodity-backed currency should be based on a broad basket of commodities, so that changes in the price of the individual commodities in the basket will even each other out and the currency will prove to be more stable than those we currently have. The commodities chosen should be those that we rely on for our daily life (food, metals, minerals, energy) and not subject to wild fluctuations. On this basis, oil and gas might not be sensible commodities to base a currency on.

Ralph Borsodi created an inflation-free currency – the constant – which circulated in the town of Exeter, New

Hampshire (population 9,000) as an experiment in 1972. Constants were sold for dollars, and the proceeds invested in a basket of 30 key commodities such as gold, silver, iron, copper, coal, oil, wheat, barley, wool, coffee, hides and sugar. Borsodi kept the value of the currency stable by arbitraging between the value of these 30 commodities on the international markets: he successfully moved his holdings in commodities whose value was changing to keep his basket stable. A constant sold for $2.18 at the beginning of the experiment paid out $2.19, at a time when inflation in the USA averaged 3 per cent (it doubled to 6 per cent in 1973, and reached 11 per cent in 1974).

The value of the constant was based on Borsodi's skill as an arbitrager, but we have seen in previous chapters that there are long-term plans for BerkShares and some of the Transition currencies to delink from backing in national currency. They may move to backing based on the value of a local basket of commodities. How well this works in practice is an issue for local experimentation.

These are not just ideas developed by local-currency enthusiasts. The eminent economist Nicky Kaldor argued for a new global commodity currency to replace the dollar as the world's reserve currency.

Energy currencies

Other valuable commodities could be used to back alternative currencies: what about power? Local currency innovator Shann Turnbull has developed proposals for 'Energy Dollars' – currencies backed by renewable energy that properly reflect the cost of generating renewable power locally. Turnbull argues that as the fuel for renewable energy is effectively free, the cost of renewable energy should be a fraction of the costs of non-renewable energy where fuel has a cost. Wind and wave power is free – you have to buy

oil, gas and coal. The reason why renewable energy is not as cheap as this line of thinking would suggest it could be, he argues, is the cost of providing the generating equipment in the first place, which is a sunk cost that needs to be funded at commercial rates of interest. If a zero-interest currency backed by the cost of generating a unit of renewable energy were established, Turnbull argues, the cost of renewable energy would plummet.

This assumes that a form of energy-based currency could be established that would be accepted by, and be spendable by, the businesses that produce the generators – a macro-economic reform that might be rather utopian at present.

Contracting and converging energy currencies

We do have a form of energy currency that is just emerging – carbon trading permits. Carbon trading requires large businesses to buy permits that enable them to emit carbon. They can trade permits that they don't need with another company that needs to emit more carbon than it has permits for. At the time of writing this applies only to very large carbon-intensive businesses such as power stations or large chemical works, but in the UK more and more companies are finding that they have to buy these permits as the Government's Carbon Reduction Commitment kicks in.

The UK economy must cut its carbon emissions by 80 per cent by 2050, and there are also targets before then. As the economy's total carbon budget reduces over time, the number of permits that can be issued will be progressively reduced under what is known as 'cap and trade'. Permits will progressively become more valuable, and will almost certainly become tradable financial products in their own right. They could evolve into a new way of valuing energy alongside conventional currencies.

Taking these arguments further, Richard Douthwaite argues for the establishment of a more robust energy-based currency based on a unit of energy generated by fossil fuels, on the grounds that sound money should be based on a resource that is, and – if we are to avoid dangerous climate change, should be – limited.[2] He proposes the global adoption of Aubrey Meyer's proposals for 'contraction and convergence'. Under these proposals, the planet's energy budget should be calculated and divided up among the world population, initially on the basis of per capita usage. But the budget for rich countries should progressively contract and that of poor countries should expand, until energy use in rich countries converges with that of poor counties on a per capita basis at sustainable levels of CO_2 emissions – 80 per cent lower than today.

Obviously, this would put a premium on the development of renewable energy, not subject to a cap as no CO_2 is emitted. This more finite currency could be traded to permit carbon emissions, but the number of credits in circulation would be far, far more limited, and hence valuable, than in the existing carbon trading system.

For more on contraction and convergence see:
www.gci.org.uk

Personal carbon credit cards

In 2006 the then climate change secretary David Miliband speculated:

> [Imagine] we carry bank cards that store both pounds and carbon points. When we buy electricity, gas and fuel, we use our carbon points, as well as pounds. To help reduce carbon emissions, the Government would set limits on the amount of carbon that could be used.

To pay for any activity that requires carbon emissions, you would need to pay in national *and* carbon currencies: for instance, filling the car with fuel might cost you £50 and 50 carbon units.

Miliband was quickly jumped on by the then Prime Minister, for whom this resonated too much with wartime rationing and austerity. But we might find that the provision of a smart card that held everyone's personal carbon allowance, and which would need to hold sufficient carbon credits for any goods or services that emitted carbon to be purchased, becomes increasingly necessary in the future to avoid dangerous climate change.[3]

High-energy users would need to purchase additional carbon credits, and low-energy users would be able to sell their surplus credits, thus incentivising energy saving and sustainable behaviour from the bottom up. People could individually decide on the trade-offs between unsustainable forms of behaviour – for example, giving up driving in return for an otherwise unaffordable, in carbon credits, flight. Each year the personal budget would be reduced, but there would be some element of personal choice in how this was accomplished.

As with any cap-and-trade scheme, personal carbon budgets would contract down to sustainable levels over time. Some argue that these units could be traded, and this would be a resource available to those who currently emit little carbon, especially those in the global South. Others are concerned that this would allow the rich to keep their profligate ways by buying credits – a strategy not open to the poor. And others say that given that domestic carbon emissions are such a major proportion of global emissions, there is no alternative to regulation of individual emissions, and the commodification of carbon emissions into a currency would be the fairest way to achieve this.

Recycling credits and rewards

At the time of writing there is no empirical evidence about how personal carbon credits as a currency could work. We can draw some lessons from experiments with recycling credits in Brazil, and 'green points' in the Netherlands (see boxes on pages 210 and 211). Carbon credits could be piloted locally, and there are plans to do this in Salford, Greater Manchester.

Community rewards

There is nothing to stop a Transition Initiative similarly connecting energy efficiency and local food production in a local reward scheme. But a number of issues would need to be overcome. Firstly, the problem of political opposition to 'rationing' and to the State having access to another way for knowing what we are doing would need to be overcome. The University of Salford's survey was undertaken just after Manchester's residents had overwhelmingly thrown out proposals for a congestion charge zone in the city, which would have seen significant new investment in public transport. The low levels of interest in paying anything at all for flood defences and for energy efficiency reflects the poverty of the area, but also needs to be put in the context of local politics.

If such a proposal were piloted at the same time as identity cards it might smack too much of 'Big Brother' micro-regulation of personal behaviour, given that, for

Green Rewards, Salford, England

A team led by Erik Bichard at the University of Salford has been investigating proposals for green points as an incentive for installing energy-efficiency and flood-prevention measures, on top of the existing incentive of lower energy bills. The greener your behaviour, the more points you earn. The team wanted to find out whether a reward scheme would be attractive, and what sort of rewards potential users would want.

It carried out a survey in a deprived part of Salford where less than 50 per cent of respondents had loft insulation, wall insulation, double glazing, efficient boilers or energy-saving appliances. Findings were mixed.

Just under half of those surveyed were unwilling to pay anything for flood-protection and energy-saving improvements to their houses. Around a quarter of respondents were uninterested in participating in any green rewards scheme. Over half would like to receive between 100 per cent and 200 per cent of the investment they would make.

However, nearly a quarter of the respondents would invest over £500, which implies that even in the areas suffering from deprivation there is a potential for the implementation of a reward scheme. Nearly 80 per cent of respondents said they would be strongly motivated by the possibility of savings on electricity bills.

Nearly half of the respondents were interested in participation in a green reward scheme for investing in flood protection or energy saving. The most popular rewards were vouchers for fruit and vegetables (52 per cent of positive answers), followed by free meals at restaurants (44 per cent), tickets for entertainment (33 per cent) and vouchers for leisure and health centres (27 per cent). The least popular reward was free bus travel, which can be expected in the area where a high proportion of people already have access to it because of their age.

The findings suggested that a reward scheme should be piloted in Salford, with fruit and vegetables being the primary reward. This would connect policies for adaptation to climate change with the promotion of healthy eating.

many, climate change is still a problem to be encountered far in the future. Marketing would be crucial. George Marshall's work on what sort of people respond to what sort of climate change message provides some valuable insights in this context.[6]

There are innumerable small-scale, hidden examples of individuals encouraging each other into sustainable forms of consumption through the use of local and alternative currencies and though conversations with friends in alternative-currency networks, through which people share knowledge and tips, and encourage and support each other to cut their personal carbon emissions. People share cars, pass around home-grown food and the seeds to grow it, grow vegetables together in shared gardens, allotments and through 'guerrilla gardening', build each other wormeries and pass on tips on successful recycling. They use Freecycle to share and reuse things that they no longer need. This is all happening anyway. Local currencies can help lubricate this, and make these hidden networks available to those outside them. The networks then benefit from the 'strength of weak ties' (see Chapter 6, page 92).

There is nothing to stop a Transition Initiative or carbon-rationing action group adopting locally defined carbon credits as a way to monitor and reduce their personal energy consumption, as a way of educating themselves about their energy use, and as a way to show others what can be done locally to combat climate change. This may not be high-tech at all.

These credits could be issued for free, and reduced over time. Or a group could insist that its members buy credits, and the money raised used to offset necessary emissions. For example, a currency has been created in New Zealand that offsets, for example, a year's driving. Of course, some people have issues with offsetting, which they see as akin to the medieval practice of selling indulgences. They argue that offsetting just rationalises unsustainable consumption. But a genuinely limited currency backed with sterling that is used to offset emissions could really make its users think about their consumption, and provide a resource to help fund the development of a local, low-carbon economy.

Community-created energy currencies
We could envisage 'Deli Dollars'-style (see page 129) local energy currencies. A community-based micro-power generation cooperative or company could sell 'energy dollars' or 'energy pounds' to its potential customers for national currency, and the cash so generated could be used to buy and install renewable energy generation. The energy dollars could then be cashed in, over time, by the holders of the energy dollars to pay their bills with an energy-generating company if the network was off-grid. It would effectively be an interest-free loan for a new energy company.

Cap and share
Proposals for 'cap and share' suggest that citizens are issued with a share of the country's carbon budget in the form of a voucher which they can then cash in, or opt to 'kill' by not cashing it. The small number of companies who introduce fossil fuels into the economy (oil, gas and coal companies) would have to buy these permits from the citizenry, thus putting democratic control over emissions. The more shares that are killed, the smaller the pot from which emissions can be purchased, and the higher the price for carbon. See www.capandshare.org

We could see photovoltaics being installed using the same means. Instead of individuals paying for the installation of solar panels themselves and just having them on one house (which can often not be very efficient or cost-effective), a group of neighbours on a terraced street or a parade of local shops, for example, could set up a cooperative and turn their roof space into a solar power station. They could use a currency that circulates amongst themselves to fund it, which is redeemed with income from feed in tariffs (money earned from selling your energy to the grid).

We have working examples of how this might happen, but without the currency. Westmill Wind Farm Cooperative in South Oxfordshire is the first 100-per-cent community-owned wind farm in the UK, established in 2004 with support from renewable energy specialists Energy4All. Half of the £7.6 million funding for the farm's five turbines came from the public issuance of Industrial and Provident Society share capital, tradable for five years. Fintry Development Trust in Scotland owns a windmill, part of a local wind farm. The Meadows Ozone Community Energy Company in Nottingham is exploring ways to fund a local windmill, perhaps through a bond. Finally, West Oxford Community Renewables is working with small local businesses to install photovoltaics on the roofs of local shops.

This model could be used to fund the development a range of local, low-carbon initiatives. For example, local currencies have been used to develop local food production. We saw in Chapter 10 how agriculture in the Berkshires was supported by the community with Farm Preserve Notes (page 129). Unicorn food co-op in Manchester was developed using LETS. A number of time banks have community gardens. Local power

Curitiba, Brazil

Curitiba is a city grown explicitly on public transport rather than the car.[4] The city has dedicated express bus lanes and specially designed bus stop 'tubes' that enable large numbers of people to enter and leave the bus quickly, and pay in advance. There is a set social fare that subsidises the poor out on the urban fringes. One fare is payable per journey (even if you change buses), and there is easy exchange between express and local feeder buses. This publicly funded infrastructure makes it easy to use public transport, so it is easy 'being green'.

The public-transport infrastructure is connected to the city's waste management infrastructure. Curitiba has 'garbage that is not garbage' and 'garbage exchange' programmes. The 'garbage that is not garbage' programme is aimed at encouraging recycling in communities that have refuse collection services. Seventy per cent of people do separate out their recyclable waste as a result.

The 'garbage exchange' programme operates in the informal settlements that do not have recycling services, as the recycling trucks can't get in because of the poor state of the roads. Without this programme residents would just dump their waste in insanitary piles in the street.

To deal with this recycling problem, and to promote social inclusion by making it easy for residents of the outer squatter settlements to get into the city on public transport, recycling and the bus system are integrated. The city 'buys' recycling with bus tickets, and dairy and agricultural produce. Thus, bus tickets and food are used to incentivise recycling in an integrated system where the provision of public transport encourages and rewards sustainable behaviour. Residents who recycle get something tangible in return – bus tickets and wholesome food.

generation is a little more complex, given the huge, multi-million cost of large-scale power generation through windmills. Perhaps the solution is to explore ways to fund community-owned micro-generation with 'Deli Dollars'-style energy currencies.

Electronic currencies

Many complementary currencies could be run electronically from a smart card. Some alternative-currency enthusiasts have long argued that paper forms of currency are very much last year's models. Credit cards and other electronic forms of payment are the high-tech solution. The business-to-business barter networks that inspired LETS have long used 'smart card' technology, as does the Swiss WIR business network, which since the 1930s has allowed businesses to exchange with each other using a low- or no-interest currency. Regiogeld's

partner local banks have provided electronic fund transfer at point-of-sale facilities.

Others are concerned that electronic currencies are a high-tech solution, beyond the means of many local Transition Initiatives and vulnerable to system collapse in a world where the availability of the fossil fuels on which our complex society is built decreases. They think that smaller-scale community-based programmes built using simple technologies are more resilient.

Business-to-business barter generally focuses on growing a business, not on building local resilience. But there have been more recent experiments with more ethically focused business exchanges that do aim to build local resilience and support local business, but using high-tech means. For example, the Vermont Sustainable Exchange is an online ethical marketplace

Rotterdam, the Netherlands

In Rotterdam the *NU Spaarpas* was a 'green loyalty point' currency that was piloted from May 2002 to September 2003. 'Green points' were earned when residents separated their waste for recycling, used public transport, or used locally owned shops. Points could be redeemed for public transport tickets or discounts on sustainable products such as organic, energy-efficient and fair-trade goods, bicycles, green financial products, renewable energy, rental, repairs and second-hand goods. Consumers could also spend points on leisure activities around the city, such as going to the cinema. Card scanners in participating shops, paid for by those businesses and managed by a partner bank, fed data into a central set of accounts.

According to the organisers,[5] by the end of the pilot period 10,000 households had the card, over 100 shops were participating, and 1.5 million points had been issued. The number of points issued and cashed was, however, much lower than foreseen because the system came up to speed much later than expected and the number of places to spend the points was still quite limited at the end of the pilot.

The main barriers to success faced during the project related to creating publicity material that successfully attracted participants, and (as has been the case elsewhere) persuading retailers to take part and to install the card scanners. A pilot of just over one year is a very short time to test a project like this, and many alternative currency projects take some time to gain wide acceptance. Furthermore, it is unrealistic to expect such a programme to be self-supporting through fees paid by participating businesses, who see little incentive in participating in something so experimental. Further development of what seemed to be a promising project was terminated through a lack of funding.

that facilitates business-to-business exchange with an agenda that seems indistinguishable from that of a Transition Initiative. Businesses pool the credit they issue to each other into a common marketplace, where local goods and services are bought and sold and loans in the electronic currency are issued to willing entrepreneurs.

The Vermont Sustainable Exchange has the following value statement, to which businesses must subscribe.

"I believe:
- in my neighbours, colleagues, and friends
- the way I do business reflects on my character
- respect and dignity are important to my business
- we can empower and trust each other to do what is right."

For more on the Vermont Sustainable Exchange see: www.changethemarket.com

Beyond having businesses exchanging virtual credits with each other over the web, the main barrier to entry for electronic currencies is the cost of the smart card and the readers. A partner like the corporate barter trade association IRTA (International Reciprocal Trade Association), which has been forging links with community currencies, might overcome this barrier.

For information on the International Reciprocal Trade Association (IRTA) – business-to-business barter – see: www.irta.com

Local currencies for students?

Dannie Grufferty, President of Liverpool University Guild of Students, is discussing piloting three complementary currencies specifically for students.

- An electronic local currency on the student's NUS cards that will hold currency that can be spent for printing, for entry to the university sports centre and for purchases in Guild shops.
- A university-sponsored paper currency that students will spend with local businesses, perhaps for ethically sourced fair-trade goods. This currency is designed to promote ethical consumption practices amongst students, and support the local businesses that students often live amongst – and to whom they are not always the best of neighbours.
- A time currency to reward students for volunteering, which perhaps can be offset against student loans.

We should also remember that many useful technologies are becoming cheaper, more accessible and easy to use, and more available than ever before. More and more people collaborate on interesting technological development using open-source approaches – they share the knowledge for free. We can use this technology for good.

Three examples of electronic currency are worthy of mention.

Ireland: the Liquidity Network

The aim of the Liquidity Network is to address the slowdown in economic activity in Ireland triggered by the credit crunch. In an economy powered by debt-based credit, individuals and businesses borrow in order to finance many of their activities. Using the credit released by these loans they employ or do business with other individuals and businesses, who in turn do business with their suppliers, and so on. When the 'seed' credit from banks dries up, as in the crisis that broke out in 2007-8, the system can break down. As Ireland is part of the Eurozone this is a particular problem for a country that has given up control of its own currency. It's economy has not been reflated by the government printing new money, as the government had given up that power. Ireland is consequently seeing 1930s-style cuts in spending, and its economy is stagnating as a result. Employees have had their pay cut in response to the crisis, and in 2009 the money supply declined by 23 million Euros.

Under these conditions, Ireland's FEASTA, the Foundation for the Economics of Sustainability, is developing proposals for a 'Liquidity Network' that will create an alternative, electronic 'liquidity stream' that is not based on debt, in the form of an electronic currency – Quids. Local authorities and participating businesses, with the consent of their workforce, would pay up to 10 per cent of salaries in Quids (as an alternative to a pay cut), while new participants in the network would be given a balance of Quids. Quids would be in electronic form, and held on a smart card or on your mobile phone: you pay by SMS.

Participating businesses would accept Quids in part payment, and councils would accept them for rates, parking charges and the like. In Ireland, car taxes are collected locally. Interestingly, the Liquidity Network would incentivise people to use Quids by rewarding active members – the more you spend, the bigger the bonus. Conversely, there is demurrage. If you don't spend credits, they rust.

Quids are just on the drawing board at the time of writing. Transition Kilkenny and Kilkenny Future Proof have been discussing the idea with Kilkenny's Green Party mayor and with Ireland's Green Environment Minister. The Kilkenny Chamber of Commerce already runs a loyalty scheme, so the local version of Quids, to be called 'Kilkenny Kats', is receiving positive interest.

Quids are seen as a temporary measure, to be withdrawn when bank lending returns and Euros re-circulate. The readers will cost about one hundred Euros. Whether businesses are prepared to pay this remains to be seen: we saw this was a problem with the *NU Spaarpas* card in the Netherlands (see page 211).

For more on the Liquidity Network see:
http://theliquiditynetwork.org

Kenya: mobile phone money

Farmers in Africa have found cheap mobile phones to be of immense benefit. Not only are tips about how to grow food and warnings of possible dangers passed around by text, but farmers can get up-to-date market prices for their crops. A currency called M-PESA (*pesa* is Swahili for 'money') has been attached to mobile phones. A registered user can put money into his or her account at an M-PESA agent and send it to other mobile phone users by SMS instruction. The recipient can then retrieve the money from another agent. These outlets include local mobile dealers, petrol stations, supermarkets and kiosks. M-PESA works where mobile phones are cheap but people don't have access to a bank. This is not a community currency – it's run by Vodaphone and financed by the British Department of International Development. But the principle of a parallel currency exchanged through SMS is interesting, and worthy of more development.

For more on mobile phone money see: http://lite.alertnet.org/db/ blogs/55868/2009/01/13-151104-1.htm

France: solidarity money

In France, an innovative and interesting complementary currency system, the SOL, has been tested in seven regions since 2004, funded by the European Social Fund. Four social economy organisations are involved: Chèque Déjeuner (a workers' cowoperative and a leading French voucher issuer), Crédit Coopératif (a cooperative bank), and MACIF and MAIF (two mutual insurers). The SOL system is an electronic card that works in Chèque Déjeuner's eftpos machines, which combines three types of complementary currency.

- The 'Co-operation SOL' is an inter-enterprise loyalty e-card created to promote the social economy. The currency unit is denominated in Euro equivalents. A social economy organisation can give SOL points to a 'solist' (someone who uses SOLs), who can use them anywhere in the SOL network. The SOL points suffer from demurrage: a solist who doesn't use his or her SOLs loses them gradually, which encourages solists to spend them instead of saving them. The SOL points that have been cancelled through demurrage are invested in a mutual fund, managed by all the solists, to support social economy projects.

- The 'Commitment SOL' is a time currency.

- The 'Dedicated SOL', a currency given by the public sector to specific target groups, allowing them to access specific goods or services. This is a tool for public authorities.

The interesting thing about SOL is its ability to combine three objectives in one smart card. SOLs can be used to stimulate local activities, to develop the social economy, and to promote sustainable consumption. The system is also focused, like time banking, on the socially and economically excluded. How successful it is in this aim will require further research. And, as with other electronic currencies, the use of smart card technology might be of interest to the not-completely-technophobic!

For more on SOLs see: http://lavieverte.wordpress. com/2008/01/02/alternative-currency-project-in-five-french-regions

Local loyalty cards

Of course, a simple local loyalty scheme need not be electronic or involve storing and spending points: it can just be a card entitling the bearer to a 10-per-cent discount at participating stores.

Local loyalty cards are local versions of store cards, and there are hundreds of examples.[7] Quick, cheap and simple to set up, a local loyalty card might be the best way to attune local businesses that are completely unfamiliar with concepts such as localisation or Transition to these ideas. Start with a loyalty card, then gift some vouchers into the economy on a time-limited basis, and see how it goes. Or follow the idea of the Manchester Green Pound, a web-based voucher scheme for local fair trade and green businesses with 5 per cent of the purchase price going towards carbon-reduction projects being run around the city. If this works, local businesses might listen to ideas about a more substantial local currency with more open ears.

For information on the Manchester Green Pound see:
www.greenpoundvoucher.com

A Christmas loyalty card from Bold Street, Liverpool.

Transition Falmouth has watched the development of Transition currencies with avid interest, but seen the idea as a step beyond its capabilities. It decided instead to work with what it had – a loyalty card developed by local business, for local business, but which still encourages people to spend their money with Falmouth businesses.

For information on the Falmouth Shopper Card see:
http://falmouthshoppercard.co.uk

Alternative financial institutions

In thinking about 'local money', you don't have to restrict yourself to creating your own currency – why not think of ways of making the conventional money we already have work for us and our community, not for things that contribute to climate change, resource depletion, war or injustice? We need a vibrant ecosystem of different currencies and financial institutions that we control that use national currency, local or regional currency, or a range of currencies. The following are some more ideas about how to use conventional money in more interesting ways.

Local banks

One thing that jumps out when comparing local currencies in the USA or German regional currencies with those in the UK is the involvement of local banks. The support and involvement of the five local banks in BerkShares is a crucial part of its success. The bank managers were central in designing the programme. Of course, our local banks have long disappeared through mergers and acquisitions, so that option is closed to us in the UK. Most of the municipal banks in England and Scotland were taken over by the Trustee Savings Bank in the 1960s and 1970s (now part of Lloyds TSB). Six municipal banks still exist in Scotland, the biggest one being North Lanarkshire, with approximately 11,000 active accounts and offices in eleven local council buildings.

It is almost certainly too much to expect a community-based group like a Transition Initiative to set up a fully-fledged local bank. Unless you have a qualified banker in your Transition group, the levels of regulation would make this very time consuming, if they didn't prohibit it completely. However, some local authorities (interestingly, Conservative-Party-controlled ones) are experimenting with the establishment of local banks to loan council funds to local businesses.

Essex

Essex County Council's 'Banking on Essex' project has developed a partnership with the Spanish multinational bank Santander. Santander provides the expertise to loan £30 million, split 50/50 between the council and the bank, as loans and overdrafts of up to £100,000 for viable Essex businesses that employ fewer than 250 people, have a turnover of less than £25 million, and who have been trading for more than a year. Santander is talking to other local authorities about similar partnerships.

For more on Banking on Essex see:
www.bankingonessex.com

Birmingham

Birmingham ran a municipal bank, which operated as a council department, for 60 years between 1916 and 1976. In 2008 the council examined reviving a Birmingham Municipal Bank to provide investment funding for Birmingham-based enterprises and banking-style services for individuals. Three elements were considered: mortgages, asset-backed loans and deposit accounts. A working group explored proposals, and decided that setting up a new institution might be too great a task to be achieved for real support to be delivered to businesses in time to make a difference.

After some consideration, it was decided that meeting the regulatory requirements of the Financial Services Authority (FSA) and recruiting suitable staff would be difficult hurdles to overcome quickly. Like Essex, Birmingham discussed a partnership with Santander, but decided to build on the local institutions it and Advantage West Midlands, the Regional Development Agency, had already established, such as the Aston Reinvestment Trust (see page 217) and another organisation, Investbx, which puts investors in touch with investment potentials. These institutions, it was felt, already had the necessary expertise to support local businesses, and putting council funding alongside the funds of other

agencies, the private sector and European funding could provide a pot of 10 million pounds to provide support investments of up to £50,000 to new firms with potential. The council is also working to support the development of banking facilities through local credit unions. Rather than set up a new agency, it decided to work with what it already had and put its finance alongside those of others in a package that included business advice, signposting to venture capital funds and connections with business angels.

In different ways, Birmingham and Essex have overcome the two key issues anyone hoping to set up a new bank will need to grapple with. First, how do you set up an institution that meets regulatory requirements quickly enough that it makes a difference while maintaining credibility? Second, how do you ensure that a new municipal bank has the expertise and the confidence to loan to local businesses where the high-street banks have refused to help? Will their loans be so loose that money is wasted on unviable businesses, or will they have the confidence and skills to spot viable firms that the banks didn't? Getting the balance right will be fiendishly difficult.

Both Birmingham and Essex decided not to try to recreate a new institution, but build on what they had locally (Birmingham) or enter a partnership with someone who has the necessary skills (Essex). But a partnership with a bank might be like putting the fox in charge of the hen coop. Might the bank be just as conservative in its lending as it was before? What would be added beyond a local face to an otherwise unchanged situation of tight credit? Might it be possible to find someone locally who used to work in the financial sector and, aware of the problems, is interested in doing things differently? BerkShares seemed to be able to identify such individuals, who might form the germ of an interesting new breed of local financial vehicles using conventional cash.

Banks with a difference

Remember that some banks and building societies, such as Triodos Bank and the Ecology Building Society, already have a commitment to working with ecologically sustainable projects. Islamic banks, the Swiss WIR and Sweden's JAK bank have also pioneered interest-free saving and lending. Local pilots originating from more developed Transition Initiatives could take these ideas much further.

Community Development Financial Institutions

It's not necessary to set up a full bank. There are other examples of local financial vehicles providing finance for local businesses, such as SHARE (see Chapter 10) or the Aston Reinvestment Trust (ART), which supports small businesses and social enterprises in Birmingham and Solihull.

ART was established by a community-based group, the Aston Commission, which involved local groups, voluntary sector organisations and businesses. Having identified the problems faced by Aston Ward in inner-city Birmingham, a key recommendation was the establishment of a community-based finance institution.

Funded with grant support, an initial feasibility study was carried out in 1989, and a business plan developed in 1992 that built on models in the USA and elsewhere. Opening its doors in 1997, it has loaned between £10,000 and £50,000 to businesses that need funds to survive or grow but have been unable to secure them from conventional sources. The loan could be for cash flow or to support a capital investment project. It could be part of a finance package with other financiers, or stand alone. Repayment terms vary from 6 months to 10 years. Between June 1997 and December 2008 ART made over 400 loans totalling over 7 million pounds, creating or safeguarding over 3,000 jobs.

For more on the Aston Reinvestment Trust see:
www.reinvest.co.uk

ART is not the only Community Development Financial Institution (CDFI). If you look at the websites of the Development Trusts Association or the Community Development Finance Association, you'll find much inspiration.

Development Trusts Association:
www.dta.org.uk

Community Development Finance Association:
www.cdfa.org.uk

Community Land Trusts

Community Land Trusts (CLTs) allow communities to take valuable land out of the reach of developers, keeping that resource in the hands of the community. This matters, as often the cost of building a new house, perhaps to very high ecological standards, will not be very high at all – it's the land that is expensive. Community Land Trusts take the land out of the equation, and ensure that people who buy houses on CLT land do not make a huge profit when they sell them. They can't rent them out. Homes are for living in, not commodities.
See www.communitylandtrust.org.uk

Credit unions

If we do not have local banks in the UK, we should work more closely with what we do have – credit unions. Credit unions are financial cooperatives owned by and run by their members, which provide finance for those who cannot get a conventional bank account, or for employees of a company.

People wishing to set up a credit union need to have what is known as a 'common bond' – something that connects them, like a common place of residence (it should be a fairly tightly drawn community, such as a district, not a whole city) or employer – or be composed of people who belong to the same association, such as a church or trade union.

Credit unions in England, Scotland and Wales provided services to over three-quarters of a million people in 2009, compared with just 325,000 credit union members in 2000. According to figures from the Financial Services Authority, there were over 655,000 adult members and over 96,000 junior savers in British credit unions in June 2008. Worldwide, there are some 118 million members of 40,258 credit unions in 79 countries.

Members save a regular small amount, and can then, in time, get a low-interest loan. Credit unions in the UK are generally quite small-scale, and in poorer, unbanked areas of cities, so they could be useful ways of getting people from these communities involved in Transition. But they provide only personal finance, not business loans. These are invaluable to people on low incomes who otherwise would be reliant on a loan shark, but it is hard to see how they might contribute to the building of a low-carbon economy unless they were able to move into the small-business support sector, or helped manage a local currency.

In the USA and Ireland, however, credit unions are much more substantial organisations offering a full range of banking services. As an alternative to a local bank this might be the aspiration for deeper Transition. In Ireland, 50 per cent of the population belongs to a credit union; in the USA and Australia the figure is around 30 per cent.

For more about credit unions in the UK see:
www.abcul.org

Microcredit

Another example of a community-based financial institution is the Norfolk-based Women's Employment Enterprise and Training Unit (WEETU), which has provided business support and small loans to women setting up businesses since 1987. WEETU is inspired by Bangladesh's Grameen microfinance bank, which provides poor women with very small amounts of money as loans, with the collateral based on a mutual agreement between a number of women to pay the loan back. If one person defaults, no one else in the network gets a loan – so the default rate is near zero.

WEETU encourages groups of four to six women to form an Enterprise Circle, to provide each other with mutual support and to combat feelings of isolation. The women then put in a collective application for finance, based on their commitment to each other – no other credit checks are carried out. Members accept responsibility for supporting other members to find a resolution to any problems and to share information and advice, but have no financial responsibility to each other.

For more on the Women's Employment Enterprise and Training Unit see: www.weetu.org

Local bonds

In the USA and other countries, where there is more of a stress on localities charting their own destinies, it is not uncommon for local administrations to issue their own bonds. They raise money from the markets with a promise to pay the money back at a certain rate of interest or at a certain time, just as companies and national governments do.

The former Mayor of London, Ken Livingstone, looking at the example of New York, suggested a bond issue as an alternative to the privatisation of the London Underground, something vigorously opposed by the then Chancellor Gordon Brown, although £600 million of bonds were issued and snapped up by investors. Colin Hines, Co-Director of Finance for the Future, has suggested the issuance of a new range of local bonds, for example a 'Brummie Bond' in Birmingham, to finance the upgrade of our urban infrastructure and to install community-level heat and power schemes to cope with climate change. Money raised through Sheffield's Green Bond is spent on environmental improvements: by 2009 some £180,000 had been raised from people and businesses across the city. A green bond is under consideration in a number of other places, including Liverpool and Cornwall. Liverpool

For more on Sheffield's Green Bond see:
www.sheffieldsgreenbond.org.uk

For Liverpool and Sefton Social Investment Bond see:
www.charitybank.org/liverpool

and Sefton Councils have a Social Investment Bond providing affordable loan finance to fund new social enterprises in north Liverpool.

Putting it all together

Now we have reviewed all the different complementary currency options and other financial vehicles that we might use to deepen Transition, it is time to start to think about how they might fit together into a wider financial ecosystem – one that provides real local resilience and helps us to generate the enjoyable, convivial forms of making a living that we want to see as we make the transition from our high-carbon, high-intensity, unsustainable world. How do the elements fit together?

We can see a LETS scheme or time bank being used for local production and exchange of things we can produce at home or in a local community – helping each other out; sharing food grown on allotments; renovating each other's houses. More complex goods would be produced by local businesses, perhaps using a local or regional scrip or at a national level, a WIR-like scheme or a business-to-business exchange. More local production could be developed using local currency loans, or through a local bank or financial vehicle. Special-purpose currencies could finance local food production and Community Supported Agriculture, and local power generation. Local bonds could finance a major renovation of our housing stock and a new green infrastructure to replace our out-of-date Victorian inheritance.

CHAPTER 17
SOME CLOSING THOUGHTS

From circulation to production – building deeper local resilience using local currencies

I hope that this book has been of use in considering how alternative currencies might contribute to the Transition process. I believe they have great potential, but it is important not to over-estimate what they can achieve straight away, or the amount of work it takes to make the currency work over the long run. Setting up a paper currency takes time and might be something for later stages of Transition, in smaller towns with lots of locally owned businesses and the potential to develop a high level of local resilience. Making a paper currency work in a large city will need the involvement of other players – the council, economic development agencies, the chamber of commerce. It will need championship by someone respected by local business owners. But setting up a LETS, time bank or a special-purpose currency is much simpler.

It's important to remember the lessons of monetary theory, which frankly were ignored by some in the early days of the development of complementary currencies, and in Argentina, with predictable results. Changing the form of money won't necessarily change the 'real' economy, although it can help to nurture things we would like to see – people's skills respected and developed; more local production, food and power.

The form of money is not set in stone. It does change over time, and we can contribute to that process of evolution by experimenting with new forms of money. It does not need to be formally backed with a commodity, with real 'stuff', but we do need to believe, and our experience needs to confirm that belief, that we can get real 'stuff' with it when we want to.

Remember that, for some, being able to pay your way is better than feeling obligated, while some want to build closer relationships and feelings of community. Money is useful in some environments. In others, national currency works just fine, while elsewhere pure cooperation is what people want, and using money may feel inappropriate.

Climate change, peak oil and relocalisation

Climate change will mean that in a post-carbon economy there will be a stronger relationship between a place and its wider ecosystem. In his book *The Long Descent*, John Greer[1] argues that we don't need to panic. Peak oil and climate change will not end in the apocalypse. Rather, he argues, complex societies like ours will go through a slow, difficult process of decline down the other side of the peak oil 'curve' until society and the ecosystem are back in balance.

He argues that some societies have handled a rise and fall better than others, comparing China's ancient civilization, with its ebbs and flows, with societies that have collapsed, like the Maya. But, he argues, even the Maya civilisation took 200 years or so to decline.

Peak oil, of course, does not mean that we are running out of oil completely – just that we are running out of cheap oil and not discovering enough new supplies to keep pace with consumption. We will see a cumulative and irreversible decline in the availability of oil but, Greer says, this will be no worse a shock than society handled in the Second World War or the 1970s. We can also look at Cuba's special period, where the loss of Soviet aid led to a resurgence of urban food production and organic gardening.[2] We can handle the change.

Moving from a large, complex integrated society like ours to one based on self reliance will take time. Greer argues that we can prepare for peak oil and climate change by radically cutting our own energy usage, living nearer to work, using sustainable locally generated fuel, and growing more of our food locally. Much more will be produced in households and a local economy. People will not be able to rely on State provision and will have to look after their own needs more through home or community provision. People will need to practise and develop new skills, developing a second, 'useful' profession producing things people use and need.

Complementary currencies such as LETS and time banking are good ways for people to share skills and resources, and learn new skills. But they aren't up to the job of developing new forms of production. Here we need paper or electronic forms of local currency that will be taken seriously as ways of exchanging resources, so we can use them to finance new forms of production.

How do we start? Ask yourself: What can we produce locally? What will always have to be produced elsewhere given their complexity and questions of

local climate and resource endowments? Perhaps we should start with what we need in our everyday life: housing, heat, clothes, furniture, food. How much of that can we produce locally?

Then look at our resources. For example, we might be living in a wooded area, but produce no wooden furniture – an obvious thing to start to produce. Or we have sheep, but make no woollen clothes. How much land can be turned over for food production without replacing parks with industrial agriculture? What attractive edible plants could we replace our current ornamental plants with? What solar, wave or wind resource have we, and how much can we generate without destroying local ecosystems to do it? What are the climatic resources we have? Can you grow grapes? Is there enough rain? Localisation perhaps means different things in different places.

What could you produce locally that you don't currently, to meet local needs? What 'factors of production' – people, resources, machines, power sources – do you have locally that you could put together using a local currency? Could you buy the wood you need to set up local furniture production locally, paying for it with local money? Could you buy your power from a local renewable source? What about the machines to turn the wood? How would you market the product? Where would you sell it? How would you get it to the customer? And – crucially – *how much of this could be lubricated by local money?* If you could buy the things you need to develop local production, could the people who accept it spend it? What about the next wave of purchasing? When does the chain break; what sort of circuits can you get going so local money passes from person to person?

Eventually, you will get to a place where you physically can't produce something locally – wheat in the desert; grapes in North Norway. What do you do then? Do

without, or trade, but sustainably and fairly? And
what sort of globally equitable and sustainable forms
of money might lubricate that?

It's clear that moving from what we have – a global
behemoth, deeply unequal, unsustainable and without
a future – to the sort of world we want to see, and the
sort of world we want to avoid, will take some time.
Local currencies and the other innovations discussed
in this book are a part of the solution, and
I hope you have as much fun on the journey of
exploration, as you investigate the potential of these
alternative currencies and financial vehicles, as I have
had over the past fifteen or so years.

REFERENCES

Introduction: The vision

1 De Goede, M. (2005). *Virtue, Fortune and Faith: a genealogy of finance*. Minneapolis, University of Minnesota Press. pp.xiii-xiv.

2 Swann, R. and Witt, S. (1995). *Local Currencies: catalysts for sustainable regional economies*. Available at: www.schumachersociety.org/publications/essay_currency.html.

3 Quoted by Houriet, R. (1973). *Getting Back Together*. London, Abacus. p.266.

4 Hopkins, R. (2008) *The Transition Handbook: from oil dependency to local resilience*. Dartington, Green Books.

5 Joseph Chamberlain was a nineteenth-century Mayor of Birmingham and influential businessman and politician. See Hunt, T. (2004). *Building Jerusalem: the rise and fall of the Victorian city*. London, Phoenix.

6 Hopkins, R. (2008). *The Transition Handbook: from oil dependency to local resilience*. Dartington, Green Books.

Chapter 1: The money we have

1 Lomborg, B. (2001). *The Sceptical Environmentalist*. Cambridge, Cambridge University Press; Lomborg, B. (2007). *Cool It: the sceptical environmentalist's guide to global warming*. London, Marshall Cavendish.

2 Stern, N. (2007). *Stern Review of the Economics of Climate Change*. London, HM Treasury / The Cabinet Office.

3 Hayek, F. (1990). *Denationalisation of Money: the argument refined*. London, Institute of Economic Affairs.

Chapter 2: What is money – and can we change it?

1 Ingham, G. (2004). *The Nature of Money*. Cambridge, Polity.

2 Smith, A. (1776/1981). *The Wealth of Nations*. London, Pelican.

3 Lapavitsas, C. (2005). 'The emergence of money in commodity exchange, or money as monopolist of the ability to buy'. *Review of Political Economy*, **17**(4): 549-69.

4 Ferguson, N. (2008). *The Ascent of Money: a financial history of the world*. London, Penguin. pp.48-51.

5 Lapavitsas, C. (2003). *Social Foundations of Markets, Money and Credit*. London, Routledge.

6 Malinowski, B. (2007). *Argonauts of the Western Pacific*. London, Read Books. pp.124-46.

7 Mauss, M. (2001). *The Gift: form and reason for exchange in archaic societies*. London, Routledge.

8 Simmel, G. (1978/1908). *The Philosophy of Money*. London, Routledge.

9 Zelizer, V. (1997). *The Social Meaning of Money*. Princeton, Princeton University Press; Zelizer, V. (2005). *The Purchase of Intimacy*. Princeton, Princeton University Press.

10 Ingham, G. (2004). *The Nature of Money*. Cambridge, Polity. pp.47-50.

Chapter 3: Localisation

1 Jacobs, J. (1961). *The Death and Life of Great American Cities*. London, Penguin.

2 Chang, H.-J. (2007). *Bad Samaritans: the guilty secrets of rich nations and the threat to global prosperity*. London, Random House Business Books.

3 Jacobs, J. (1984). *Cities and the Wealth of Nations: principles of economic life*. London, Penguin.

4 See Bhagwati, J. (2004). *In Defense of Globalization*. Oxford, Oxford University Press;
Friedman, T. L. (2006). *The World is Flat: the globalized world in the twenty-first century*. London, Penguin;
Norberg, J. (2003). *In Defense of Global Capitalism*. Washington D.C., The Cato Institute;
Stiglitz, J. and Charlton, A. (2005). *Fair Trade for All: how trade can promote development*. Oxford, Oxford University Press;
Wolf, M. (2005). *Why Globalization Works*. New Haven, Yale Nota Bene.

5 Shuman, M. (2001). *Going Local: creating self-reliant communities in a global age*. London, Routledge.

6 For a deeper analysis, see North, P. (2010). 'Eco-Localisation as a progressive response to peak oil and climate change – a sympathetic critique'. *Geoforum* (issue to be confirmed).

Chapter 4: A brief history of complementary currencies
1 Dana, C. (1896). *Proudhon and his 'Bank of the People'*. New York, Benjamin R. Tucker.

2 Kantor, R. (1972). *Commitment and Community: communes and utopia in sociological perspective*. Cambridge, MA, Harvard University Press. p.391;
Woodcock, G. (1962/1986). *Anarchism: a history of libertarian ideas and movements*. Harmondsworth, Penguin.

3 Ferguson, N. (2008). *The Ascent of Money: a financial history of the world*. London, Penguin. pp.93-8.

4 Ferguson, N. (2008). *The Ascent of Money: a financial history of the world*. London, Penguin. p.98

5 Galbraith, J. (1975). *Money: whence it came, where it went*. London, Andre Deutsch. pp.93-110.

6 Goodwyn, L. (1976). *Democratic Promise: the populist moment in America*. Oxford, Oxford University Press. p.26.

7 Gesell, S. (1958). *The Natural Economic Order*. London, Owen.

8 Fisher, I. (1933). *Stamp Scrip*. New York, Adelphi. p.25.

9 Fisher, I. (1933). *Stamp Scrip*. New York, Adelphi.

10 Douglas, C. H. (1937). *Social Credit*. London, Eyre and Spottiswoode.

11 Drakeford, M. (1997). *Social Movements and Their Supporters: the Green Shirts in England*. Basingstoke, Macmillan.

Chapter 5: Local Exchange Trading Schemes
1 Stott, M. and Hodges, J. (1996). 'LETS: Never knowingly undersold?' *Local Economy* **11**(3): 266-8.

2 For more on the performance of LETS as a tool to help people into paid work see: Williams, C. C. et al. (2001). *Bridges into Work: an evaluation of Local Exchange Trading Schemes*. Bristol, The Policy Press.

Chapter 6: Time banking
1 Cahn, E. (2000). *No More Throw-away People*. London, HarperCollins.

2 Putnam, R. (2001). *Bowling Alone*. London, Simon and Schuster.

3 Granovetter, M. (1973). 'The strength of weak ties'. *American Journal of Sociology*, **78**(6): 1360-80.

4 nef (2008). *The New Wealth of Time: how time banking helps people build better services*. London, new economics foundation.

5 nef (2008). *The New Wealth of Time: how time banking helps people build better services*. London, new economics foundation.

Chapter 7: Ithaca and other 'hours'
1 See www.visitithaca.com/press/13.html.

2 Maurer, B. (2005). *Mutual Life, Limited: Islamic banking, alternative currencies, lateral reason*. Princeton, Princeton University Press.

3 Douthwaite, R. (1996). *Short Circuit: strengthening local economies for security in an uncertain world*. Dartington, Green Books. For more on Ithaca Hours see also: Boyle, D. (1999). *Funny Money: in search of alternative cash*. London, HarperCollins; Glover, P. (1995). 'Ithaca Hours'. In S. Meeker-Lowry, *Invested in the Common Good*. New York, New Society Publishers. pp.72-80.

Chapter 8: Argentina's barter networks

1 For a fuller analysis see North, P. (2007). *Money and Liberation: the micropolitics of alternative currency movements*. Minneapolis, University of Minnesota Press. (Chapter 8).

2 Blustein, P. (2005). *And the Money Kept Rolling In (and Out): Wall Street, the IMF and the bankrupting of Argentina*. New York, Public Affairs;
Rock, D. (2002). 'Racking Argentina'. *New Left Review* **2/17**: 55-86.

3 Auyero, J. (2000). *Poor People's Politics: Peronist survival networks and the legacy of Evita*. London, Duke University Press.

Chapter 11: The Totnes Pound

1 Lietaer, B. (2001). *The Future of Money*. London, Random House.

2 As reported by Schamotta, J. (2009): *Alternatives to the Pound: local currencies compete with sterling*. Available at http://personalbudgeting.suite101.com/article.cfm/alternatives_to_the_pound#ixzz0OA3Naybc.

3 See www.pdsr.co.uk/shopimages/prtotnespound.pdf.

Chapter 13: The Stroud Pound Co-op

1 See http://gaianeconomics.blogspot.com.

Chapter 14: The Brixton Pound

1 Sassen, S. (1991). *The Global City: New York, London, Tokyo*. Princeton, Princeton University Press.

Chapter 16: Towards a deeper ecosystem of currencies and local finance

1 BoBo: 'Bourgeois Bohemian'. Having a TV or a car is vulgar, but locally sourced vegetables are a sign of good taste and status. See: Brooks, D. (2000). *Bobos in Paradise: the new upper class and how they got there*. London, Simon and Schuster.

2 Douthwaite, R. (1999). *The Ecology of Money*. Dartington, Green Books.

3 Seyfang, G. (2007). *Personal Carbon Trading: lessons from complementary currencies*. Norwich, Centre for Social and Economic Research on the Global Environment.

4 Rabinovitch, J. (1992). 'Curitiba: towards sustainable urban development'. *Environment and Urbanization*, **4**(2): 62-73.

5 van Sambeek, P. and Kampers, E. (2004). *NU-Spaarpas: The Sustainable Incentives Card*. www.nuspaarpas.nl/www_en/pdf_en/NUspaarpasEN-GCH6.pdf. Stiching Points. Amsterdam.

6 Marshall, G. (2007). *Carbon Detox: your step-by-step guide to getting real about climate change*. Stroud, Gaia Books Ltd.

7 Worthington, S. (1998): 'Loyalty cards and the revitalisation of the town centre'. *International Journal of Retail & Distribution Management*, **26**(2): 66-77.

Chapter 17: Some closing remarks

1 Greer, J. (2008). *The Long Descent: a user's guide to the end of the industrial age*. Gabriola Island, BC, New Society Publishers.

2 See www.powerofcommunity.org.

RESOURCES AND FURTHER READING

This section provides a range of accessible books and articles, details of organisations working on the issues discussed in this book (including groups described in this book) and websites. If you do wish to contact the groups described in this book, please remember that often the people running these projects are doing it for the love of it: they are not paid. So please be economical in your requests for help and information, and respect their time. These days so much good information is available online that there shouldn't be much need to approach voluntary organisations for information.

Contents

Localisation

Books

Boyle, D and Simms, A. (2009). *The New Economics: a bigger picture*. London, Earthscan.

Cavanagh, J. and Mander, J. (eds) (2004). *Alternatives to Economic Globalization*. San Francisco, Berrett-Koehler Publishers.

DeFilippis, J. (2004). *Unmaking Goliath: community control in the face of global capital*. London, Routledge.

Douthwaite, R. (1996). *Short Circuit: strengthening local economies for security in an uncertain world*. Dartington, Green Books. (O/P)

Estill, L. (2008). *Small is Possible: life in a local economy*. Gabriola Island, BC, New Society Publishers.

McKibben, B. (2007). *Deep Economy: the wealth of communities and the durable future*. New York, Times Books.

Shuman, M. (2001). *Going Local: creating self-reliant communities in a global age*. London, Routledge.

Organisations promoting localisation

Business Alliance for Local Living Economies (BALLE) (USA)
Bellingham, Washington
(+1) 415 255 1108
www.livingeconomies.org

North America's fastest-growing network of socially responsible businesses, comprised of over 80 community networks with over 21,000 independent business members across the USA and Canada.

The E. F. Schumacher Society (USA)
Great Barrington, Massachusetts
(+1) 413 528 1737
www.smallisbeautiful.org
A long-standing resource building on E. F. Schumacher's ideas, including a very comprehensive library and a range of localisation initiatives, from community supported agriculture through land trusts to local currencies. Probably the best-developed set of ideas you will find.

FEASTA: The Foundation for the Economics of Sustainability (Ireland and UK)
Dublin
(+353) (0)1 661 9572
www.feasta.org
Based primarily in Ireland, but now working across all of the British Isles, FEASTA has a wealth of resources that will help in the journey to resilient, low-carbon local economies.

Living Economies (Aotearoa/New Zealand)
Carterton, Wellington
(+64) (0)6 379 8034
http://le.org.nz/tiki-index.php
A wonderful source of information on localisation and alternative currencies run from, but not limited to, New Zealand.

Localise West Midlands
Digbeth, Birmingham
0121 685 1155
www.localisewestmidlands.org.uk
A network doing good work to develop local economies in the West Midlands. Other regions could replicate this model as a way to pull together the different strands explored in this book.

new economics foundation (nef)
London
020 7820 6300
www.neweconomics.org
The UK's premier 'think and do' tank, which is developing a wonderful range of ways to build resilient local economies.

Limits to growth

Books

Daly, H. (1996). *Beyond Growth: the economics of sustainable development*. Boston, Massachusetts, Beacon Press.

Douthwaite, R. (1999). *The Growth Illusion: how economic growth has enriched the few, impoverished the many and endangered the planet*. Dartington, Green Books.
Meadows, D. H. et al. (2005). *Limits to Growth: the 30-year update*. London, Earthscan.

nef (2007). *The European Unhappy Planet Index: an index of carbon efficiency and well-being in the EU*. London, the new economics foundation and Friends of the Earth.

Simms, A. (2005). *Ecological Debt: the health of the planet and the wealth of nations*. London, Pluto Press.

Supermarkets

A key aim of local currencies is to protect local shops and high streets from the predations of supermarkets.

Books and articles

Mitchell, S. (2006). *Big-Box Swindle: the true cost of mega-retailers and the fight for America's independent businesses*. Portland, Beacon Press.
(Stacy Mitchell's website, supporting the above book, can be found at www.bigboxswindle.com.)

Ritzer, G. (2004). *The McDonaldization of Society*. Thousand Oaks, CA, Pine Forge Press.

Simms, A. (2007). *Tescopoly: how one shop came out on top and why it matters*. Constable & Robinson, London.

Worthington, S. (1998). 'Loyalty Cards and the revitalisation of the town centre'. *International Journal of Retail and Distribution Management* **26**(2): 66-77. An exploration of the value of local loyalty cards in revitalising town centres under threat from supermarkets.

Websites
www.ilsr.org
The website of the Institute for Local Self-Reliance, promoting localisation generally and vibrant local high streets in particular.

www.tescopoly.org
This is NOT Tesco's website – despite the look and feel. It's a site for campaigners opposed to supermarkets.

Peak oil

Books
Astyk, S. (2008). *Depletion and Abundance: life on the new home front*. Gabriola Island, BC, New Society Publishers. (Sharon Astyk's blog is worth a look: see http://sharonastyk.com.)

Greer, J. (2008). *The Long Descent: a user's guide to the end of the industrial age*. Gabriola Island, BC, New Society Publishers.

Heinberg, R. (2004). *Powerdown: options and actions for a post-carbon world*. Forest Row, Clairview Books.

Heinberg, R. (2007). *Peak Everything: waking up to the century of decline in Earth's resources*. Forest Row, Clairview Books.
(See also Richard Heinberg's website: www.richardheinberg.com.)

Kunstler, J. (2006). *The Long Emergency: surviving the end of oil, climate change and other converging catastrophes of the twenty-first century*. New York, Grove Press.

Websites
www.peakoil.net
The site of the Association for the Study of Peak Oil & Gas – full of useful information on peak oil.

www.postcarbon.org
The site of the post carbon institute, bringing together a range of resources on post-carbon economies.

Climate Change

Books
Hulme, M. (2009). *Why we Disagree about Climate Change: understanding controversy, inaction and opportunity*. Cambridge, Cambridge University Press.

Lynas, M. (2007). *Six Degrees: our future on a hotter planet*. London, Fourth Estate.

Marshall, G. (2007). *Carbon Detox: your step-by-step guide to getting real about climate change*. Stroud, Gaia Books Ltd.

Monbiot, G. (2006). *Heat: how to stop the planet burning*. London, Allen Lane.

Neale, J. (2008). *Stop Global Warming: change the world*. London, Bookmarks.

Websites
www.capandshare.org
www.gci.org.uk (Global Commons Institute)
These are two websites that discuss two ways of sharing the world's limited resources and carbon budgets on an equitable basis. See page 206 on energy currencies.

www.realclimate.org
This is by far the best site to get accurate information on climate change from climate change scientists – not the spin.

Conventional analyses of how money works

Books

Boyle, D. (ed.) (2003). *The Money Changers: currency reform from Aristotle to e-cash*. London, Earthscan.

Ferguson, N. (2008). *The Ascent of Money: a financial history of the world*. London, Penguin.

Galbraith, J. (1975). *Money: whence it came, where it went*. London, Andre Deutsch.

Hart, K. (2001). *Money in an unequal world*. London, Texere.

Hutchinson, F., Mellor, M. and Olsen, W. (2002). *The Politics of Money: towards sustainability and economic democracy*. London, Pluto Press.

Ingham, G. (2004). *The Nature of Money*. Cambridge, Polity.

McMillan, J. (2002). *Reinventing the Bazaar: a natural history of markets*. London, W. W. Norton & Co.

Simmel, G. (1978/1908). *The Philosophy of Money*. London, Routledge.

Zelizer, V. (1997). *The Social Meaning of Money*. Princeton, Princeton University Press.

Zelizer, V. (2005). *The Purchase of Intimacy*. Princeton, Princeton University Press.

Useful money-related websites

http://projects.exeter.ac.uk/RDavies/arian/llyfr.html
Roy and Glyn Davies's website at Exeter University.

http://thememorybank.co.uk
The website of Keith Hart, one of the world's most interesting anthropologists of money – well worth a dabble, even if at first it does not seem directly money-related.

Social capital

Books and articles

Fukuyama, F. (1995). *Trust: the social virtues and the creation of prosperity*. London, Penguin.

Granovetter, M. (1973). 'The strength of weak ties.' *American Journal of Sociology* **78**(6): 1360-80.

Putnam, R. (2001). *Bowling Alone*. London, Simon and Schuster.

Historical examples of alternative currencies

Robert Owen

Bickle, R. and Scott Cato, M. (2008). *New Views of Society: Robert Owen for the twenty-first century*. Glasgow, Scottish Left Review Press.

Donnachie, I. (2000). *Robert Owen: Owen of New Lanark and New Harmony*. Phantassie, East Lothian, Tuckwell Press.

Robert Owen Society
Leominster, Herefordshire
01568 615510
www.robertowen.org
The Robert Owen Society is a modern cooperative organisation: a good source if you want to follow up Owen's ideas.

Proudhon and the anarchists

Dana, C. (1896). *Proudhon and his 'Bank of the People'*. New York, Benjamin R. Tucker.

Woodcock, G. (1962/1986). *Anarchism: a history of libertarian ideas and movements*. Harmondsworth, Penguin.

Populism

Goodwyn, L. (1976). *Democratic Promise: the populist moment in America*. Oxford, Oxford University Press.

Social credit

Douglas, C. (1937). *Social Credit*. London, Eyre and Spottiswoode.

Drakeford, M. (1997). *Social Movements and their Supporters: the Green Shirts in England*. Basingstoke, Macmillan.

www.kibbokift.org
The website of the Kibbo Kift Foundation (archives of the Green Shirt movement). If you want to learn more about social credit, this rather esoteric site is a good place to start.

The Great Depression

Books
Alter, J. (2006). *The Defining Moment: FDR's hundred days and the triumph of hope*. Simon and Schuster, New York.

Fisher, I. (1933). *Stamp Scrip*. New York, Adelphi.

Fisher, I. (1934). *Mastering the Crisis: with additional chapters on stamp scrip*. Allen & Unwin, London.

Shaeles, A. (2007). *The Forgotten Man: a new history of the Great Depression*. HarperCollins, London.

Alternative currencies

Boyle, D. (1999). *Funny Money: in search of alternative cash*. London, HarperCollins.

Boyle, D. (2009). *Money Matters: putting the eco into economics – global crisis, local solutions*. Bristol, Alastair Sawday Publishing.

Greco, T. H. (2010). *The End of Money and the Future of Civilization*. White River Junction, VT, Chelsea Green.

Kent, D. (2005). *Healthy Money, Healthy Planet*. Nelson, New Zealand, Craig Potton.

Lietaer, B. (2001). *The Future of Money*. London, Random House.

North, P. (2007). *Money and Liberation: the micropolitics of alternative currency movements*. Minneapolis, University of Minnesota Press.

Offe, C. and Heinze, R. (1992). *Beyond Employment*. Cambridge, Polity Press.

Solomon, L. (1996). *Rethinking Our Centralised Money System: the case for a system of local currencies*. London, Praeger Publishers.

Websites
www.lietaer.com
Bernard Lietaer's website

www.reinventingmoney.com
http://beyondmoney.net
Tom Greco's websites

The above websites are by interesting local currency advocates and are full of useful information.

www.cc-literature.org
The Bibliography of Community Currency Research.

www.complementarycurrency.org
The online Complementary Currency Resource Center.

The above two websites attempt to pull together written research on alternative currencies.

www.uea.ac.uk/env/ijccr
The International Journal of Community Currency Research – An online, open-access, academic but accessible journal of recent research on alternative currencies.

LETS

Books and articles

Aldridge, T. and Patterson, A. (2002). 'LETS get real: constraints on the development of Local Exchange Trading Schemes'. *Area* **34**(4): 370-81.

Croall, J. (1997). *LETS act locally: the growth of Local Exchange Trading Systems*. London, Calouste Gulbenkian Foundation.

North, P. (2006). *Alternative Currencies as a Challenge to Globalisation? A case study of Manchester's local money networks*. Aldershot, Ashgate.

Pacione, M. (1997). 'Local Exchange Trading Systems as a Response to the Globalisation of Capitalism'. *Urban Studies* **34**(8): 1179-99.

Stott, M. and Hodges, J. (1996). 'LETS: Never knowingly undersold?' *Local Economy* **11**(3): 266-8.

Williams, C. C. et al. (2001). *Bridges into Work: an evaluation of Local Exchange Trading Schemes*. Bristol, The Policy Press.

Organisations

LETSlinkUK
London
www.letslinkuk.net

Système d'Échange Locaux (SEL)
France
www.selidaire.org (in French)

Tauschringe
Germany
www.tauschring.de (in German)

The above are organisations for a range of LETS schemes in other countries where they are strong. If you live in one of these countries, these sites will help you to find out more about how to set up a LETS scheme.

Time banking

Books

Cahn, E. (2000). *No More Throw-away People*. London, HarperCollins.

nef (2008). *The New Wealth of Time: how time banking helps people build better services*. London, new economics foundation.

Organisations

Time Banking UK
Stroud
01453 750952
www.timebanking.org
The primary organisation for time banks in the UK. A good place to start for resources for time banks.

TimeBanks USA
Washington, DC
(+1) 202 686 5200
www.timebanks.org
The primary organisation for US time banks.

Websites

The following are the websites for a range of particularly active time banks.

http://growingnewsome.wordpress.com
Growing Newsome

www.isleofavalon.co.uk/community/AFS.html
Avalon Fair Shares

www.lyttelton.net.nz
Lyttelton Time Bank, New Zealand

www.peckhamsettlement.org.uk/Hourbank.htm
Peckham HOurBank

www.rgtb.org.uk
Rushey Green Time Bank

www.skillsharenetwork.org
Denver SkillShare, Colorado, USA

Ithaca Hours

Books
Glover, P. (1995). 'Ithaca Hours'. In *Invested in the Common Good*. S. Meeker-Lowry. New York, New Society Publishers.

Maurer, B. (2005). *Mutual Life, Limited: Islamic banking, alternative currencies, lateral reason*. Princeton, Princeton University Press.

Organisations
Ithaca Hours Inc.
Ithaca, New York
(+1) 607 272 3738
www.ithacahours.org

Websites
www.ithacahours.com
Paul Glover's website.

For links to a wide range of hour-based currencies in the USA see **www.ithacahours.com/otherhours.html**

Argentina

Books and articles
Auyero, J. (2000). *Poor People's Politics: Peronist survival networks and the legacy of Evita*. London, Duke University Press.

Blustein, P. (2005). *And the Money Kept Rolling In (and Out): Wall Street, the IMF and the bankrupting of Argentina*. New York, Public Affairs.

López Levy, M. (2004). *We are Millions: neo-liberalism and new forms of political action in Argentina*. London, Latin America Bureau.

Rock, D. (2002). 'Racking Argentina'. *New Left Review* 2/17: 55-86.

Websites and contacts in Spanish
www.trueque.org.ar
The website for PAR, originators of the Global Barter Network (RGT).

www.trueque-marysierras.org.ar
This is the website of the Mar-y-Sierras barter network in Mar del Plata, Argentina. It is one of the most resilient and well managed of the RTS schemes. If you read Spanish, you will find access to a wide variety of resources here.

heloisa.primavera@gmail.com
Heloisa Primavera is a contact for the Solidarity Barter Network (RTS). She speaks good English and is a good source for up-to-date information on alternative currencies in Argentina, as well as more widely in Latin America.

Regiogeld

Regiogeld e.V.
Magdeburg, Germany
(+49) 0391 5058116
www.regiogeld.de (in German)
Although in German, this website is the best resource for exploring the many different approaches to regiogeld across Germany.

BerkShares

www.berkshares.org
Run by the E. F. Schumacher Society, this site is a good place to find out more about some of the practicalities of BerkShares and get up to date with the latest developments. It has some good links to YouTube films about BerkShares, which give you more of a flavour of how it works.

Transition currencies

Brixton Pound
http://brixtonpound.org

Lewes Pound
www.thelewespound.org

Stroud Pound
www.stroudpound.org.uk
Contacts: John Rhodes, 01452 812709; Bernard Jarman, 01453 757436

Totnes Pound
http://totnes.transitionnetwork.org/totnespound/home

The Transition movement

Books
Chamberlin, S. (2009). *The Transition Timeline: for a local, resilient future*. Dartington, Green Books.

Hopkins, R. (2008). *The Transition Handbook: from oil dependency to local resilience*. Dartington, Green Books.

Pinkerton, T. and Hopkins, R. (2009). *Local Food: how to make it happen in your community*. Dartington, Green Books.

Organisations
The Transition Network
Totnes, Devon
01560 531882
www.transitionnetwork.org

Websites
www.transitionnetwork.org
The main website of the Transition movement.

www.transitionculture.org
The website of Rob Hopkins. "An evolving exploration into the head, heart and hands of energy descent."

www.transitionbooks.net
The website of Transition books, an imprint of Green Books.

Building resilient local economies

As part of the wider project of building resilient localised economies, these resources can help take forward some of the ideas in Chapter 16.

Books and articles – carbon trading and energy currencies
Douthwaite, R. (1999). *The Ecology of Money*. Dartington, Green Books.

Rabinovitch, J. (1992). 'Curitiba: towards sustainable urban development'. *Environment and Urbanization* **4**(2): 62-73.

van Sambeek, P. and Kampers, E. (2004). *NU-Spaarpas: The Sustainable Incentives Card*. www.nuspaarpas.nl/www_en/pdf_en/NUspaarpasENGCH6.pdf. Stiching Points. Amsterdam.

Seyfang, G. (2007). *Personal Carbon Trading: lessons from complementary currencies*. Norwich, Centre for Social and Economic Research on the Global Environment.

Books – community businesses and the social economy
Amin, A. et al. (2002). *Placing the Social Economy*. London, Routledge.

Amin, A. (ed.) (2009). *The Social Economy: International Perspectives on Economic Solidarity*. London, Zed Books.

Gibson-Graham, J. (2006). *A Post Capitalist Politics*. Minneapolis, University of Minnesota Press.

Mackintosh, M. and Wainwright, H. (eds) (1987). *A Taste of Power: the Politics of Local Economics*. London, Verso.

de Sousa Santos, B., (ed.) (2006). *Another Production is Possible: Beyond the Capitalist Canon*. London, Verso.

Organisations

Association of British Credit Unions
Manchester
161 832 3694
www.abcul.org
Offers support and advice for those who want to develop credit unions.

Aston Reinvestment Trust
Birmingham
0121 359 2444
www.reinvest.co.uk
Provides support to small businesses in inner-city Birmingham who are unable to get help from conventional sources.

Community Development Finance Association
London
020 7430 0222
www.cdfa.org.uk
The trade association for Community Development Finance Institutions, which provide loans and support to businesses and individuals that have had difficulty getting finance from the usual sources.

Community Land Trusts
University of Salford
0161 295 4951
www.communitylandtrust.org.uk
A resource to help develop a community land trust, which takes land out of development in perpetuity, allowing its value to be retained by the community.

Development Trusts Association
London
0845 458 8336
www.dta.org.uk
The leading network of community enterprise practitioners, dedicated to helping people set up development trusts and helping existing development trusts learn from each other and work effectively.

Social Enterprise Coalition
London
020 7793 2323
www.socialenterprise.org.uk
Promotes and helps develop community-based and socially responsible social enterprises, from the very large (the John Lewis Partnership) to the more local.

Women's Employment Enterprise and Training Unit
Norwich
01603 230625
www.weetu.org
A project helping women to develop their own small businesses through 'microcredit'-style peer lending. Women in the network guarantee each other's loans.

Banks and building societies
Ecology Building Society
Keighley, West Yorkshire
0845 674 5566
www.ecology.co.uk

Triodos Bank
Bristol
0117 973 9339
www.triodos.co.uk

Triodos Bank and the Ecology Building Society are long-established businesses offering finance for sustainable development.

Local bonds

Liverpool Sefton Social Investment Bond
01732 774040
www.charitybank.org/liverpool

Sheffield's Green Bond
Sheffield
0114 263 6420
www.sheffieldsgreenbond.org.uk

Two examples of local bonds, designed to raise finance for sustainable development in Sheffield and on Merseyside.

Websites

www.bankingonessex.com
A partnership between Essex Council and Santander Bank to provide support for businesses in Essex.

www.changethemarket.com
Vermont Sustainable Exchange, an interesting network linking local community-focused and sustainable businesses to each other for mutual aid.

www.greenpoundvoucher.com
Manchester Green Pound, an online network enabling people to support certified sustainable and ethical businesses in the Manchester region.

www.irta.com
International Reciprocal Trade Association, the trade association for the multi-million pound business-to-business barter industry, now looking to develop relations with more local currencies.

www.jak.se (in Swedish)
JAK Bank, an innovative model for an interest-free bank.

www.libertydollar.org
If you hate our paper, 'fiat' money and would like to see a return to hard gold and silver money, this is the site for you.

http://theliquiditynetwork.org
Based in Ireland, the Liquidity Network is a project developed by FEASTA and Transition Initiatives to provide an electronic currency that will help some of Ireland's communities to weather financial crises.

www.wir.ch (in German)
With a history going back to 1934, WIR is the Swiss 'business ring' enabling Swiss businesses to trade with each other using WIR credits.

INDEX